MEDITATION IN MODERN BUDDHISM

In contemporary Thai Buddhism, the burgeoning popularity of *vipassanā* meditation is impacting upon the lives of those most closely involved with its practice: monks and *mae chee* (lay nuns) living in monastic communities. For them, meditation becomes a central focus of life and a way to transform the self. This ethnographic account of a thriving northern Thai monastery examines meditation in detail, and explores the subjective signification of monastic duties and ascetic practices. Drawing on fieldwork done both as an analytical observer and as a full participant in the life of the monastery, Joanna Cook analyses the motivation and experience of renouncers, and shows what effect meditative practices have on individuals and community organization. The particular focus on the status of *mae chee* – part lay, part monastic – provides a fresh insight into social relationships and gender hierarchy within the context of the monastery.

JOANNA COOK is George Kingsley Roth Research Fellow in Southeast Asian Studies, Christ's College, University of Cambridge.

MEDITATION IN MODERN BUDDHISM

Renunciation and Change in Thai Monastic Life

JOANNA COOK

CAMBRIDGE
UNIVERSITY PRESS

32 Avenue of the Americas, New York NY 10013-2473, USA

Cambridge University Press is part of the University of Cambridge.

It furthers the University's mission by disseminating knowledge in the pursuit of education, learning and research at the highest international levels of excellence.

www.cambridge.org
Information on this title: www.cambridge.org/9781107660557

© Joanna Cook 2010

This publication is in copyright. Subject to statutory exception and to the provisions of relevant collective licensing agreements, no reproduction of any part may take place without the written permission of Cambridge University Press.

First published 2010
First paperback edition 2014

A catalogue record for this publication is available from the British Library

ISBN 978-0-521-11938-2 Hardback
ISBN 978-1-107-66055-7 Paperback

Cambridge University Press has no responsibility for the persistence or accuracy of URLs for external or third-party internet websites referred to in this publication, and does not guarantee that any content on such websites is, or will remain, accurate or appropriate.

Contents

Acknowledgements		*page* vi
List of map and figures		viii
Notes on language		ix
1.	Meditation and monasticism: making the ascetic self in Thailand	1
2.	Meditation and religious reform	26
3.	The monastic community: duty and structure	51
4.	Meditation as ethical imperative	70
5.	Language and meditation	96
6.	Monastic duty, mindfulness and cognitive space	116
7.	Money, *mae chee* and reciprocity	135
8.	Hierarchy, gender and mindfulness	151
9.	Monasticization and the ascetic interiority of non-self	173
Appendix	*Ordination transcript for an eight-precept nun* (mae chee)	195
Bibliography		198
Index		210

Acknowledgements

I would like to thank all those who helped me during the fieldwork on which this book is based, which was conducted in northern Thailand in Wat Bonamron, a meditation monastery just outside the city of Chiang Mai, between 2002 and 2007.

Phra Ajharn Sila was a caring teacher and mentor throughout my time in the monastery. I am humbled by his unfailing generosity and guidance. He welcomed me into the community as a daughter and I am deeply indebted to him. As my *mae chee pi liang* (mentor and advisor), Mae Chee Or guided and supported me with compassion and taught me how to be a *mae chee* through counsel and example. Mae Chee Im, Mae Chee Suey, Pi Deng Noi and Khun Jeng were a constant source of good humour and companionship. Phra Neo has been a true and valued friend to me throughout my years of involvement in Wat Bonamron as a brother and a conversation companion for thinking through the challenges of monastery life. Lisa Tsen and Maggie Methschild, during their time in the monastery, provided good company and great tea-breaks, for which I am very grateful. I must express a collective thanks to the religious community of Wat Bonamron, which has been unreservedly open and helpful.

In Cambridge the lion's share of my gratitude must fall at the feet of James Laidlaw. As an advisor, colleague and friend he has been a guiding inspiration. He has generously commented on every part of this book in all the stages of its development. His measured insight and humour have informed my thinking about and enjoyment of the process of writing this book over the past five years. As has that of Cahir Doherty. I cannot begin to count the ways in which his support, encouragement and care have impacted upon this work.

The book has benefited from the comments, corrections and criticisms of a number of people. I am particularly grateful to Justin McDaniel and Steven Collins for reading and commenting on earlier drafts of the manuscript. I am very grateful to Julene Knox for exceptionally diligent copy editing. The following people have read parts of one or more of the many drafts of the book and I am grateful for their advice and critical eye: Susan Bayly, the late Sue Benson, Barbara Bodenhorn, Matei Candea, Hildegard Diemberger, Laura Jeffery, Tom Lee, Nick Long, Tanya Luhrmann, Sophie Read, Gwyn Williams. Thanks also for academic guidance to Marilyn Strathern and David Gellner. I am also unquantifiably indebted to my family, Marcus Cook, Sally Burnley and David Cook, for unfailing love and support.

Much of the early research for this work was conducted with the financial support of the Economic and Social Research Council. It has also benefited from support from a British Academy Small Research Grant and the Evans Fund.

In Christ's College I found an intellectually stimulating environment in which to settle and write. I am grateful to the college for the community of support that I continue to find there.

List of map and figures

MAP
1. Map of Thailand — *page* x

FIGURES
1. Phra Ajharn giving a *dhamma* talk to lay meditators — 46
2. The *vihāra* — 54
3. Mae Chee Im working in the monastery shop — 59
4. Mae Chee Poy and Mae Chee Suey working in the office — 59
5. The author having her eyebrows shaved by Mae Chee Suti on the morning of ordination — 63
6. Mae Chee Or giving the basic meditation instruction to new meditation students — 76
7. The sitting posture showing the twenty-eight touching points — 77
8. *Mae chee* offering alms to monks on the morning alms round — 144
9. A money tree (*pha pa*) before it is offered to the monastery — 146
10. Mae Chee Pon preparing floral offerings for senior monks — 158

Notes on language

Thai is a tonal language with a number of vowel and consonant sounds not found in English. While Thai has its own phonetic script, there is no generally agreed system for transcribing Thai words using the Roman alphabet. In this book a modified version of the Royal Thai General System of Transcription (RTGS) from the Royal Institute is adopted. I have transliterated words from standard Thai without the use of diacritic marks. Tones are not marked and vowel lengths are not distinguished with the exception of certain long vowel sounds. In order to avoid confusion, in some cases *ee* is used to transcribe the long vowel sound written as *i* in the Royal Institute System. For example the title for a Thai Buddhist nun is written *mae chee*, not *mae chi*.

Buddhist terms are based on Thai transcriptions of Pali. Diacritical marks are included for the Pali wherever possible. Pali and Thai words are italicized (e.g., *wat*, *kamma*) throughout the text.

It is customary for Thai names to be arranged alphabetically by first name, not surname. All Thai titles are prefixed to given names rather than surnames (e.g., Dr John, not Dr Smith). Bibliographies in Thai-language publications also reflect this, while most English-language publications follow the English system. In this volume Thai authors are entered into the bibliography and text according to their first names.

The name of the monastery has been changed, as have all names of individuals. I have chosen to use pseudonyms in order to preserve the anonymity of those who have shared information with me that was not in the public domain or that might cause embarrassment if its source were to be identified.

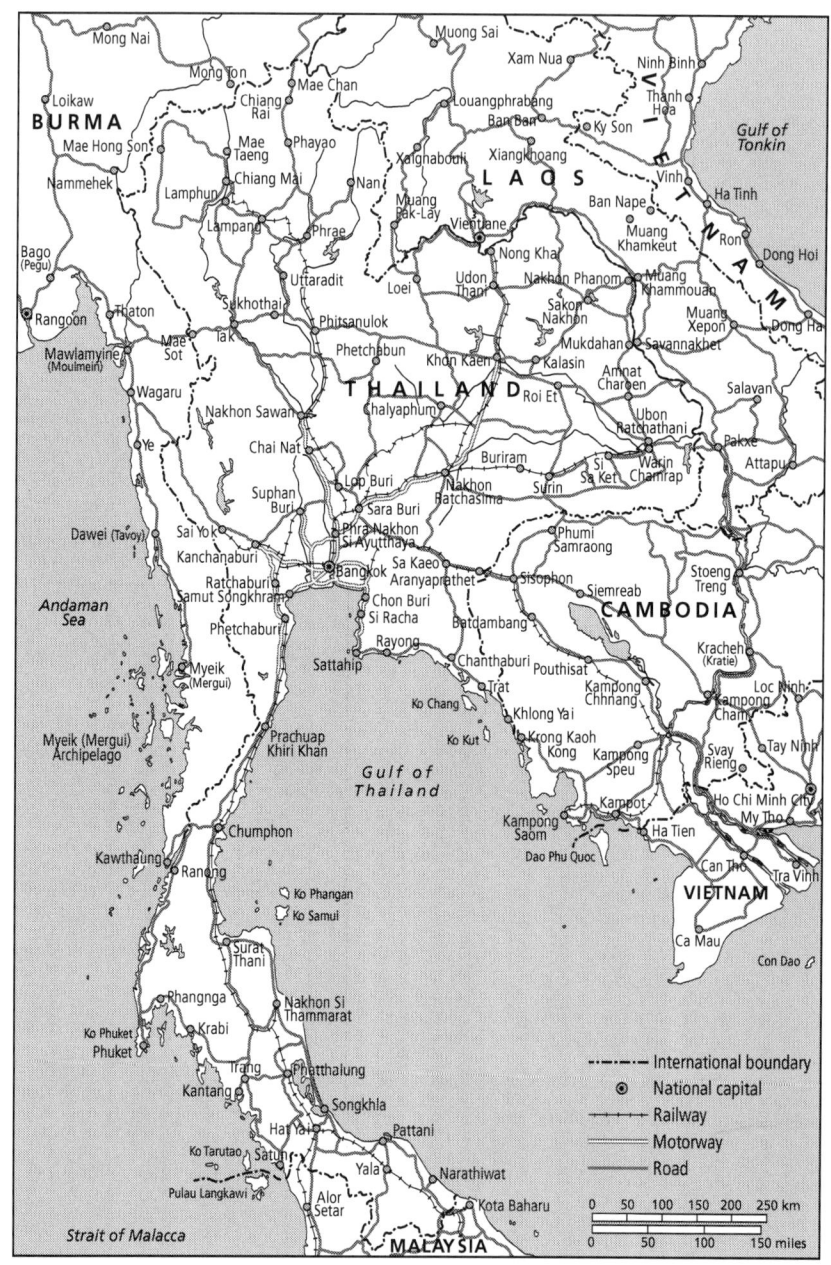

Map 1: Map of Thailand

CHAPTER I

Meditation and monasticism: making the ascetic self in Thailand

Meditation practice has only become available to large numbers of Thai laity since the 1950s. In that time Buddhism in general and meditation specifically have been incorporated as representative markers in the presentation of Thailand as a modernizing nation state and a self-consciously 'traditional' kingship. The widespread adoption of meditation by the laity since the 1950s is identified by some scholars as the greatest single change to have come over Theravāda Buddhist countries since the Second World War (Gombrich and Obeyesekere 1988: 237). Today meditation is taught in monasteries throughout Thailand, Sri Lanka, Burma and, latterly, Nepal and is a widely popular and influential movement. Furthermore, the global interest in meditation practice is leading to its inclusion in varied syncretic and often secular practices. However, such inclusion is also feeding and informing the ways in which such practice is understood and propagated in the emblematic religious institutions of Buddhist monasteries.

I take the ethnographic study of a meditation monastery in northern Thailand, Wat Bonamron, as my window on the process of renunciation, forms of which are found in all major religions. This study analyses the impact and meaning of renunciatory moral practice from the perspective of the Buddhist renouncer. I consider monastic practitioners' experiences and understandings of themselves, the significance of renunciation, ascetic discipline, rituals and duties as well as the place of community in the renunciatory project and the historical development and changes in monasticism and meditation.

THE PROPAGATION OF *VIPASSANĀ* MEDITATION

Theravāda Buddhism has been a powerful influence in Thailand for over 700 years. Thailand has a population of 69 million, the majority of whom are ethnic Thais. While there is total religious freedom in Thailand, Buddhism is followed by over 90 per cent of the population. Buddhism is also closely associated in the minds of Thai people with Thai national identity and it is an important part of Thailand's self-representation to outsiders. There are approximately 33,000 Buddhist monasteries in Thailand, which act as the focal point for the formal practice and reproduction of Thai Buddhism. As Kirsch (1985: 305) puts it, the practices of almsgiving and ordination are 'key socialisation mechanisms for the introduction of abstract Buddhist values into the everyday life of ordinary Thais'.

In many ways the monastery where I lived and carried out fieldwork is a typical Thai monastery where monks and *mae chee* (Thai Buddhist nuns) live lives of renunciation and contemplation. The idea of detachment is central to the monastic community's imagining of itself. At the same time, much daily activity surrounds collective commitment to the monastery's well-being and observance of monastic hierarchy. Moreover, Wat Bonamron is set apart from other similar institutions in Thailand by the teaching of *vipassanā* meditation. It has functioned as a *vipassanā* meditation centre since it was re-founded in the 1970s. It has a stable monastic community, the largest *mae chee* population in the region and each year thousands of lay people attend the monastery to do a retreat. For individual monastics, periods of retreat are tempered by long periods of time in which they work and teach. The scale of teaching, and the work involved, makes extended periods of isolation difficult for members of the community and as such monastics have relatively little opportunity to do retreat themselves, though all work in the monastery ideally provides an opportunity to develop the state of mind engendered by meditation: mindful awareness. The work of teaching also fosters a great sense of community among people who feel that they are doing good by combining engagement with and withdrawal from the world.

The burgeoning popularity of *vipassanā* practice as both a lay and a monastic responsibility has had important implications for the ways in which monastic subjectivity and community are understood. Rather than revealing meditation practice as a predefined entity, I begin Chapter 2 by tracing the historical development of Thai lay meditation practice in its current form. Processes of nationalism, internationalism and engagement with practice have made meditation what it is. This should seem obvious, but it is often the case that meditation (certainly in the popular imagination) is presented as timeless and without history. In contemporary meditative practices, as in Yoga (Alter 2004), we see a historically specific converging of religion, cosmology and philosophy with concerns for physiological and psychological well-being. I trace the historical context in which some monasteries in Thailand became devoted to the propagation of meditation to the laity and I locate this in the context of hybrid processes of reform in Thai Buddhism. I begin with a historical account of the introduction of Burmese *vipassanā* to Thailand in the 1950s in the context of sectarian rivalry and the popularization of alternative forms of meditative discipline in a changing religious landscape. The Mahanikai sect of the Thai ordained monastic community (sangha) has enlisted monasteries as 'satellites' in its project of promoting meditation as a practice appropriate for lay people as well as monastics since the 1950s. This intensification of lay practice was linked to increasing standards of literacy and the rise of a nascent middle class. Many urban meditators became attracted to meditation because it was promoted as a Buddhist intellectual response to Western Scientific theory. Meditation centres were modelled as 'research centres' and meditation was presented as a 'rational' and 'authentically' Buddhist practice for salvation.

Subsequent decades have witnessed a proliferation of diverse religious movements within and peripheral to the sangha. Through providing a brief overview of the reformist trends that have characterized Thai Buddhism in recent decades I account for the concurrent patterns of localism, commoditization, engagement and soteriological imperative. Trends have included a critique of Buddhism by reformist thinkers, fundamentalist movements, the commercialization of Buddhist practices, the decentralization of religion, increasing numbers of spirit-cults, and social and environmental reform movements based upon Buddhist ethics. Such trends are often accompanied by discourses of localism, in which Buddhist practice and philosophy are interpreted as an 'authentically Thai' response to the pressures of the capitalist world economy. Locally relevant forms of economic development and self-sufficiency are promoted as being founded on core Buddhist values.

Religious resurgence and revival can be seen in the increasing popularity of alternative forms of religiosity. With such variance in practice and focus, the concerns of the laity and monastics become to discover the moral purity of 'true' Buddhism and the extent to which individual monastics are able to embody the *dhamma* (teaching of the Buddha; lit.: law/truth). The laity seek out monastics who are renowned for their ethical and ascetic purity. The relatively recent meditation movement is incorporated into a landscape of localist and nationalist concerns. The shift towards lay proselytizing is reflected in different Buddhist traditions around the world (Gellner and LeVine 2005; Gombrich and Obeyesekere 1988; Houtman 1990). The meditation movement has led to a changing responsibility and role for the laity and monastics. In the plurality of practices and statuses in contemporary Thai Buddhism it is possible for people outside the official sangha hierarchy to be defined as 'monastic' without this calling into question the authority or hierarchical superiority of the official institutional sangha.

MONASTIC COMMUNITY AND THE CHANGING STATUS OF *MAE CHEE*

In Chapter 3 I focus in detail on Wat Bonamron. I examine the monastic routine and the duties of monastics, considering the daily routine of the different members of the community and the very differently structured routine of those doing retreat. Of significant interest in Thailand is the part that women, in the ambiguous role of 'nuns' (*mae chee*), are now playing in monastic religion. The twentieth century saw rising numbers of women, particularly young women, becoming precept-holding 'nuns' (on Thailand see Collins and McDaniel 2010; on Nepal see Gellner and LeVine 2005; on Sri Lanka see Gombrich and Obeyesekere 1988). The monastery on which this work is based has the largest *mae chee* community in the north of Thailand. I argue that the propagation of meditation to the laity has been crucial in the development of monastic identity for these *mae chee*. I show that these changes offer a radical reform and may be interpreted as the monasticization of popular Buddhism. A marginal and institutionally unrecognized group, *mae chee* have been gaining growing respect and prestige in recent years and are increasingly recognized as monastics, even though they are debarred from full ordination.

Although full ordination for women, known as *bhikkhunī* ordination, was once widespread in Theravāda Buddhism, the practice died out around the tenth century and has never existed in Thailand. *Bhikkhunī* ordination was only to be found in the Mahayana countries of Korea, Vietnam, Taiwan and China. In order for a woman to receive full ordination it is formally necessary to have a quorum of fully ordained monks and a quorum of fully ordained nuns to conduct the ritual. Because the Theravāda order had died out it was believed to be impossible to find the *bhikkhunī* to perform the ordination ceremony.[1] Women who wish to take ordination in Theravāda traditions do so by taking 8 or 10 precepts rather than the 10 for novice monks, the 227 precepts taken by monks, the 311 precepts taken by fully ordained Theravāda nuns, or the 5 observed by lay people (lay people may also take 8 or 10 on religiously significant occasions). In Thailand these precept-holding nuns are known as '*mae chee*': they commit themselves to a life of renunciation, living in monasteries and nunneries. This commitment is also marked on their bodies: they shave their

---

[1] As we shall see in Chapter 8 a new movement is currently under way to introduce *bhikkhunī* ordination in Theravāda countries.

head and eyebrows once a month, wear a white shirt and skirt with a large white robe over the top, which goes underneath the right arm and pins on top of the left shoulder. Collins and McDaniel (2010: 7) report that the word *mae chi* (Romanized here as *chee*) consists of the word *mae*, mother, often used as an honorific in hierarchical as well as familial relationships and the word '*chi/ji*', an honorific used for persons who occupy positions of respect, including male and female ascetics. The first records of *mae chee* date from the seventeenth century when their presence was noted by a French missionary (La Loubere 1986 [1691]: part 3, p. 113).[2] Today, there are perhaps twenty thousand *mae chee* living in temples or nunneries throughout Thailand (Lindberg Falk 2007). The monastic office of '*mae chee*' is complicated. It is conveyed through the ritual adoption of religious vows and is usually undertaken for life. However, *mae chee* ordination is only partial and its status is far below that of monks. In Thai law *mae chee* are regarded as pious lay women (*upāsikā*) and the Department of Religious Affairs does not mention them in its annual report. Because of this they do not receive the same benefits as monks, such as reduced fares on public transport. Even so, because they are said to have renounced the world they do not have the right to vote.

There is variance in the practice and status of *mae chee* throughout Thailand. While some *mae chee* go on daily alms rounds, others are debarred from doing so. The institutional marginalization of *mae chee* means that their options are considerably more constrained than those of monks. On the one hand monastic practice seems to confirm dominant modes of gender difference and separation, while on the other it dissolves them. *Mae chee* engage positively evaluated Buddhist practices that confer prestige and respect: meditation (Tambiah 1984: 38), controlled comportment, shaving the head, continuing commitment to the sangha (religious community), and wearing white robes, all are expressions of purity and renunciation of sexuality (Tambiah 1970: 104; Keyes 1986: 73, 78).

Whereas some reports of *mae chee* give information on groups of women living as 'temple-servants' (Sanitsuda 2001), living lives of 'hardship and poverty' (Barnes 1996: 268), more recent research has revealed that the status of *mae chee* is influenced by age, social background, educational level, aspirations and motives (cf. Collins and McDaniel 2010; Lindberg Falk 2007; Seeger 2009). There is variance in the roles and

---

[2] I have never found reference to either vernacular or foreign-language texts prior to this time. The lack of evidence of *mae chee* prior to the seventeenth century is perhaps telling of the historical lowliness of the institution.

responsibilities of *mae chee* throughout Thailand. *Mae chee* are taking active roles as meditation teachers and practitioners (see Adiele 2004; Brown 2001; Van Esterik 1996), in social welfare work (McDaniel 2006a) and as teachers (Brown 2001; Collins and McDaniel 2010; Lindberg Falk 2000; 2007). These developments are related to a broader expansion of educational and professional possibilities for women in Thailand (cf. Van Esterik 1996; Mills 1999; Wilson 2004; see also Ockey 2005).

While monastic identity and ascetic practices such as *vipassanā* meditation have historically been the preserve of monks, requiring full ordination and celibacy, in contemporary Thailand 'monastic' and 'lay' are not fixed or mutually exclusive categories: temporary ordination for short periods of time has always been available to Thai men; large numbers of laity now enter monasteries as meditation students for short periods and accept monastic precepts for the duration of their retreat; and finally, the subsequent monasticization of popular Buddhism is enabling *mae chee*, though outside the ordained monastic community (sangha), to define themselves in ways which are, critically, religious, monastic *and* associated with prestige. Moreover, as this ethnography will show, *vipassanā* is providing a vehicle for the actualization of renunciation through the monastic duty to teach and embody the principles of meditation. The involvement of *mae chee* in teaching and practising meditation is leading to the incorporation of women in religious and monastic roles; *mae chee* are able to define themselves and be defined by others as monastics. While monks are controlled by the 227 precepts of the *vinaya*,[3] the relative lack of formal rules for *mae chee* means that their *performance* of monastic identity is crucial in their self-placement between the sangha and the laity. Even though or indeed partly because the status of *mae chee* is ambiguous, they are playing a decisive role in transformations in Thai Buddhism.

I examine the heterogeneity of the monastic community by looking at the difference between the ordination rituals for monks and *mae chee*, some of the diverse reasons people choose to ordain, variance in age, educational attainment and social background prior to ordination and the ways in which such prior experiences influence ordination and the distribution of monastic duties. For all members of this community, however, ordination is conceptualized as an opportunity to 'do work' on oneself through meditation.

---

[3] Literally: discipline, training, guidance; the monastic precepts; the first 'basket' of the *Tipiṭaka*. The *Tipiṭaka* (Pali: *ti*, 'three', + *piṭaka*, 'baskets'), or Pali Canon, is the collection of primary Pali-language texts which form the doctrinal foundation of Theravāda Buddhism.

PRACTISING AND LEARNING

This book aims to examine the ethical significance for monastic practitioners themselves of teaching wide swathes of people. A nexus of community, individual and lay interests, I argue that meditation practice is also the fulcrum around which this religious monastic community is structured and by which the monastic self is formed. Through an examination of meditative practice I examine the domain of 'the self' as it is meaningful for Thai monastics in the context of rapidly developing global and national discourses about the benefits of meditation for all. It is an account of the ways in which people come to understand themselves through ascetic practice and of how subjectivity is reshaped through religious experience. I argue that meditation, which is often thought of as an asocial activity, has an important social dimension and that this profoundly influences the psychological benefits that people experience and intend to experience as a result of practice.

In Chapter 4 I examine the practice of *vipassanā* meditation in the monastery in order to understand what it is that people do when they meditate, why this is an appropriate practice, what is achieved by it and what changes are effected by it. Meditation practice is intended to bring about a change in perception in the meditator, one that is consistent with Buddhist ethical principles. In order to understand these principles and their significance for individuals in other areas of monastery life it is necessary to understand how these specific bodily and mental practices bring about the experiences that are recognized and valued as religious in this context. I consider in detail the very specific techniques by which the religious tenets that inform practice are actualized through the meditation practice. A central argument of the book is that monastics learn to engage with experiences in specific ways: they learn to reinterpret subjective experiences and responses in ways that are consonant with religious principles. These principles then become the context in which all apperceptions of phenomena are carried out and the renunciate learns to experience her activities, both physical and mental, as evidence for the importance of renunciation.

I begin with the basic meditation course, the first introduction to meditation that most people in the monastery have, both lay and monastic. I describe the experiences of the basic meditation course as it would be learnt by a novice meditator. It is through these introductory disciplines that the compelling importance of renunciation is first realized for those who later come to understand their renunciation in terms of the imperative to cultivate mindfulness. I examine meditation as a 'technology of the self', a practice through which people intend to effect a change upon themselves that is consonant with religious tenets. The practitioner wills, observes and experiences the changing nature of the mind and the body through a very conscious process of self-fashioning. I focus on the paradox of will and spontaneity in religious attainment. I demonstrate that the spontaneous experience of meditative attainment at the end of a meditation retreat is an embodiment of the ideal telos of Buddhist practice. The insight into non-self, impermanence and imperfection that is thought to be attainable through the retreat provides an experiential resolution between Buddhist soteriology and ascetic practice for meditation practitioners.

In Buddhist philosophy all things are thought to be 'causally interdependent': everything is interconnected and everything affects everything else. Thus, no phenomena are independent or self-originating. This principle extends through all things, and all aspects of existence are thought to be connected and interrelated, from physical conditions, to events in a person's life, and happiness or suffering in the mind. Thus, how the world is experienced and lived is, in part, how it is created; acting in a morally good or bad way creates the conditions and causes for future experiences and actions.

The three tenets at the heart of Theravāda Buddhism are impermanence, suffering and non-self (Pali: *anicca, dukkha, anattā*):

- Impermanence: *Anicca* refers to the ever-changing nature of all phenomena. All conditioned things are in a state of flux and eventually cease.
- Suffering: Sometimes translated as suffering, pain or unsatisfactoriness, *dukkha* is philosophically closer to disquietude. Nothing in the physical or psychological realms can bring lasting satisfaction or happiness.
- Non-self: Not only does Buddhism teach that there is no external salvation (no theistic deity) but also that there is no essential core of identity (no soul). What is normally thought of as 'self' is revealed through Buddhist teaching and practice to be a conglomeration of changing mental and physical constituents. Clinging to a delusional sense of self is thought to lead to unhappiness and suffering. The Buddha declared that all things are not-self (*anattā*).

These three principles are thought to characterize all phenomena. By bringing the three characteristics (as they are referred to) into their awareness on a moment by moment basis through the mental discipline of meditation the Buddhist monastics with whom I work explicitly intend to change their world view, cut attachment to a sense of self and thereby attain enlightenment, the perfect peace of a mind that is free from craving, aversion and anger. It is believed that through the practice of meditation it is possible to realize and experience ultimate truth: that there is no self that exists, that all things are imperfect and impermanent.

These Buddhist renunciates *learn* to recognize the principles of Buddhism in their bodies and in their minds. Of interest to me were the ways in which people learn to use cognitive concepts to interpret their experiences and responses. For example, as an interpretation of physical sickness or mental restlessness, impermanence, suffering and non-self come to be compellingly in evidence: the uncontrollability, imperfection and transience of mental and bodily states are readily enough available. Interestingly, through the dedicated practice of meditation each mental and physical movement becomes evidence of religious principles at the same time as people actively learn to interpret their subjectivity through such principles. People engage in specific practices in order to change their experiences in relation to religious concepts, that is, they learn and practise with intent and in so doing, religious tenets become real.

The experience of non-self arises through meditation as it is taught and learnt. Practitioners are encouraged to interpret the everyday flow of their own awareness in terms of impermanence, suffering and non-self and to see in it evidence of these religious truths. Thus, people are encouraged to experience moments of their own subjectivity as illustration of religious concepts. Life in this monastery is centred on a specific practice that is focused upon developing awareness of interiority. The meditation technique is intended explicitly to enable the practitioner to attend to internal phenomena and to cut involvement in external or sensorial stimuli. The practitioner learns to engage with and interpret internal and external sensory phenomena in specific ways. The development of monastic identity and meditative discipline involves a process of both learning to reinterpret subjective experiences and learning to alter subjectivity. On the one hand, monastics recognize their pre-trained experiences to be replete with the suffering brought by ignorance and attachment, and on the other, they recognize that their subjectivity has changed as a result of the practice.

The point of *vipassanā* meditation for these monastics is to achieve awareness of the tenets of Buddhism, such that one experiences that there is no self which exists and that attachment to a delusional sense of self is the result of ignorance and the cause of all suffering in the world. Thus, the goal is to develop a very specific and vivid subjective awareness. This meditative development occurs in the context of community interaction. I consider narratives of the lives of monks and nuns within the larger context of social norms, monastic duties and discourse in Thailand, taking into account theoretical considerations of renunciation as a practical and ongoing process.

In Chapter 5 I examine understandings of language in ritual, meditation and daily monastic life. I consider in more detail the cognitive impact of meditative practice for monastics and laity through a consideration of the advanced meditation technique. I examine understandings of Pali and language use in the monastery more broadly and I then consider the ways in which use of Pali is understood as a method for self-improvement. Pali language is thought to have an immediate physical and psychological effect upon meditators. Each time the practitioner does retreat he or she gains more insight into the nature of the words summoned in Pali, through cultivating mindful detachment. The cultivation of mindfulness is understood as an ongoing fostering of forms of perception. Practitioners intend to move progressively towards a realization of ultimate truth. This requires particular subjective responses to the experiences of meditation in the ongoing cultivation of such perceptual capacities.

Use of language in the monastery reflects an emphasis on non-verbal or non-conceptual knowing. On the one hand, meditation is learnt and becomes important through solitary practice and in this sense language is insufficient as a pedagogic aid. On the other, Pali provides the meditator with an unmediated experiential access to ultimate truth. The experience of truth through Pali language is distinct from the rationality or irrationality of beliefs in that truth. This reflects broader culturally specific distinctions between the heart/mind (*jai*) and the brain, knowledge and wisdom, behaviour and speech. I suggest that belief may not always be prior to religious experience and that private meditative experience is often taken as persuasive evidence of changes in and by the meditator.

A central focus of the book is the ways in which monastic involvement becomes compelling. I consider how becoming a monastic changes one's relationship with mental, physical and emotional processes as well as how one interprets subjective experiences. My argument is that in this monastery monastics' subjectivities are shaped by the 'work' that they do on themselves and that this creates a personal commitment to practice, precept and community that operates simultaneously on several different levels – psychological, social and political – as understanding of the ascetic self and relation to others (both at close quarters and more widely) develop. In some ways these changes are similar to those engendered by ascetic practice for laity, but there are also ways in which they are crucially different.

While renunciation constitutes a removal from the world and meditation is conceived of as a solitary practice, asceticism and renunciation are necessarily shaped by social dimensions.

In considering how we might explore the processes through which monastics make of themselves the kinds of people who, on reflection, they think they ought to become I employ Foucault's writings on ethical self-formation. I argue that Buddhist renunciation may be understood as a process of self-formation even though the end result, the ideal 'telos' of practice, is the realization of 'non-self': to completely cut attachment to all sense of self. Thus, I argue that it is through ascetic practice that the ascetic self is made.[4] Through religious training monastics learn to experience the world around them and all internal states (such as emotions, desires, thoughts, aversions and physical sensations) as that from which ascetic discipline brings detachment. It is through strict discipline in intensive retreat periods, in daily practice, and in the conscious effort to imbue all daily activity with the same quality of mental being found in intensive retreat, that monastics develop a change in interpretations, perceptions and dispositions – a transformation of subjective experience that is understood by monastics themselves to indicate a progressive and embodied realization of Buddhist soteriological principles. The monastics with whom I work understand the process of religious formation as a shedding of a delusional perception of 'self', the ultimate conclusion of which is the realization of enlightenment: the cessation of suffering and the cycle of rebirth.

PARADOX AND BEHAVIOUR

Having examined meditation in detail I return my focus to monastic identity at a time when the techniques for attaining meditative detachment are increasingly available to people who are not themselves renouncers. What, in such a situation, is becoming of monastic identity? Moving away from a rules-based understanding of morality I analyse the impact and meaning of renunciatory moral practice from the perspective of the Buddhist renouncer. Chapter 6 examines monastic practitioners' experiences and understandings of themselves, the significance of renunciation, ascetic discipline, rituals and duties as well as the place of community in the renunciatory project. The mindfulness engendered in meditation is

---

[4] The focus upon ethical self-formation as a means of understanding the psychosocial experience of monasticism also resonates with a broader emerging field in the anthropology of ethics (cf. Hirschkind 2006; Lester 2005; Mahmood 2005; Robbins 2004).

articulated and embodied by monastics in the wider context of intersubjective relationships. If meditation and meditative attainment are available to all people irrespective of ordination status, in what ways are monastics distinct from laity? I demonstrate that the performance of religious identity is one way in which the moral self is formed and communicated. I examine the way through which monastic performance may actualize the Buddhist principle of non-self (*anattā*) while simultaneously being a question of social hierarchy, judgment and duty. I examine the practice of mindfulness in monastic duty and the relationship between this and the social transfer of merit and individual morality.

During fieldwork and analysis it became apparent that there appeared to be a paradox between internal processes of renunciation for individual monks and *mae chee* and the importance of public demonstrations of 'non-self'. As shall be explored in more detail later, *vipassanā* meditation involves a process of detaching from a sense of self. Such detachment is evidenced through the level of sartorial neatness exhibited by the individual. The appearance of the body of the monastic reveals an inner state of moral attainment: others bear witness to moral qualities and virtues in monastic physical performance. Sitting up straight, speaking quietly, eating slowly, and so on, therefore become a question of morality for the monastic. Ideally, appropriate emotional and physical control comes as an automatic result of ascetic practice. Yet by refining behavioural characteristics and holding them up as indicative of a virtuous state of mind, one's behaviour becomes not only a question of individual morality but also social responsibility.

Members of the laity relate to monastics as those who have renounced a sense of self but there is necessarily a discrepancy between this and one's own awareness of the ongoing process of renunciation: between oneself as a spectacle of asceticism and the reality of one's own imperfection. Monastics are 'on show' to the laity for much of the time. If the monastic appearance communicates how the monastic is to be treated *by* the laity then it also communicates how the monastic is to behave *for* the laity. The appearance of the monastic both physically and performatively acts as a buffer zone between the social world and the bounded self. It is the space in which lay impressions of renunciates are realized, and where renunciates communicate themselves to others in the light of the religious ideal. The body may speak to others about one's personhood but after ordination one's body becomes part of the public domain – one has a moral duty to behave in an appropriate way.

Multiple displays of sensory and physical control become a central focus in renunciates' lives, but this necessarily creates a dynamic paradox between understandings of self and the moral context of public action. My aim in this book then is to examine the ways in which individuality, subjectivity and interiority stand in relation to social and monastic duty in the context of the propagation of meditation to the laity by monastics in contemporary Thailand. I argue that ascetic practice gains its force as the means by which individual monastics develop subjective processes of interiority within the context of the monastic community, which ultimately lead to the *removal* of individuality. In Dumont's terms it is through ascetic practice that people become 'individuals' (1980 [1966]): they develop a 'self', which it is their duty to patrol and fashion. At the same time, however, it is through such practice that the person cultivates, what Flood (2004) terms, an 'ascetic interiority' through which self, desire and volition are eradicated. This ethnography focuses on how ascetic practice becomes meaningful for practitioners; that is, what is meant by the renunciation of self for these Buddhist monastics.

The monastic body becomes a spectacle of religious perfection for the laity, and as such it is never appropriate to see a monastic body misbehaving or in the wrong place. The morality of monastics paradoxically presents a process of self-aware reflection, on the one hand, and, on the other, absence of self in the performance of one's moral duty to the laity. Monastics may be restricted in their emotional expression by cultural conventions prescribing appropriate behaviour, but the extent to which people's behaviour is influenced by such restrictions or the points at which one may choose to express emotion depend upon personal placement and negotiation. Mindful awareness emerges as a moral injunction: a way of establishing who one is in the moral landscape of intersubjective relationships. Crucially, the duty to behave in accord with such an ideal creates the cognitive space required to actualize spiritual development and it is through such a performance that people become members of a community of practice.

COMMUNITY CONCERNS

I concentrate both on the formation of a community of practice through the monastic duty to teach and practise meditation and on the experience of individuated ascetic discipline. In so doing, I consider the ways in which the personal process of becoming a monastic is in direct dialogue with the concerns of community living and the broader issues of modernization and cultural change in Thailand. In the community on which this study is based *mae chee* are afforded considerable veneration and respect. However, their involvement in monastic practice and duty is highly qualified and without question they are hierarchically inferior to monks. I argue that the propagation and practice of meditation by *mae chee*, among other factors, is leading to their inclusion as religious professionals within the community, while also maintaining their hierarchical inferiority.

In Chapter 7 I examine the ways in which the inclusion of women within the monastic community is reflected in the emblematic religious practice of alms donations. *Mae chee* in this monastery are debarred from going on the morning alms round. They also donate alms to individual monks and to the monastery, as do laity. However, they receive alms from laity on both an individual basis and as an important part of many rituals. They also handle lay alms donations on behalf of the monastery. By donating alms to monks, *mae chee* appear to reaffirm their status of partial ordination, yet in order for them to be able to receive alms and handle the alms donation on behalf of monks they must see themselves, and be recognized by the laity, as an integral part of the monastic community. I consider the alms donations in detail, questioning how we might understand such gifts. I argue that in their highly qualified involvement in alms donation, *mae chee* mediate between monks and laity in a process of generalized exchange. They understand their donations of alms as both a way of making merit and also a way to cultivate the ethical virtues of generosity (Pali: *dānapāramī*). *Mae chee* understand the practice of receiving alms from the laity as an opportunity to cultivate non-attachment in order to offer a fertile 'field of merit' for lay donors.

In considering *mae chee*'s involvement with religious practice my primary focus is upon women's engagement with particular forms of life rather than the degree to which women's subordination is legitimated through particular practices and institutional structures. I argue that understanding the forms of practice that *mae chee* engage in on their own terms enables insight into the choices and motivations of monastics. The moral imperative to behave mindfully is the result of self-monitoring and entails particular ways of relating to the self, to the body, to emotional responses and thought patterns requiring constant analysis and reinterpretation in the light of religious ideals. This points towards an analysis of the work that such practices do in the formation of subjectivity.

In Chapter 8 I examine the gendered hierarchy of the monastic community in more detail, asking how we might understand women's involvement in practices and institutional structures that appear to reaffirm their subordination. I argue that cultivating the virtues of mindfulness and equanimity should not be understood as a performance of identity, but, rather, as the ongoing experience of shaping the ethical self through ascetic practice. It is through repeated mental and bodily acts that one learns how to be moral. This is highlighted in the understandings of monks and *mae chee*, located within a gendered hierarchical community, of enlightenment as a non-gendered state. I argue that the transformations that we are seeing in the position of *mae chee* in Thai monasticism must be considered with reference to the specific practices that make particular modes and presentations of subjectivity possible. Thus, *mae chee*'s embodiment of the virtues of humility, selflessness and service may be understood as a positive and affirmative way of acting in the world.

To conclude, through a consideration of the preceding ethnography I question what is meant by 'individuality' for renouncers, in what ways the self and the person are distinct and in what ways they may be related. I analyse the ascetic self as it is formed in monastic practice and ask what it is about ascetic practice that may produce a unique or differentiated 'self'. As a consequence of the propagation of *vipassanā* meditation to the laity, ascetic practice is becoming the responsibility of all, without the social and cosmological hierarchy of Thai Buddhism being overtly questioned. At the same time duty, hierarchy and performance are focused upon individual liberation for the monastics with whom I work. I argue that the often powerful experiences of meditation and the changes they effect and are intended to effect within the person are connected to the moral duty of mindful performance, through which monastics cultivate an ascetic interiority, creating the cognitive space in which spiritual development may be actualized. I revisit the scholarship of Dumont, central to academic understandings of renunciation, and I argue that the renouncer has a singular agency, which Dumont fails to problematize: he writes as if renunciation were accomplished once and for all through the act of retreat from the world. I propose that renunciation may fruitfully be considered as an ongoing project irreducible to the moral rules which inform it. As such, I argue that the challenges of ascetic practice are the means by which the religious self is formed.

ASCETICISM IN THE MONASTIC CONTEXT

I interpret the intended shaping of the monastic self through disciplined meditative work in this monastery as a form of ascetic practice. Buddhist monasteries in Thailand vary widely in focus and institutional organization and we must be careful not to assume a necessary correlation between monasticism and asceticism, or indeed between meditation and asceticism, in any given context. Only a small minority of monastics in Thailand are focused on the *vipassanā* meditation that is the central concern of the people on whom this book is based. I do not use the term 'ascetic' to describe all people who 'renounce the world' or become monastics: to be a monastic one does not have to engage in ascetic practices and vice versa. It is not necessarily the case at all that monastics, though they have renounced home, sexual activity and marriage, are necessarily then to be understood as engaging in ascetic practices.

I employ an analysis of 'asceticism' in the Greek sense of '*askesis*', or way of life by which some forms of activity are inhibited, while others are developed, through specific strenuous forms of religious discipline (cf. Brown 1988; Flood 2004; Ishwaran 1999). I understand asceticism to be the disciplined practices and forms of self-regulation that become imperative for practitioners as they cultivate an understanding and experience of what Hick (1995: ix) has termed a 'believed in sacred reality'. The focus of a study of asceticism rests upon the training involved in becoming virtuous: the personal development of particular virtues, more than adherence to moral laws or the avoidance of vice. Freiberger (2006: 6–7) defines asceticism as 'the enduring performance of practices that affect bodily needs for religious purposes'. It is understood as enduring because it is understood as a lifestyle rather than a mode of religious practice (which could be adopted temporarily). It suggests a particular attitude to life and to the futurity of the self: what the practitioner imagines their self to be and the self that is to be realized in the future.

In a comparative analysis of Buddhism, Christianity and Hinduism, Flood (2004) argues that the subjectivity of the ascetic self must be located in accordance with the goals and practices of a religious tradition. 'Claiming that constraints within scriptural traditions form the ascetic self is not simply to give an account of a cultural construction but is also to give an account of the discovery or opening out of an interior world' (Flood 2004: ix). He understands asceticism as the internalization of tradition, in which the ascetic life is shaped in accordance with tradition and tradition is performed through the ascetic body. Flood highlights the necessary paradox of ascetic practice: the eradication of the will through the affirmation of will in ascetic practice (see Nietzsche 1996). He argues that the performance of the ascetic self both looks back to an origin and forward to a future goal firmly located within traditional religious cosmology. For Flood, asceticism entails subjectivity and a self who renounces, but after renunciation the self is expressed through the structures of tradition. 'The ascetic submits her life to a form that transforms it, to a training that changes a person's orientation from the fulfilment of desire to a narrative greater than the self. The ascetic self shapes the narrative of her life to the narrative of tradition' (Flood 2004: 2).

Flood argues that, 'The ascetic conforms to the discipline of the tradition, shapes his or her body into particular cultural forms over time, and thereby appropriates the tradition. This appropriation of tradition is a form of remembrance, the memory of tradition performed through the body, and is also the vehicle for change or transformation' (Flood 2004: 6). The change that Flood speaks of in this context is internal rather than external: it is through submitting to the discipline of a predetermined cultural form external to the ascetic that her body becomes a vehicle for internal transformation. While the willed practice of asceticism seeks its own destruction this is enacted through the performance of tradition.

This highlights the tension identified in the Thai Buddhist context between the intention to eradicate the will through meditative practice and the experience of the dissolution of the will as a result of that practice. I will argue that through ongoing mindful self-examination, the permanent mental articulation of all bodily and mental processes and sensations, the meditator creates a hermeneutic relationship with herself (Foucault 2000b). During the retreat mindful vigilance becomes an ethical imperative, and enlightenment is potentially attainable in the final hours when ideally the purchase of self-identification on the meditator is loosened and, if possible, extinguished. The paradox of the eradication of the will through self-willed practice is addressed through the use of Pali in the retreat context, believed to bring about the spontaneous experience of enlightenment. Meditative attainment then is understood here as the spontaneous extinction of volition and a result of concerted and willed discipline.

Flood's focus is the ascetic self as it appears in historical, textual accounts. His assumption, therefore, must be that textual accounts are faithful representations of cultural practices, and that it is tradition as found in the text that is 'remembered' and performed through ascetic practice. When reading Flood's account we must be aware that the Buddhist textual record may not be wholly divorced from the vested interests of its writers, and that within it specific groups of people or employments of practices may remain muted, without ever being compliant with or resistant to historical representations of power.[5]

---

[5] In basing an analysis on text alone, as does Flood, there is a danger that the illusion of continuity with past tradition may be maintained, such that what has always been done is done now, or, conversely, what is done now is what has always been done. Ascetics from diverse cultural and temporal locations are understood by Flood to affirm the continuity of a cultural past. This being so, the cultural others of Flood's account take current events (though each is presumably at a temporal distance to the other) and subordinate them within the structures of tradition. Flood identifies a contrast between 'tradition' and 'modernity' and thus creates an ideological structure against which to ground the novelty of the modern cultural moment. If textual examples are made to stand for 'what we do now' it is easy to see

Asceticism incorporates the whole realm of methods and disciplines, including fasting, celibacy, obedience as well as formal meditation and monastic duty that are employed in the project of cultivating purity, mindfulness and self-discipline understood by monastics in this context to be necessary for realizing the ultimate truth of 'non-self' in their own bodily concerns. In this monastery, I identify asceticism in the quite extraordinary forms of self-control and self-restraint that are intentionally cultivated by monks and *mae chee*. This is a small group of religious professionals who do not assume that the majority of people will have the opportunity to achieve the specific social, religious and personal goals that they progressively work towards (Olivelle 2006). This distinguishes monastic practice from that of the laity who enter the monastery for given periods of time in order to do intensive meditation retreats. Though such periods may be important and transformative for lay practitioners they are understood by the monastics teaching them to be so because they enable laity to live more harmonious familial lives, to which they will return. Through working towards the cultivation of mindfulness, monastics intend to renounce personal satisfactions in order to better appreciate the *dhamma* (truth) and this is not a focus that they expect to share with the laity (which is not to say that it may not be the case).

'EFFING' THE INEFFABLE

One cannot overestimate the importance of meditation in this monastery. It is the activity around which the entire daily schedule, spatial layout, bureaucratic organization and social interaction of the monastery are centred. It is understood as the central act of life: activities such as listening to music, chatting and entertainment are minimized in order that monastics are not distracted from meditative practice. Meditation is the means by which one comes to understand oneself. It is said that one should try to maintain meditation at all times. The state of mind – mindfulness – cultivated in formal meditation practice should, ideally, develop and become a continuous state of mind in all activity, waking and sleeping. And while few in the monastery feel that they are actually able to maintain this at all times, they recognize it as an achievable goal and something towards which one should strive.

how this reality may then be contrasted with 'modernity' in Flood's work. This comparison creates a friction and contrast where contemporary ascetic practitioners may not necessarily feel one. Flood's conclusion that texts reveal 'how the ascetic self is set within a cosmological tradition that runs against contemporary sensibilities' may itself be the result of his focus on text rather than the reality of contemporary ascetic practice.

The experiences of meditation can be described and identified; they are vivid and emotive and must be made sense of by the experiencer as she makes sense of herself and the changes that she effects, and intends to effect, through meditation practice. Talking about meditation in the monastery is frowned upon. It is considered that learning is by doing, not by talking and there is a limited amount that can be transmitted verbally. Meditation may be understood as a prescribed embodied practice. It is associated with psychological states, such as 'mindfulness', that are the result of physical and mental discipline. And, it may be considered through the terms by which these states and practices are articulated and understood by individuals.

For me as an anthropological fieldworker, experiential knowledge of meditation was of paramount importance if I was to have any understanding of how meditation becomes meaningful and why people commit themselves to what is often a gruelling practice. In order to translate theoretical issues of individuality, renunciation and practice into researchable empirical questions I spent fifteen months in Wat Bonamron and for one year of this time I took ordination as a *mae chee*.

I had some experience of my field site before I began research. While travelling around Southeast Asia at 21 I did a one-month meditation course at the monastery and ordained as a *mae chee* for a subsequent four months, taking a vow of silence for much of this time. As a child my parents had taught me various different meditation techniques and our family holidays were often organized around meditation retreats in a variety of traditions. Thus, when I first entered the monastery I already had some experience of meditation and the tenets of Buddhism. I took ordination at this time because I saw it as a way of developing my meditation practice and I disrobed in order to complete my undergraduate degree. My later research work on meditation presented a way of returning to the monastery and taking ordination for longer.

Prior to embarking upon my first serious, long-term, research I imagined that ordination and my life as a *mae chee* would be straightforward. Having had a brief flirtation with ordination a few years previously, I naively thought that I knew what it entailed. However, nothing prepared me for the effect and challenges of the relative longevity of my second ordination period. My ordination as a *mae chee* was both central to my research and a monumental personal commitment. It was understood by people in the field and by me as a demonstration of respect for monasticism and the monastic project.[6] My religious position was unambiguous. I was a

---

[6] I do not want to suggest that an ethnographic study of religion by the uninitiated would be impossible or insufficient, only that this approach was fitting for me.

Buddhist and I was committed to the ordination and meditation. It was known in the monastery that my ordination would be limited to one year[7] and that I would be doing anthropological research. My interest lay in finding a way to understand not only the monastic code, but also the practices, patterns, responses and experiences of monasticism: to know why people do what they do, to describe human action as it is variously motivated, the cognitive force of meditation as well as the ascetic interiority engendered by monastic duty and discipline.

Through a combination of extensive participation, socialization and formal and informal interviews I began to understand how monastics come to find their meditation practice engaging. As a *mae chee* my explicit duty was to offer an example of monastic piety for the laity and to act as daughter to senior monks and *mae chee*. Learning what was appropriate in my behaviour with particular people was also central to learning about what it means to be a monastic in Thailand. It was through this process of 'gradual familiarization' (Hastrup and Hervik 1994: 7) that I learnt how to act and behave sensitively and become aware of the feelings of those around me.

The emphasis placed upon the experiential dimension of meditation makes it a particularly thorny challenge for anthropology: in many ways research about meditation is an attempt to 'eff' the ineffable. In translating the daily instructions of the meditation teacher I was struck by the number of questions that were met with responses such as 'acknowledge' or 'meditate and you will know'. Houtman found that because of similar strictures in a Burmese meditation centre, cultivating social contacts was difficult. Houtman makes the further point that, in comparison with a monastery not focused on meditation, in the meditation centre the pursuit of a very limited type of knowledge was encouraged:

> In the monastery my every question was taken seriously by the monks, but in the meditation centre questions about the organisation of the centre, and the way people experienced meditation, were all considered tangential to the knowledge they thought I *should* be seeking – 'If you meditate yourself you will find all answers to your questions'. (1990: 131)

---

[7] Temporary ordination is common in Thailand and remains an important part of the life cycle of most men. As a cultural ideal every Thai Buddhist man should ordain as a monk as a rite of passage between adolescence and marriage, usually for one *phansa*, or Buddhist Lent of three months, during the rainy season (Tambiah 1970). Men at this age or later are granted paid leave from government employment in order to ordain temporarily. Both monk and *mae chee* ordination are considered as temporary in the first instance, even if the ordinand remains in the robes for a lifetime. This is fitting with the Buddhist principle that all things are impermanent.

The knowledge engendered by meditation is highly valued and considered the only appropriate area of enquiry for meditation students: 'While in the monastery knowledge can be received in a social context and transmitted between people, in the meditation centre knowledge is not conceived in its "received" form but only as an experiential knowledge derived from lengthy private dedicated "work"' (Houtman 1990: 156). By choosing to ordain and practise meditation I experienced the effects of religious practice on my own feelings and sense of self. Long-term participant observation enables the anthropologist to think about a multiplicity of bodily practices in order to examine cultural processes of physical learning. This emphasizes 'a mode of fieldwork that focuses on the mediations of corporeal experience and that locates what has been called "the mind" ... in the body' (Fernandez and Herzfeld 1998: 110). I suggest that, while being careful not to generalize from the individual to the collective, the anthropologist who wholeheartedly participates in cultural practice can draw on such experiences when reflecting on their stated impact for other people. As Luhrmann writes,

> often human experience is stimulated in similar ways by similar activity. Being deprived of food in an initiation ceremony, undergoing group-led imaginative 'journeys', dancing until exhausted in a group ritual – all these have a significant subjective impact upon the participants, and some features of the subjective response to each will be common to many. (1989: 14–15)

Through one's own involvement one can begin to understand what others may have been experiencing. Without resorting to assumptions about mental actions one may cautiously develop some awareness of the psychological landscape in which assertions are made.

In order to understand what it is like to be a monastic and the way monastic identity is formed through ascetic practice it was necessary for me to ordain *and* to practise. A combination of in-depth and long-term participant observation with formalized research methods provided me with abundant and varied data on the lives of renunciates. As well as ordaining, meditating, striving to cut attachment to a sense of self, I busied myself conducting surveys, employing questionnaires, doing formal and informal interviews, collecting life-histories, documenting rituals, researching the meaning of symbols, writing everything down in notebooks of varying sizes, and so on. I undertook regular intensive meditation retreats, as all monastics do in Wat Bonamron, going for up to five days without sleep, and cultivating mindfulness, the state of mind sought in meditation. The research incorporated the narratives and life stories of members of the monastic community, a group of people seldom accessible to research because of the community's focus on meditation and monastic detachment from lay concerns. I was able to explore understandings about the propagation of meditation to the laity, gender hierarchy and the changing roles of *mae chee*, as well as engaging directly with the duties and responsibilities of a *mae chee* myself: I had shaved my head, renounced the world and strove in all things to cut attachment to a sense of self, as do all monks and *mae chee* within the community.

Throughout fieldwork I was fully involved in life at Wat Bonamron, performing my daily monastic duties and participating in rituals as a monastic. I would wake at 4 a.m., meditate or chant for two hours before breakfast, work in the office during the morning giving information and meditation instruction to foreigners. I observed fast for eighteen hours a day (from noon until 6 a.m.) and conditioned myself to sleep for six hours a night. I translated the Abbot's meditation teaching for foreigners during the daily meeting between teacher and meditation students. I received alms from the laity and donated alms to the monastery and monks.[8] I tried to maintain six hours of daily meditation practice when not on retreat. I also assisted in the meditation retreats of large groups of Thai laity, usually comprising school children, university students or work colleagues. My duty was to speak on the microphone about the benefits of meditation. At such times my status as a young scholar from Cambridge was always emphasized and it was suggested that my level of education at a renowned institution and my ordination directly resulted from my meditation practice. I was thus endowed with symbolic capital that reflected well on the monastery, the community and the monastery's project to teach meditation to large numbers of people.

During fieldwork I participated in numerous meditation retreats both as a personal practice and that I might develop more understanding about meditation. Initially, this process was greatly aided by personal conviction and faith in the technique and the teacher. Intensive embodied practice of this sort provided a way of understanding abstract concepts of 'truth' in the field while remaining 'true' to the roles of *mae chee* and meditator adopted in the field: alternative 'me's' in relation to the cultural world I had come to inhabit. Through executing my duties to behave impeccably, practise meditation and observe monastic hierarchy, I was taught how to be a *mae chee*.[9]

---

[8] For a discussion on the qualified involvement of *mae chee* in giving and receiving alms see Chapter 7.
[9] On a similar 'action-oriented pedagogy' in Sri Lankan Buddhism see Samuels (2004).

My fieldwork was distinctive in that I committed myself to ordination as a Buddhist nun and to intensive meditation practice. However, my experience of being a *mae chee* was coloured by my reasons for ordaining and my experiences of meditation in the past. I understood the different meditation techniques that I had learnt from an early age as options that I could draw upon depending on how I felt and this mix and match approach to meditative practice was very different to the belief in the monastery that *vipassanā* meditation is the only path to enlightenment. This presented a clear contrast between my own understandings of meditation and those of the people around me. Surprisingly, given the hybridity of the Thai religious landscape (examined in the next chapter), I never encountered monks or *mae chee* in the monastery engaging in or promoting any other meditative techniques. While other techniques, traditions and religions were discussed they were understood to be inferior to the practice of *vipassanā* and it was thought that, as such, practising them would be a waste of time. Even common Thai Buddhist meditations such as *samatha*[10] techniques were discouraged in discussions with meditation students. In contrast, while I had practised *vipassanā* intensively for five years I had not conceived of this to be at the exclusion of other possible techniques on anything other than a temporary basis.

Although my fieldwork involved a heavily participant form of participant observation it had limits: it was informed by my doubts as to whether or not I could remain as a *mae chee*; that these appeared as doubt is indicative of the degree to which I committed myself to participating as a *mae chee*. Thus, my doubts were less a question of belief – whether or not meditation 'works', whether the principles of Buddhism are true – than a question of my own commitment to Buddhist monasticism as a vocation.

For me, the greatest trial of the fieldwork period was lack of exercise. Prohibition on exercise is intended to enable monastics to cut attachment to the body. Prior to entering the monastery I was surfing and dancing regularly and I found that after a number of months of ordination without exercise my body became sluggish, my skin became sallow and I had very low energy. Furthermore, though it is prohibited to eat solid food after noon,[11] every evening a group of *mae chee* and I would have sweet tea with condensed milk. By the end of my ordination my blood sugar was

---

[10] The effect of *samatha* meditation is to calm the mind and develop one-pointed awareness and concentration. It is often associated with the development of supernormal powers.

[11] The monastic precept to refrain from eating at wrong times prohibits consuming solid foods after noon.

fluctuating wildly and I frequently felt hypoglycaemic. When I expressed concern about my health to a *mae chee* the same age as me, she responded that if we were crippled later in life it would not matter because we would have no attachment to our physical form; I was not so convinced. I tried to improve my physical condition by doing the exercise that *is* appropriate for monastics. I swept the paths of the monastery vigorously and hand washed my robes and towels more than I needed to. Towels were particularly useful because once wet they took effort to lift. When I disrobed I went on holiday in the south of Thailand. I relished the sheer physicality of Frisbee, swimming in the sea, the sun on my skin and eating green vegetables regularly. But how I perceived my own and other people's bodies changed dramatically during fieldwork. I was given a photographic atlas of the body as a meditative tool to assist me in cutting attachment to the body. At first I found the images of dissected corpses upsetting but soon I became fascinated by the construction of the human body and the ways in which the pictures on the pages corresponded to my own imagining of my body. In a short time this coloured my perception of other people as well: I would be aware that their skull was made up of plates that meshed together, or that with a turn of the head countless tendons and muscles were activated in the neck. I was encouraged, and was keen, to view the corpses at funerals I attended.[12] In ways I had never experienced before I became imaginatively aware of not only other people's mortality but my own also. In the context of the meditation this was a fascinating experience: I felt as though I was experiencing and accepting the Buddhist principles of non-self, impermanence and suffering (*anattā, anicca, dukkha*) in my own self-perception.

If we assume that the anthropologist is affected or changed by the process of participant observation this does not necessarily suggest a before and after, so often seen in the narrative structures of entry stories such as the flight from the cock fight immortalized by Geertz (1973). As Beatty has argued (1999), such epiphanic immersion stories do nothing to hint at the confusion and incompleteness of formative processes of participation. My emotional commitment to ordination positioned me in relation to monastics and laity but my ultimate withdrawal from the monastic project, my inability to understand my doubts about my vocation and *vipassanā* as my sole practice as a site for meditative awareness, in some ways placed me in opposition to people in the monastery. In different ways, then, during fieldwork, I both shared in and resisted religious experience. However,

---

[12] In this monastery this meditation technique (*asubha kammaṭṭhāna*) is used as an aspect of *vipassanā*. See Klima (2002) for an interesting discussion of *asubha kammaṭṭhāna*.

this ambivalence was fruitful and interesting in and of itself and my involvement in the monastery, robes and all, led to ways of understanding both my self and monasticism through the learning process of fieldwork.

This book focuses on the experience of monasticism for monks and *mae chee* as they practise and teach meditation. It is concerned with the processes by which ascetic discipline creates meaning in the context of a rapidly developing Thailand. In order to open up a theoretical consideration of asceticism, the self and the reform and revival of religious practices, I address a variety of issues currently at the fore of the anthropology of religion and ethics: the construction of identity; the processes by which the religious self is formed; the personal significance of religious practice for practitioners; the relationship between men and women and the ways in which gender differences are negotiated and negated in a community where religious hierarchy is clearly inscribed in bodily practice. Drawing on a broad spectrum of anthropological literature I situate the popularity of meditation practice in Thailand within trends of increasingly syncretized and secularized Buddhist popularity. It is through the shifting and situated negotiation of the ascetic self in the contemporary context that ascetic practice finds its significance: that is, how it becomes meaningful for people.

CHAPTER 2

Meditation and religious reform

In contemporary Thai Buddhism there is massive variation in the foci of Buddhist practice. While some monastic and lay organizations focus on ascetic discipline, others focus on ritual practices, social welfare projects or wealth creation. In Thailand modernist Buddhist movements have elaborated Buddhist responsibilities as both a social concern and a personal responsibility of purification. Furthermore, with the proliferation of practices and foci of monastics and laity it is possible for practitioners to incorporate diverse perspectives and motivations into their understanding of Thai Buddhism. This book is an analysis of the cultural elaborations of *vipassanā* meditation and an examination of the ways in which this specific practice has implicated monastic subjectivity and community at this historical juncture. The burgeoning popularity of *vipassanā* meditation as a practice available to all people, lay or monastic, is fast becoming a verifying technique by which people seek and often find the experiences of the religious tenets of impermanence, suffering and non-self. The focus of some monasteries on *vipassanā* propagation is a recent development in Thai Buddhism and has occurred in tandem with hybrid processes of reform, localism and commoditization. In this chapter, I locate the monastery on which this book is based in the history of the Thai *vipassanā* meditation movement and the broader reformist landscape that has characterized recent decades of religious change.

The nationwide movement to popularize meditation among both monastics and laity was instigated by Phra Phimolatham (1903–89) in the 1950s. Phra Phimolatham was ecclesiastical minister of the interior and the abbot of Wat Mahathat,[1] the largest monastery in the country and the principal monastery of the Mahanikai sect. The *vipassanā* technique that Phra Phimolatham promoted was developed by the renowned Burmese

---

[1] This is the more commonly used abbreviated name of Wat Mahathat Yuwarajarangsarit Rajaworamahavihara.

meditation master Mahasi Sayadaw (1904–82).[2] Phimolatham travelled to Burma more than a dozen times in his attempts to introduce the Burmese meditation technique and focus on *Abhidhamma*[3] study to Thailand (Jordt 2008; see Jordt 2007b for the development of the Burmese practice during the U Nu period). Though it was developed by the time of Buddhaghosa in AD 500 as an orthodox method for the attainment of enlightenment, it was only during the twentieth century that *vipassanā* became widely available in its current form. Mahasi Sayadaw's technique has been widely adopted in Thailand, Sri Lanka[4] and Nepal. Mahasi Sayadaw emphasized the importance of the *Mahāsatipaṭṭhāna Sutta* on which the practice is based (see Nyanaponika 1973; Sayadaw 1971; Sayadaw 2000; Van Esterik 1977). The technique accords with the canonical *satipaṭṭhāna* discourses on the Four Foundations of Mindfulness (Nyanaponika 1973: 61; Silananda 1990; Soma 1999 [1941]: 43). Drawing his method from the canon, rather than traditional practices within Buddhism, Mahasi Sayadaw instigated a modern meditation movement that claimed its antecedent roots in the canonical word of the Buddha. It was this practice that inspired Phra Phimolatham to promote *vipassanā* in Thailand. As we shall see, his efforts were deeply influenced by the conflicting forces of sectarianism and centralization that crosscut Thai Buddhism at the time.

There was massive variance in doctrinal and monastic practice throughout Thailand prior to the twentieth century (Tiyavanich 1997: 3), and 'Each abbot was to a large extent master of his own realm ... The quality of monastic leadership in combination with the attention the monastery received from the community determined its prosperity and influence' (Reynolds 1972: 26). During the nineteenth and early twentieth centuries, the kings of the Chakri dynasty established themselves through increased centralization and absolutism. In a politicized move and in response to what he saw as the lax practices of the existing sangha, Mongkut founded the Thammayut sect in 1830, which was subsequently given recognition and autonomy as part of the national sangha in the reign of King Chulalongkorn (1868–1910).[5] The order emphasized mastery of the *vinaya* and Pali studies.

---

[2] See Silanandabhivumsa (1982) for a bibliography of Mahasi Sayadaw (see also Kornfield 1993 [1977]).
[3] The third 'basket' of the *Tipiṭaka*; Buddhist philosophy and psychology; metaphysical teachings which deal with the ultimate nature of things.
[4] The practice was introduced to Sri Lanka from Burma in 1955 by Prime Minister Sir John Kotelawala at a time when all three governments were preparing to celebrate the twenty-five hundredth anniversary of the death of the Buddha (Gombrich and Obeyesekere 1988: 238).
[5] Thammayut means 'those adhering strictly to the monastic discipline'. The term 'Mahanikai', meaning the 'large order' of monks, was coined in response to the establishment of the Thammayut order to refer to the existing sangha. Mongkut ruled as King Maha Mongkut (Rama IV) 1851–68.

Lay people performed duties such as distributing monks' food, cleaning living quarters and washing robes. Mongkut introduced a new way of wearing the robe, new ordination rituals, new pronunciation of Pali scriptural language, new routines and new religious days (Tiyavanich 1997: 6). The greater emphasis on Pali studies came at the expense of practices such as meditation which he viewed as mystical, asserting that 'true religion was a matter of rational doctrine and belief' (Tiyavanich 1997: 6). Tiyavanich (1997: 7) suggests that Mongkut's interpretation of religion was heavily influenced by Christian missionaries' judgments that traditional Buddhism was too superstitious. Mongkut sought to demythologize the *dhamma* and emphasize its compatibility with empirical science. His Thammayut monks were to preach in the vernacular as part of a missionizing project, each of them acting as 'exemplars of disciplined conduct, and they would be the agents who would transform the religion among monks and laity alike' (Tambiah 1984: 161).[6]

Mongkut's 'rationalizing' and 'reforming' work was further developed by his son Wachirayan, who in the time of King Chulalongkorn, his half-brother, became the abbot of Wat Bovonniwet, head of the Thammayut sect, and Supreme Patriarch of the sangha. Wachirayan too sought to educate the laity and worked with King Chulalongkorn in a programme to promote primary education through monasteries. In order to do this it was necessary to attempt to unify the national sangha, which was not tightly centralized in precept or practice, monasteries often observing heterogeneous practices in line with local or regional traditions. The Sangha Act of 1902 promoted the Thai sangha as a national hierarchy controlled from Bangkok and modelled upon the development of a centralized patrimonial-bureaucratic structure of provincial administration (Tambiah 1984: 162).[7] Whereas previously no one tradition had dominated, now it was intended that Buddhist monks become part of a religious hierarchy, having to adhere to standard texts and practices.[8] Wachirayan also created a monastic

---

[6] As we shall see, a distinction between 'rational' and 'superstitious' has remained unclear in practice ever since.
[7] As Tambiah writes, 'The Thammayut brand of central Thai Buddhism was to be the criterion of pure Buddhism, and regional traditions of Buddhist practice, worship, and identity were to be obliterated in favour of a Bangkok orthodoxy and of central Thai language as against variant languages, such as the Tai Yuan of the North and its associated script' (1984: 162).
[8] Of course, there were oppositional responses to the process of unification. I will mention only one monk here as his presence extends beyond the politics of history and is felt in the monastery today. Phra Siwichai (1878–1937), a renowned *khru ba* ('esteemed teacher') from Northern Thailand, defied the Bangkok hierarchy and using his massive popularity and charismatic qualities presented a significant, if temporary, challenge to the project of national sangha unification. He challenged the

education system and his interpretations of Pali canonical works in Central Thai language were printed as authoritative.⁹ The system still exists today and is based on degrees, examinations and ranks in the sangha hierarchy. 'It defines the ideal Buddhist monk as one who observes strict monastic rules, has mastered Wachirayan's texts, teaches in Bangkok Thai, carries out administrative duties, observes holy days, and performs religious ritual' (Tiyavanich 1997: 9). The subsequent 1941 Sangha Act may be seen as a bid to bring the sangha into line with the then political system. Through the agencies of monastic schools and centrally administered exams, titled ecclesiastical positions and the royal monasteries of both the Thammayut and Mahanikai sects, attempts were made to unify the sangha under the control of the official sangha centred in Bangkok.

The degree to which centralization was successfully achieved has been questioned by some scholars. McDaniel (2006a; 2008) demonstrates that elite reform movements had influenced Buddhism since the thirteenth century: 'Siamese kings and high-ranking monks saw it as their duty to collect and edit Buddhist texts, rewrite Buddhist history, purge the community of monks (sangha) or corrupt persons, and rein in renegade

---

assertion that a monk required entitlement from the national sangha before he was able to instruct and ordain novices, claiming that even though he had not received the appropriate entitlement from the sangha, he ordained noviciates according to the pristine tradition of the Buddha, thereby asserting an authoritative spiritual lineage for himself which ran contra to that of the official sangha. He was accused by the national sangha of not complying with government regulations, not discouraging rumours of his supranormal powers and for encouraging schism. However, aware of Siwichai's massive popularity the Bangkok authorities absolved him of all charges on two occasions. The first time he returned from the trial to a hero's welcome. As Thompson writes, 'A crowd of ten thousand gave the hero-priest an enthusiastic welcome, all nationalities vying with each other to do him honor. He walked on a carpet made of the silk head-dresses of his Shan advisers, who carried him over the muddiest passages' (1941: 642, cited in Tambiah 1984: 304). The second time he signed an agreement that he would abide by the Sangha Act of 1902. After this he focused his energies on raising money and building projects, including the road from Chiang Mai to Wat Doi Suthep, a famous temple standing on the mountain overlooking the city (for more detailed studies of Khru Ba Siwichai see Keyes 1981; Tambiah 1984). Today this massive achievement of fundraising and labour mobilization is credited to Siwichai's personal power as a result of his ascetic practice, and he is widely considered to be an *arahant* (an enlightened person who has eradicated defilements). As a young novice the founder of Wat Bonamron worked on the road-building project, itself something that is considered to be highly meritorious. A statue of Khru Ba Siwichai stands next to the *stūpa* (a mound-like structure that usually contains Buddhist relics) in the grounds of the monastery and is solicited with gifts and prayers by monastics and laity in the early morning.

⁹ One of the greatest obstacles to King Chulalongkorn's consolidation of power was the linguistic diversity within the borders of Siam. Bangkok Thai became the national language and a 'focus of identification for the modern Thai state' (Tiyavanich 1997: 7). Later, the promotion of Central Thai during the first regime of Prime Minister Luang Phibunsongkhram (1938–44) still required enforcement as large numbers of people considered, and still do consider, their domestic language to be other than Central Thai (Diller 2002). This is a fine example of the project of national culture and nation building masking cultural and ethnic heterogeneity (Smalley 1988: 246). Nonetheless, the standardized form of Central Thai is widely held as a symbol of national unity.

independent-minded practitioners' (2006a: 102). While such techniques had become more efficient and widespread under the Chakri kings, he questions the efficacy of their education policies. He demonstrates that, despite the royally stated focus on the Pali Canon, there is no evidence to suggest that it was available to the majority of Thais in or prior to 1902 (McDaniel 2006a: 103). The Canon was rarely found as a set in one monastery and there has never been agreement on the authoritative parts of the Canon at any point in Thai history (McDaniel 2008: 102–3). He argues that centralist policies did not present a radical breach with earlier forms of education, that they were not effectively carried out in the rural north and northeast, and that education remained idiosyncratic and to a large extent influenced by the charisma of local monks. Although regional monasteries have pledged allegiance to the Thai government in Bangkok since the early twentieth century, they have also been able to maintain diverse local pedagogical traditions (McDaniel 2008: 92).[10]

It was in the context of a fierce rivalry between the Mahanikai and Thammayut sects that a national campaign to promote *vipassanā* in Thailand was introduced. Tambiah tells us that rivalry between the Mahanikai and Thammayut sects crystallized in the vying for ecclesiastical posts as a consequence of the resultant enactment of an elected Ecclesiastical Assembly and Ecclesiastical Cabinet under the control of a Supreme Patriarch, who was to be appointed by the king (Tambiah 1984: 166). This is clearly illustrated in the rivalry between Phra Phimolatham and Somdet Phra Mahawirawong of Thammayut affiliation. Both sought to sponsor and promote meditation but the authoritarian Prime Minister Sarit Thanarat and his military government construed the popularity of the Mahanikai meditation programme as a political threat and Phra Phimolatham's activities as 'politically subversive' (Tambiah 1976: 260–1). Phra Phimolatham was disrobed and incarcerated in 1955 and the previous democratic 1941 Act was replaced by the authoritarian Sangha Act of 1962, which gave power to the Supreme Patriarch and his advisors in the Council of Elders (Mahatherasamakhom), the position of Supreme Patriarch now being inhabited by Phimolatham's Thammayut rival,

---

[10] McDaniel proposes an examination of 'curricula' as an interpretive category for the history of religions. He suggests that a curriculum both reacts to and constitutes cultural and historical forces. In so doing he is able to demonstrate that monastic educators are not passively influenced by centralized government forces but are active agents 'who often operate outside and in direct opposition to ideological nation-building coercion' (2008: 18). In tracing the history of curricula, textual practices, pedagogical methods, local rituals and continuities in monastic education throughout the period he is able to demonstrate that dichotomies between engaged/ascetic, scholarly/magic, urban/forest, while important at the level of discourse were never clearly drawn in practice.

Somdet Phra Mahawirawong. However, by this time many monasteries around the country had become satellite meditation 'branches' of Wat Mahathat. The popularization of meditation continued in the 1970s and Phra Thepsiddhimuni continued the work of Phra Phimolatham.

Tambiah tells us that the promotion of the meditation movement was achieved through the 'enlisting of numerous urban and village *wat* to teach meditation not only to monks and nuns but also, and perhaps more importantly, to pious laymen of all ages and occupations' (1984: 167). The promotion of *vipassanā* meditation to the laity was presented as a way to find relief from worldly concerns by enjoying the benefits of meditative exercise. Tambiah tells us that from its inception the participation of laity in the programme was substantial and that with time laity came to outnumber monks (Tambiah 1976: 259). The intensification of meditation for the laity was linked to developments in standards of literacy and education and the translation of Pali texts into Thai, as well as the development of an urban middle class. Meditation instruction was given at monasteries usually, though not always, by monks, and collective meditation sittings became increasingly popular. Tambiah highlights the effect that this had upon the religiosity of the laity:

> In a sense, then, when increasing numbers of laymen observe the eight or ten precepts on *wan phra*, and congregate at *wat* for meditational sittings, the layman–monk distinction as portraying totally different regimes and styles of life is blurred. Nevertheless, there is a striking contrast between the forest ascetic monk totally devoted to meditation and the search for liberation on the one hand, and on the other hand the educated informed layman practicing occasional meditation to lend him some tranquillity and detachment from the cares, stresses, and involvements of a layman's life in the world. (1984: 168)

The evangelism of those involved in the meditation movement in the 1970s sought to extend lay involvement in Buddhism. In her study of urban monastic organization in central Thailand, Bunnag suggests that in Ayutthaya in 1966–7 *vipassanā* was less highly regarded than the study of Pali texts because success within the former was the less tangible (1973: 54). Less than one-third of her monastic informants in Ayutthaya reported an interest in *vipassanā* practice and she reports that it was regarded as an activity more appropriate to *mae chee*, monks who practised magic and *thudong* monks (Bunnag 1973: 54).[11] However, she notes that,

---

[11] The *thudong* tradition celebrates the forest and wandering monks. It places emphasis on meditation and ascetic practice over scholarly pursuits. On this see Tiyavanich 1997.

there is some evidence of a trend towards extending the *bhikkhu*'s pastoral role, by encouraging the householder to take a more active part in religious activities. One manifestation of this new emphasis is that some monks are starting classes to teach laymen how to meditate, as it is felt to be easier for them than scriptural study. This ruling also applies to mae chi or nuns who are encouraged to join these meditation courses, some of which are set up by *bhikkhus* sent by the Department of Religious Affairs from the Buddhist Universities in Bangkok. (1973: 54, fn. 7)

We can see from Bunnag's account that at its inception the *vipassanā* movement was considered most appropriate for *mae chee* and monks 'peripheral' to the central sangha administration. Subsequent developments in the 1970s made *vipassanā* a more visible landmark on the Thai religious landscape.

During the 1970s the Mahachulalongkornrajavidyalaya Buddhist university at Wat Mahathat began to hold lectures on meditation and the *Abhidhamma* for Thai and foreign laity and monks (Van Esterik 1977: 56). Tambiah tells us that the sessions that he attended were 'addressed solely to a lay audience, which was orderly, urban, educated, and of middle-class status' (1984: 178). An important aspect of the Burmese practice, which accounted for its appeal among intellectual and elite Thai laity, was the practice of combining it with the study of *Abhidhamma*. The *Abhidhamma* is a section of the Theravāda Buddhist canon that focuses on the psychological nature of the individual and its links with actions and potentials. Mastery of the *Abhidhamma* is understood to be a mark of ethical and social prestige. The *Abhidhamma Jotika* handbook is used at the central monastic universities and is designed as a written guide to oral expositions that incorporate 'Western' science and Buddhist notions of birth and death (McDaniel 2008: 245). Urban meditation movements of the 1970s responded to an environment that involved Western education and scientific ideology, the meditation groups modelling themselves as 'research centres' and *Abhidhamma* 'foundations'.

One significant attribute of the *vipassanā* meditation propagated by Wat Mahathat and its branch monasteries around the country was the ease and safety with which it could be practised independently by laity after a relatively short period of intensive training. Previously, within Thai Buddhism emphasis had been placed on the efficacy of *samatha* meditation in the development of magico-religious powers and transformation. In the promotion of *vipassanā* since the 1950s Wat Mahathat and its satellites argued that *vipassanā* is farther-reaching and easier to control than *samatha* meditation. The effect of *samatha* meditation is to calm the mind and develop one-pointed awareness and concentration but, as the practitioner continues, he or she will pass through increasingly deep 'absorptions' (*jhānas*) attained through the development of concentration (*samādhi*) and through entering these trance-like states it is possible to develop powers such as clairvoyance, transubstantiation, clairaudience, and so on. Those who are believed to have attained such powers are given great respect. Writing in 1970, Spiro suggested that it was precisely these powers, cultivated by monks, that were respected in Burma: 'It is the supernatural products of meditation which they view as holy and for which they venerate monastic meditators who, allegedly, have achieved these supernormal states' (1970: 51 fn. 21). It was considered that progress in this form of meditation required intensive practice over a period of years under the constant supervision of a meditation master (see Gombrich and Obeyesekere 1988: 237). The practitioner might have numerous experiences of visions, sensations and extra-normal phenomena, which can be frightening and dangerous without the guidance of an experienced teacher. Many monastics in Thailand are able to recount stories of people they know who have gone into meditative absorptions and 'got lost'. This, coupled with the traditional inclusiveness of ascetic discipline within renunciate communities, made it very difficult for meditation to be accessible to many lay people.

Thus, the propagation of meditation by the Mahanikai sect was presented as a move away from 'esoteric' meditative practices towards a more 'rational' and 'authentic' practice for salvation, available to monastics and laity. In the promotion of *vipassanā* as against *samatha* it was argued that as meditative power increases in *samatha* practice so does the practitioner's attachment to *jhanic* absorption. In Spiro's words, 'The meditator prefers to perpetuate his *jhanic* pleasures rather than proceed to *nibbana*' (1970: 51). The deep levels of concentration (*samādhi*) developed through *samatha* meditation are not necessarily beneficial for the *vipassanā* practitioner. The principle of *vipassanā* is to develop awareness of the conditions of the body and the mind in the present moment, thereby gaining insight. This is done by maintaining a level of mindful awareness in which 'one attends to, and is self-consciously aware – in the minutest detail – of one's every act, thought, sensation and emotion' (Spiro 1970: 51). Thus, the propagation of meditation in the 1970s widened the gap between different meditation techniques.

Urban lay practitioners found a response to 'the materialistic, scientific theory of life' (Van Esterik 1977: 55) through the combination of *Abhidhamma* and meditation while remaining grounded in their own religious tradition. However, the concerns of these groups to find a Buddhist intellectual response to Western Scientific theory were not necessarily mirrored by the interests of village and rural meditators (Van Esterik

1977: 46). In the 1970s lay meditation practitioners in the village where Van Esterik conducted his research made two kinds of claims: first, as a result of the Thai political and religious elite demonstrating that meditation was an appropriate practice for the laity, village lay men were able to reveal their own worth by engaging in the valued practice of meditation, traditionally associated with monks; and, second, lay meditators also claimed supernormal or magical powers as a result of their practice. 'They have associated themselves with the intellectual *vipassanā* and *Abhidhamma* movement but they have also accepted the traditional ritualistic Samadhi meditation and the powers as one major goal of their practice' (Van Esterik 1977: 62).

It is worth saying a few words about the effect that the popularity of *vipassanā* meditation had on peripatetic (*thudong*) monks and lay interest in other types of meditation practice. Tiyavanich (1997: 287) cites Phra Ajharn Thet's assertion that it was only with the success of this movement that the meditation practice of Thammayut *thudong* monks became popular, whereas previously their practice had been viewed as an insignificant part of the order. With the success of the popularization of *vipassanā* practice by the Mahanikai order, the Thammayut order began to celebrate the forest meditation masters; thus different types of meditation within Thai Buddhism began to gain followers as never before. Whereas at the turn of the century ascetic monks and practice were perceived by many educated urbanites as 'backward, uncivilized, old-fashioned, and standing in the way of westernization and modernization' (Tiyavanich 1997: 286), by the 1960s they had become firmly located within the centralized sangha bureaucracy, and by the 1970s the royal family had visited some of the more famous forest monks, thereby giving them and their practice popularity nationwide. 'Within less than a century, *thudong* monks had risen from the bottom of the national sangha hierarchy to the top, and from being despised as vagabonds (by urban elites) to being venerated as saints' (Tiyavanich 1997: 288).[12]

---

[12] Whereas previously a diversity of regional Buddhist traditions had flourished, the bid for centralization and administrative control decreed many of the more peripatetic and meditative aspects of Buddhism, traditionally associated with the forest ascetic tradition, to be inauthentic. The forest-monk tradition was partially co-opted by Mongkut's reformist Thammayut sect and some of its adherents were thereby incorporated within the sangha establishment. At the same time, however, the formation of a national sangha hierarchy and the bureaucratization emanating from Bangkok provided no place for forest monks who did not conform to either side of the two major divisions of the Thai sangha. As Tambiah notes, the Sangha Act of 1902 does not appear to have given forest monks any administrative recognition: 'The act changed the previous central division of the forest-monks into a central geographical division of the Mahanikai sect; thereafter, until today, the forest-monks have not enjoyed a separate administrative recognition in either the Mahanikai or Thammayut sects' (1984: 71).

Furthermore, the distinction between 'science' and 'superstition' was rarely maintained in practice. For example, the forest monks Phra Ajharn Man Bhuridatto and Phra Ajharn Sao Kantasilo are often portrayed as symbols of authenticity who did not concern themselves with scholarship, magic or rituals, and yet, as McDaniel (2006a: 105–6) points out, they are significantly associated with both the state centralization project and the marketplace of amulets and fortune-telling.

These wandering teachers were seen as reformers and purveyors of a rational, canonical Buddhism, and their popularity was due to widespread belief in their superior healing powers. They were social activists and serious ascetics. They lived in rural areas, but their lineage and early training were sponsored by royal temples in Bangkok. (2006a: 107)

ALTERNATIVE RELIGIOSITY AND LOCALISM

As we have seen, royal reformist movements that have sought to reorganize and structure the sangha have influenced forms of practice and interpretation of doctrine.[13] We have also seen that this was not a totalizing or uncontested influence and we have focused on some of the dynamic and shifting interpretations and continuities in Buddhist practice on both local and national scales.

The increasing prevalence of meditation practice for the laity and the changing roles of monastics who teach and practise meditation have occurred in tandem with a proliferation of alternative practices and movements. The 'turn to the self' prevalent in many religious movements in the contemporary world demands that we consider the degree to which previously demarcated scholarly distinctions, such as this-worldly and other-worldly, sacred and secular, material and spiritual, are being transgressed by increasingly transnational and modernist discourses and religious movements.[14] In many of these religious developments we see a focus upon capitalist success as reflective of the ongoing religious or spiritual work that the practitioner is doing and their efficacy in cultivating virtues in outlook and subjective experience.[15]

---

[13] See also Jackson (1999) in which he argues that this reorganization mirrored movements in the changing structures of secular power.

[14] For the rise of subjectivized and democratized religious practices in other contexts see Coleman (2006); Heelas (1991; 1992; 1996; 2002); Luhrmann (2009). I hope to show that this 'turn to the self' is also reflected in Thai Buddhism in the increasing emphasis being placed on the interiorization and experience of soteriological Buddhist principles that are increasingly the responsibility of more and more people, monastic and lay, as the meditation movement gains momentum.

[15] In Thailand this move towards the marketplace has been combined with the processes of capitalist and expansionist economics and the mass media. Jackson (1997: 83) demonstrates that with the emergence of new expressions of religiosity, the market has penetrated religion. For example, we see the

The fast-paced social and cultural changes that Thailand has undergone as a result of modernization, urbanization, as well as social and economic migration, have led to analysts exploring questions of the ways in which people maintain meaningful identities and social practices in the face of what has been understood by some as the 'crisis of modernity' (Tanabe and Keyes 2002: 6). It is argued that the 'decentralization of religiosity' (Jackson 1997: 76) and the subsequent decrease in the moral authority of the sangha have led to a questioning of the authority and relevance of mainstream Buddhism and a burgeoning of alternative forms of religiosity, thought to speak more directly to current societal needs.[16]

Buddhism, as well as being closely associated with Thai national identity in the minds of Thai people, is an important part of Thailand's self-presentation to outsiders. Today meditation and Buddhism are incorporated into the tourism project of the Thai government as a presentation of the modern state and nationalism. Grounding the nation on the traditions and practices of Buddhism as signifiers of authenticity, meditation is presented as an attractive, accessible and authentically Thai experience for foreign and Thai tourists. The Tourism Authority of Thailand now presents meditation as 'one of the most popular aspects of Buddhism, [it] is practiced regularly by numerous Thai as a means of promoting inner peace and happiness. Visitors, too, can learn the fundamentals of this practice at several centres in Bangkok and elsewhere in the country' (TAT 2004). Along with other tourist activities such as cookery courses, massage courses and treks to the hill tribes, meditation is being encouraged as a distinctly Thai experience. For example, an article in TAT's E-Magazine states that,

---

'commodification of religion' leading to individualization (Jackson 1997) and the commercialization of Buddhism (Pattana 2005a: 461), clearly in the phenomenally popular Thammakaai movement (Swearer 1991; McCargo 2004). In 1988 this massively wealthy movement won an award from the Business Management Association of Thailand for its religious market planning strategies. Taylor argues that the Thammakaai movement has gained massive support because it 'provides a constructed hetero-space for an exclusive (re-) disciplined community in a (post-) modern context where a sense of community nowadays is much-needed' (2001: 140). The Thammakaai movement, which claims 100,000 members, most of whom are urban-based and middle-class, is an explicitly modernist movement that engages with both political liberalism and domestic capitalism.

[16] For example, Phothirak set up Santi Asoke, an independent ascetic Buddhist movement, in the 1970s. He argued that his authority for doing so derived from Buddhist scriptures and as such state sanction was neither necessary nor relevant. In the 1980s Santi Asoke became the focus of much debate in Thailand about the legality of Phothirak's secession from state control. In 1989 a trial was set up to defrock him, but it quickly lost momentum. He agreed to change the colour of his robes from brown to white as a compromise, thus dissociating him from the status of fully ordained monk, but he refused to have a formal defrocking. For many, the trial was interpreted as a power play between the corrupt sangha, attempting to maintain its stranglehold on religious power, and an ascetic and ethically virtuous renunciate attempting to purify the religious order.

'Thailand's reputation as a safe and peaceful destination is attracting thousands of foreigners from all over the world to learn more about the 2,547-year-old Buddhist faith and one of its most famous practices, the art of meditation' (Anisa and Krittaya 2004). The rhetoric surrounding meditation practice draws on localist discourses on globalization and the limited satisfaction provided by 'capitalism' and 'consumerism'.[17] This is a moralizing project in which the authentic simplicity of meditation as an integral part of Thai culture is read against the uncertainty and cultural fragility of the putatively insatiable 'Western' appetite for hedonism and consumption.[18] As a fundraising pamphlet for the meditation monastery on which this book is based states,

> The idea of globalisation has strong effects upon our minds in general. Therefore, our mental tranquillity and purity is very important as well as our need for enjoyment and peace. Staying in the *Wat* for meditation practice is like resting in the shade of a big tree on a long and hot journey, and drinking refreshing water.

The diversification of Buddhist practices has been informed, in part, by localist discourses on the need for an authentically Thai and Buddhist response to the pressures of modernity. As Parnwell and Seeger (2008) argue, it is the image of the *wat*-centred village religion that localists engage when they seek an answer to the crises of modernity and economic insecurity. A critique of Thailand's involvement in the capitalist world economy and a discourse of localism that emphasizes a need to return to agrarian roots has flourished in Thailand particularly since the Asian financial crisis of 1997. Such discourses often look to hold global forces – such as the World Bank, the IMF and, more broadly, the West and globalization – responsible for Thailand's economic problems. In such discourses globalization is often treated as an active entity wilfully subordinating Thailand to forms of economic colonialism. McCargo argues that while both strands of discourse are presented as populist, in fact they reflect the elitist and statist rhetoric of official Thai nationalism. For example, localist responses to the 1997 economic crisis blended elements of official nationalism with a romanticized

---

[17] This is a perennial theme in Asian nationalisms, see for example Chatterjee's discussion of Indian Nationalism as derivative discourse (1993). See also Carrier (1995).

[18] Interestingly, in this instance, the message of Thai identity and authenticity is aimed at Thai people *through* foreigners – the testimony to Thailand's cultural greatness being its international appeal rather than prestige that is attributed to it by Thais for Thais. Reynolds makes a similar point in his discussion of the gendering of nationalist and post-nationalist selves and the celebrity status accorded Thai nationals who succeed in international competitions: 'Such people are national heroes, because they are deemed to have enhanced Thailand's image (*phap-phot*) and reputation (*cheu-siang*) on the international stage' (1999: 270).

notion of Thai people 'as village-dwelling farmers, buffeted by the storms of global capital' (McCargo 2001: 89). Hewison (2001) argues that since the Asian crisis, opposition to neo-liberalism in Thailand has taken the form of a broad localist reaction and conservative populism.[19] Media and political discourse in Thailand often presented the 1997 economic crisis as symptomatic of the ineffectual and ultimately rapacious nature of capitalist-driven development, after which theories of development based on self-sufficiency became increasingly popular. In response to what was felt to be the erosion of Thai identity by Western forces many called for a return to Thai-ness, and looked to Buddhism as offering the answers. For example, Sanitsuda (2001: 11), a journalist for the English-language *Bangkok Post*, writes that, 'Thailand can choose to follow the Way chosen by the Buddha and work toward mutual respect and simplicity, or it can continue on its current path of exploitation and greed'.[20]

In response to the 1997 crisis His Majesty the King of Thailand developed the policy of 'sufficiency economy'. This was intended to reduce reliance on exports, and promote localized economic systems in which at least 25 per cent of production was destined for local needs. The policy was intended to stimulate economic self-discipline at the individual level. The balance between economic growth and sustainability developed as a Thai response to the Asian crisis by HM the King has been promoted as a potentially global policy in response to the global economic crisis a decade later. At the United Nations General Assembly 2009 in New York, Thai Prime Minister Abhisit Vejjajiva used the 'sufficiency economy' model to propound development that was both 'qualitative and quantitative', highlighting the improvement of education, healthcare and welfare services as well as economic development. Since the economic crisis of 2007/8 'sufficiency economy' and its correlate 'moderation society' have been widely promoted within Thailand (Abhisit 2009). For example, a high-profile campaign in 2009 run by the Army and the Internal Security Operations Command (ISOC) led with the motto 'Mindfulness + reason = immunity'. Immunity here refers to immunizing the national economy against shocks. This campaign promoted guidelines for

---

[19] He further notes that such 'progressive nationalism' prevents consideration of the causes of exploitation in capitalist processes and that the national/global dichotomy at the heart of such an approach is insufficient for thinking through capitalist production and globalization.

[20] The links between responses to global economic crisis and Buddhist teaching were the subject of a themed panel of the International Buddhist Conference on the United Nations Day of Vesak Celebrations in May 2009. This panel proposed different approaches to a Buddhist Economic Ethic that could offer solutions and remedies towards solving the crisis (UNDV Conference Volume 2552/2009).

life: accessing news with mindfulness, spending money reasonably, carrying out one's job with perseverance and making one's family sufficiently happy.

Localism vaunts locally controlled and locally relevant forms of economic development and self-sufficiency that are based on traditional and indigenous core values.[21] Such localist discourses have presented Thai culture and identity as under threat from the rapacious forces of global capitalism and the seductive lure of rampant consumerism. These forces were to be countered by a return to the morals of village community, the basis of traditional Thai cultural values (Parnwell and Seeger 2008: 84). This representation of rural Thai life has been criticized for its romanticization of rural and village life that is both populist and nationalist (McCargo 2004). In many instances this localism has been promoted in critiques coming from non-governmental organizations and social movements (Hewison 2000).

The particularly Buddhist character of Thai localist discourse is summed up by Parnwell and Seeger (2008: 86):

Buddhism is central to localist discourse, which in no small measure is also a culturalist discourse. In part this is because the civil religion is presented, or at least imagined, as a cornerstone of Thai culture, and Buddhism is also a key referent in the distillation of a sense of 'community culture' and its operationalization within the alternative development movement. Buddhism is the embodiment of the Thai cultural capital that localists envision will provide the heartbeat of future development in reaction to the forces of globalization and capitalist modernization.

In a consideration of the localist and Buddhist responses to what were perceived as the amoral and impersonal forces of globalization, Taylor (2001) argues that religious discourses about bodily well-being and disease have been used since the economic crash in imagining the symbiotic relationship between the body-politic, the social body and the individual. For example, the fundraising campaign, 'Thais help Thais', spearheaded by the monastic saint Luang Ta Mahabua, called for the protection of the social body against the impersonal forces of globalization. In this campaign the health of the sangha was explicitly linked to the health of the nation: the bodies of national subjects, the religious body and the body of the nation being mutual interdependencies (Taylor 2001: 137).

Parnwell and Seeger (2008) demonstrate that localism has become an important part of socially engaged Buddhism and that the democratization of religious practice and 'relocalization' of the ideas of prominent Buddhist

---

[21] Localism is of course a global rather than a local phenomenon. On localist responses to globalization in France see Williams (2008).

thinkers have resulted in a proliferation of interpretations as to the appropriate practices and priorities of Buddhist monastics and laity. Through three case studies in the northeast of Thailand, they demonstrate that the teachings of influential Buddhist thinkers are interpreted, adjusted and implemented by local monks in response to local needs and realities. Their case studies, combined and compared, provide a subtle, considered and insightful representation of the changes taking place in and around mainstream Buddhism. Parnwell and Seeger (2008) argue that Thai Buddhism is in a process of, what they term, 'relocalization'. Their ethnography suggests that the diversification and fragmentation of Buddhism as it is locally interpreted do not present us with a 'crisis' in Buddhism, but, rather, point towards the progressive and innovative interpretations of Buddhist practice by individual monastics.

Parnwell and Seeger's case studies reveal different approaches in practice to the roles and responsibilities of monastics in relation to the laity. They suggest that the debate concerning the appropriate engagement of monastics in social welfare campaigns is fed by localism in contemporary Buddhist practices and discourses (Parnwell and Seeger 2008: 80). While some have argued that Buddhism has been increasingly strained in the face of globalization, hybridization, syncretism and a proliferation of alternative religiosity, as well as suffering a crisis of relevance and moral authority in the light of public scandals and commoditization of religion, it has also been at the heart of a localist discourse in reaction to these same challenges and obstacles. Those people feeling disenchanted with Buddhism have been the driving energy behind reformist trends that seek a return to the fundamental teachings and core values of the religion. As Parnwell and Seeger's case studies clearly demonstrate, these currents have led to reconsideration of the roles of monastics, whether the monastic has a responsibility to strive exclusively for the soteriological telos of enlightenment or to confront the challenges of modern life on behalf and for the benefit of the laity.

ENGAGED BUDDHISM

In this context of political, economic, environmental, cultural and social change several kinds of developments, in addition to what I understand as the monasticization of popular Buddhism (see below), have taken place within Thai Buddhism. Trends have included a critique of Buddhism by reformist thinkers, fundamentalist movements and social and environmental reform movements based upon 'Buddhist ethics'. Buddhism has been interpreted in a socially, economically and politically active manner producing a form of Buddhist social activism which incorporates Buddhism within a global socio-developmental position. One result of this has been the validation of monastic and lay work in the advancement of social welfare.

Darlington (2000) cites the fight against a proposed cable car up Doi Suthep mountain and through Doi Suthep-Pui National Park in Chiang Mai (1985) as one of the first instances in which Buddhist monks took an environmental position. Opposition to the cable car was framed in terms of sanctity and a threat to Buddhist heritage. A link was articulated between Buddhism and preserving trees beyond the concern for a pilgrimage site. Though the motivation of the monks involved was connected to protection of a sacred Buddhist site 'it was the first time that Thai monks articulated the relationship between Buddhism and the natural environment as a motivation for social and political activism' (Darlington 2000; cf. Darlington 1998).[22]

Reformers have presented Buddhism as a form of beneficial scientific rationality and exercise, and thereby invoked religious pluralism in Buddhism's applicability (if Buddhism is a philosophy that transcends all religions then it is of benefit to all those who practise it, irrespective of their

---

[22] Though this represented a new link between monks and environment, there were precedents for monks being involved in state-endorsed development work. For example, empowered by the 1962 Sangha Act, Prime Minister Sarit Thanarat incorporated the centralized sangha administration into a campaign of development. Presenting national integration as the enhancement of traditional values represented by the monarchy and Buddhism, Sarit promoted agricultural intensification and expansion towards an export-orientated, industrial economy (Darlington 2000). Monks were employed in development programmes that aimed to strengthen a sense of national identity through Buddhism as well as campaigning to counter communism: through missionary programmes, such as the *thammathud* programme, which sent monks to politically sensitive and economically marginalized border areas, and the *thammacarik* programme, which sent monks, under the control of the Department of Public Welfare, to missionize and develop the hill tribes and propagate the political values of national unity, including loyalty to the king and government (Tambiah 1976: 434–71).

Later administrations have continued Sarit's agricultural intensification policies and aggressive industrial and export-orientated development. Darlington tells us that the results of such policy have been mixed:

> Thailand's growth until the economic crisis of 1997 was phenomenal, but the rate of environmental degradation, especially forest loss and pollution levels, was among the highest in Asia. The gap between rich and poor widened, and consumerism spread ... Through the use of a national, centralized concept of Buddhism, local culture and regional diversity were devalued. (2000)

Subsequent Thai governments have seen communism as the potential destroyer of Buddhism and national unity. During the Cold War and civil wars of Vietnam, Laos and Cambodia, the threat of communism amounted to a threat to the foundations of the Thai nation and the monarchy. Communism in Thailand, then, was anti-Buddhist, as Buddhism was anti-communist (Jackson 2003). However, it is important to note that Thailand remains unique as the only Buddhist kingdom to have avoided colonialism, communism, civil war and genocide.

lower-level religious beliefs).[23] The call is often for practical programmes and an ethic of wealth creation to counterbalance the exploitation of the natural world as a result of the capitalist ethic (Harris 1995: 179–80). As Gombrich and Obeyesekere (1988: 222) argue, reformist Buddhists thus 'lift Buddhism out of the ruck of religions by claiming that it is not a religion but something else; and sometimes they further claim that all mere religions are compatible with this something else. Sometimes the something else is a practice. But the commoner claim is that Buddhism is rational, scientific'. Since the early 1970s the rationalist and reformist views of the Buddhist monk Buddhadasa have become a major focus of debates surrounding Theravāda Buddhist doctrine and practice in Thailand. The majority of his supporters were members of an urban elite of military and government bureaucrats, businessmen, teachers, students, writers and artists, who, while numerically small, dominated the country politically, economically and culturally (Jackson 2003: 49). Buddhadasa's modernist critical reforms were understood as outside the system of sangha, monarchy, military and bureaucratic alliances by the rising middle and intellectual classes, who took them up as a component of an alternative Buddhist ideology. Buddhadasa attempted to shift the focus of Thai Buddhism from the transcendent to this-worldly concern by conferring religious value on action in the social world through a theoretical re-evaluation of Buddhist doctrine (Jackson 2003: 3). His reinterpretation was grounded first in a desire to conform to what he understood as rational and scientific methodology and reasoning, as can be evidenced in his reduction of non-empirical entities and supernatural powers to psychological states, and secondly in his desire for Buddhism to remain relevant in the face of massive social, economic and cultural change.[24] Buddhadasa emphasized *vipassanā* as the most important aspect of Buddhist spiritual practice and denounced *samādhi* as central to a supernaturalist view of Buddhism (Jackson 2003: 158–9). In his analysis Buddhadasa proposes a vision of Thai Buddhism removed from all non-scientific influences (such as the transferral of merit, rebirth, heavenly beings, and so on), which may act as a model for progressive social development and individual spiritual

---

[23] Interestingly, Gombrich and Obeyesekere demonstrate that the history of Buddhism as 'philosophy not religion' in Sri Lanka stems from the contrast drawn by Christian missionaries between Christianity as theistic and resting on faith and Buddhism as atheistic and resting on reason and ethics. While this was historically the case, its annunciation was a new phenomenon: 'earlier no need had been felt to justify the rationality of Buddhism, let alone to posit a contrast between religion and philosophy: the *Dhamma* was both' (1988: 221). See Bayly (2004) for a comparative case of reflective analysis as a distinct mode of religious experience in Vietnam.

[24] Subsequent reformers, such as Sulak Sivaraksa (Swearer 1996), have encouraged environmental activism as a means towards developing a more ethical Buddhist society.

attainment.[25] It is interesting to note, however, that many of Buddhadasa's supporters believed that he had attained high levels of spiritual power and insight and as such it was especially meritoriously accumulative to donate alms to him.

In Thailand the development of reformist movements that appeal to a rationalist ethic are rarely primarily motivated by soteriological ethics. Rather, what is sought is an effective means to change the world for the better. Such an emphasis on world engagement and social development has become an important aspect of many Thai Buddhist practices at the same time as increasing numbers of people are engaging with the ascetic imperative implicit in Buddhist soteriology (see Chapter 4).

DECLINE AND HYBRIDITY

McCargo argues (2004) that the relationship between the state and the sangha in Thailand has confined Theravāda Buddhism to the role of legitimating state power and its teachings have been subordinated to nationalist ideology (2004: 155). He argues that state support of Buddhism has encouraged a form of Buddhism that is authoritarian, orthodox and conservative, and he notes that such subordination has occurred at the same time as a decline in the numbers of monks, the rise of commercialized Buddhist practices, and scandals about the financial and sexual misdeeds of monks. For example, the widespread public anxiety surrounding the scandals centred on Ajharn Yantra and Phra Bhavana highlighted the perceived decline in ethical standards for monks and a perception of moral crisis in the sangha (Jackson 1997: 81; see also Keyes 1999; McCargo 2004). The moral purity of individual monks became a question of great concern as a result of the indiscretions of the few. The personal ethics of the individual monk are of great concern to the laity. It is only by donating to spiritually pure monks that alms donations may be meritoriously accumulative. Also, reformist Buddhist thinking holds that it is only through the cultivation of morality and virtue that social and economic domains will be transformed. Such moral purity is reflected in the extent to which monastics are able to embody the principles of the *dhamma*. In parallel with the undermining of confidence in the institution of Buddhism as a result of such public scandals, laity have sought out those

---

[25] Laidlaw (2008) provides an interesting point of comparison in his discussion of the inclusion of Jain teachings of non-violence into global movements for animal rights and environmentalism by the Jain Diaspora.

monks who are reputed to be ethically strict. It is common for people to travel great distances to meet with monks who are renowned for their ethical purity and ascetic restraint. As Jackson writes, 'the growing prominence of charismatic clerical figures can also be seen as marking a return to the historical emphasis placed on individual ascetics as sites of sacral power, a traditional form of religiosity that was often suppressed in earlier decades of this century as part of the state's attempt to institute a centrally controlled religious structure' (1997: 82–3). It is in this context that monks, both at the periphery and the centre of the official sangha, may rise to prominence.

The perceived crisis in Buddhism and the decline in centralized monastic authority has led to the professed need for a socially relevant, lay ethic beyond traditional patronage of the sangha. While Jackson (1997) and others have commented on the 'withering' health of institutional Buddhism, such concerns have also led to variety in the focus and practice of Buddhist monasteries. Along with trends towards decentralization and personality-focused religiosity, other foci have meant that Buddhism still retains a political, social and religious relevance for contemporary Thais. For example, recent years have seen a mushrooming proliferation of magical monks and popular spirit-medium cults influenced by mass media and religious commodification (Pattana 2005a; 2005b; Morris 2000; Tanabe 1991). Such developments cannot be understood without contextualizing them firmly in socio-economic and political changes in Thai culture and society, rapid urbanization and massive rural–urban migration (see also Mills 1999). Pattana (2005b) steps away from analyses of spirit mediums and magic monks as responses to dystopian religious crises or the result of the rupture of modernity. He argues that popular religion has always been hybridized in Thailand and that the current proliferation of such practices is evidence of the negotiations of existing religious and socio-economic structures, reflecting concerns for material wealth and mundane success, rather than resistance to or rebellion against engagement with modernity and capitalism. Pattana argues for a conceptualization of Thai religion as a 'subtle hybridization' in popular beliefs and religiosity (2005a: 461; cf. Taylor 2001).[26] The concept of hybridization captures the dynamic picture of Thai religion: the ever changing involvement of diverse aspects of the religious system. He identifies what he terms 'third spaces', to account for the worship of diverse religious deities, in which

---

[26] For similar reasons Thai religion is described by Keyes as 'complex' and 'confusing' (1978). The complex intermingling of Theravāda Buddhism, folk Brahmanism and animism in Thai religion was understood by Kirsch (1977) to constitute a syncretic system.

'conventional Theravāda Buddhism, state and sangha authorities, multi-original religious beliefs and the drive for material success in the capitalist market all come to coexist and produce a hybrid moment of religious change' (Pattana 2005a: 468).

In contrast to the attempted centralizing, nation-building projects of the nineteenth-century sangha reformers, the late twentieth century saw a changing landscape of Thai Buddhism shifting into a diversity of competing and compelling interpretations of what Buddhism might be as instantiated at the local level. While scandals of corruption, commercialization and declining authority are concerns, I suggest that these are balanced by significant emerging processes of religiosity either through the charisma of individual monks, the shared focus of particular religious movements, or the sharing of common goals that religious practices and networks are expanding and proliferating.

MEDITATION AND MONASTICIZATION

In Thailand the importance and propagation of *vipassanā* meditation is instilled predominantly through the guidance of monasteries. The centrality of the monastery and the historical roles of monks have not been challenged by the propagation of meditation to laity. Rather, in those monasteries given over to teaching meditation to the laity (by far the minority), their role has been augmented and the order is maintained by the aspirations of meditation students. This is further illustrated by the continued support of Thai meditation monasteries by the laity through alms donations. However, as we shall see in Chapter 7, the way in which this historically significant relationship is negotiated in a meditation monastery with a large population of *mae chee* must be understood through a nuanced analysis of broader hierarchical relationships.

As part of his PhD thesis Houtman (1990) draws a comparison between a Burmese monastery not involved in the teaching of meditation, and a Burmese monastery which has been given over to teaching *vipassanā* meditation. Houtman argues that it is useful to examine the way meditation students become 'monasticized' rather than focus on the 'laicization' of Buddhism (Houtman 1990: 124). As I shall argue below, such a focus is important in an account of the changing status of *mae chee* in Thailand as a result of lay meditation practice, through the teaching of which they are able to define themselves, and be defined by others, as monastics.

Houtman's ethnography demonstrates that in the Burmese case lay meditators aspire to the ideal of the Buddhist monastic order by adopting monastic language and classification (Houtman 1990: 133). This includes

Figure 1: Phra Ajharn giving a *dhamma* talk to lay meditators

conceiving of the meditation centre as a monastery, the meditator as a 'monk', property as 'monastic property' and gifts to lay meditators as the meritorious equivalent of monastic 'offerings'. *Yogi* (meditation students) may be classified as 'monks of the ultimate truth', or members of 'the monastic order of the ultimate truth' (Houtman 1990: 136), claims which do not occur in Thailand. In the Burmese case lay *yogi* within the meditation centre consider themselves to be a part of the sangha: 'the concept of the *than-ga* [sangha] has been changed, including not only those ordained into the monastic order wearing robes and having a shaven head but also all those who practice WM [*vipassanā*]' (Houtman 1990: 138). Houtman suggests that by classifying themselves in this way lay meditators are upholding the belief that religious action may only be properly performed by members of the monastic order, in its widest sense (1990: 138). As Houtman argues, the claim to monastic status may stem from 'a deeply rooted view that monkhood is about implementing the Buddha's teachings, and as meditation is the crux of this, monastic status can be claimed by all who pursue meditation' (1990: 134). Of course, the view that meditation is the crux of the Buddha's teachings is not uncontroversial.

Houtman's thesis is that this does not present a revolutionary breach from the discourse of the Buddhist order. When applied to the Thai case, however, this raises two interesting points. On the one hand, the Thai instance is one of relative religious conservatism. Laity and *mae chee* do not make claims to the monastic status of monkhood. Indeed, the role of monks is important to both as the paragons of religious professionalism; by paying respect to such a paragon one is able to act meritoriously. The distinction is a necessary part of *mae chee*'s conceptions of themselves and their role in the monastic community (this will be explored in subsequent chapters). On the other hand, the Thai case suggests that by comparison the Burmese laity are indeed making claims to religious status which would have been unthinkable prior to the advent of lay meditation or in a different context (Houtman tells us that in fact, outside the meditation community such claims are still controversial). In the Thai monastery, donations made by laity to the monastery are considered to be meritoriously accumulative in the same way as donations to individual monastics; money and property is then considered to belong to the monastery under the control of the Abbot and committees.[27] Yet there is no instance in which lay meditators consider themselves to be monks, in speech or action. However, as we shall see below, what is striking and may stem from the same intention is the monastic status claimed by and for *mae chee* who practise and teach meditation, and do not receive full ordination.

Houtman tells us that in the Burmese case the criteria by which different people constitute religious membership are varied: 'Monks use the criterion of ordination by an unbroken lineage of monks; nuns use the idea that they have renounced the world, shaved their heads, taken up robes, and have a Pali "title" as the criteria. Lay *yaw"gi* [*yogi*], on the other hand, use the practice of WM [*vipassanā*] as the criterion of membership' (1990: 139). What is interesting is that all are making claims to religious membership on their own terms and Houtman emphasizes that the monastic rules remain the yardstick by which all measure their morality, while continuing to offer alms to and receive teaching from monks (1990: 140).

Gombrich and Obeyesekere identify the widespread practice of meditation by the laity in Sri Lanka as the 'laicization of meditation'. Meditation comes to be seen as an instrumental tool for the improvement of lay life as well as a way to salvation. Their suggestion is that the development of lay meditation created an inherent contradiction for world-involved laity, a contradiction which was predicted in the scriptures and which has created

---

[27] The bureaucratic structure of the monastery will be examined in the next chapter.

some anxiety among practitioners.[28] They argue that the involvement of laity in meditation creates psychological problems because, as it is a non-theistic, non-essential (no-soul) practice done on one's own, Buddhist meditators 'must feel themselves spiritually lonely and isolated' (Gombrich and Obeyesekere 1988: 452).

While Gombrich and Obeyesekere may well be right about Sri Lanka, when applied to the Thai case the distinction between monastic and laity appears overdrawn. This distinction may have always been sharper in Sri Lanka where there is no tradition of temporary initiation, as there is in Thailand. However, I would argue that Buddhist meditation is physically and emotionally challenging for all who practise it to any serious level, irrespective of their ordination status. Gombrich and Obeyesekere appear to assume that making meditation available to laity results in them aping what monastics do rather than genuinely engaging in meditative practice. As we shall see, doing a meditation retreat in Wat Bonamron constitutes considerably more than dabbling. Some people take to meditation while others do not, and the criterion for this is not necessarily ordination status.

Furthermore, Gombrich and Obeyesekere suggest that 'Modern bourgeois Buddhists attempt to reconcile radical Buddhist meditation with the ordered reality of everyday social life, a reconciliation that is theoretically impossible in Buddhist doctrinal terms' (1988: 15; cf. Weber 1948). This implies that the project of reconciliation is unique to non-monastics. I would point out that a similar project of reconciliation must always have occurred for monastics as well (this theme will be greatly developed later in the volume). I refer not only to the fact that in Thailand the institution of temporary ordination must influence reconciliation between monastic practice and everyday social life, but also that such a reconciliation must occur in the daily lives of monastics both because meditation is a challenging activity for everyone, irrespective of ordination status, and because this must be reconciled with social life by monastics as well as laity. As we shall see in Chapter 6, this reconciliation is itself a crucial aspect of monastic practice. As Tambiah and others have reminded us (Burghart 1983; Tambiah 1982), although ascetics may in some sense be 'outside the world', they still live social lives.

A discrepancy between the ideal monastic and individual monastic's experience of his or her own approximation to such an ideal may remain

---

[28] They suggest that the traditional positions of laity and sangha as mutually exclusive and appropriately supportive show a 'realistic appraisal of the needs of the society and polity' (Gombrich and Obeyesekere 1988: 451) and that the traditional division demonstrated 'a realistic acceptance of the emotional needs and capacities of mankind' (1988: 451).

hidden from the laity because of the monastic duty to behave in a religiously consistent and appropriate way, something which Gombrich and Obeyesekere identify as the hallmark of monasticism (1988: 232). This, in fact, is the foundation of the distinction between the two groups: monastics have a duty to behave in a morally perfect way as paradigms of virtuosity and self-control for the laity whose concomitant duty is to support the sangha. Yet Gombrich and Obeyesekere believe that the consequence of the 'laicization' of meditation may be the replacement of the monastery with the meditation centre in Sri Lanka, if not physically then certainly in significance (1988: 240).[29]

Some monks and *mae chee* in Thailand are adopting roles of social involvement (see above) but, certainly in the Thai case, I would question the extent to which such activist roles have come to replace more traditional monastic duties. Such developments have been in addition to, rather than in place of, monastic responsibilities. The monastic structure of Wat Bonamron that we shall examine in the next chapter may be used as an illustration of the continuity between the two types of Buddhism identified by Gombrich and Obeyesekere. The involvement of religious institutions in the propagation of meditation is enabling those outside the ordained sangha, such as *mae chee*, to define themselves in ways which are religious and associated with prestige. A parallel result of this change has been a more religious role for the laity, a role that emulates the monastic ideal. This is understood by Gombrich and Obeyesekere to be the result of the laicization of religious practice. As I have argued, following Houtman, another equally valid interpretation is to understand the changing nature of monastic–lay interaction as the result of the monasticization of popular Buddhism. Similarly, Holt cites the examples of observance of '*sil*' (moral conduct) on religious days, the routines of lay meditation centres being modelled on the monastic routine, and the increasing presence of monks at rites, the increasing public display of the Buddha image as effecting a form of temporary monasticism for laity. These processes and practices may be understood as instances of 'monasticization' rather than laicization (cf. Drougge 2007; Holt 1991).

I understand the increasing numbers of people practising meditation and the changing status and responsibilities of different monastics as instances of the monasticization of modernist Buddhism, but I do not propose such an

---

[29] 'The Venerable Balangoda Ananda Maitreya ... has predicted that in twenty years there will be no more monasteries (*pansal*), only meditation centres. Literally, this may be an exaggeration; symbolically, it puts the matter in a nutshell' (Gombrich and Obeyesekere 1988: 240).

interpretation in opposition to processes of 'laicization'. Rather, I suggest that it might be profitably understood as one identifiable trend in the context of the plurality of practices and statuses in contemporary Thai Buddhism. Among all the calls for doctrinal reform and the involvement of laity in monastic practice there are no calls for a Protestant-like reform of Thai Buddhism. No lay Buddhists or *mae chee* have attempted to appropriate full religious authority to themselves. The greatest religious status remains with those who most strikingly follow the *vinaya* code, and that remains the monks. Lay religious practice may be consonant with the social aspirations of a modernized and developed Thailand, but monastic religious practice remains the ideal of moral perfection. While a distinction between lay and monastic statuses is an important feature of Buddhist thought, we have seen that this is variously interpreted in practice.

CHAPTER 3

The monastic community: duty and structure

I flew into Chiang Mai late one night in October 2003. As I waited to collect my luggage on the carousel I could see a group of half a dozen monks and *mae chee* waiting for me through the doors to the arrival hall; sitting in two separate groups, the respective orange and white of their robes created blocks of colour amidst the chaos of the airport. I was greeted with huge smiles, myself and my friends meeting each other with happy wai's.[1] I was returning to the monastery after an absence of a few years to ordain as a *mae chee* and spend fifteen months conducting participant observation. I was whisked through the streets of Chiang Mai high up in the comfort of the monastery's air-conditioned mini-van. I enquired about the health of monks and *mae chee*. It had been a few years since my last three-month stay in Wat Bonamron and I learnt that my arrival had been much anticipated and talked about. We rolled into the sleeping monastery and I was shown to my room in the *mae chee* quarter behind the kitchen and left for the evening. My room was basic but very comfortable with a wooden bed, a bedroll, blanket and pillow, a Buddha image and a bathroom. I unpacked my bag as the monastery slept, listened to the occasional dog barking at the night and the industry of the insects in the bamboo outside my door.

I wake at 4 a.m. to the morning bell and the smells of breakfast coming from the kitchen as *mae chee* work in diligent silence, the chatter of the late afternoon forgotten in the dark of the early morning. Cocks are beginning to crow and as I walk in the pre-dawn air, white-clad meditation students shuffle sleepily towards the meditation hall to begin a day of practice. In the

---

[1] A '*wai*' is a traditional gesture of respect, greeting and farewell in Thailand. The palms are placed together and brought towards the chin with the head bent slightly forward. Respect and deference are shown to someone by proffering the initial *wai*. This is responded to in kind but the person showing deference (in this case, me) will *wai* with slightly higher hands and lower head than the person receiving his or her respect. The word *wai* is used as a noun when referring to the gesture and as a verb when referring to the act of gesturing.

two halls at the heart of the monastery monks and *mae chee* begin the morning chants. As the sun rises and the mist clears around the orange stone of the *stūpa* at the centre of the monastery, cocks crow in earnest and the sound of sweeping can be heard as the fallen leaves of the night are tidied into small piles and collected in preparation for the new day. Monks move silently and barefoot in twos and threes as they leave for their morning alms rounds. The bell chimes for breakfast at 6 a.m. and monks and meditation students make their way to the dining room, while other monastics break their eighteen-hour fast in their rooms. A new day has begun in the monastery, a compound that houses a large number of monastics, and, for the brief period of their stay, a transient population of lay people, for all of whom daily activity is, in different ways, focused around the practice of *vipassanā* meditation.

ENTERING THE MONASTERY

On 15 March 2518 BE (1975)[2] the abbot and head meditation teacher of a monastery in Chiang Mai[3] re-established Wat Bonamron on the outskirts of the city as a meditation monastery and branch of Wat Mahathat with himself as head and acting abbot. The monastic compound itself was ensconced in the quiet woods and fields on the outskirts of Chiang Mai in an area believed to be dangerous and frequented by thieves and bandits. A foundation-stone inscription in the grounds of the monastery dates back to AD 1492. At the top of the stone is a horoscope that indicates the position of the sun, the moon, Mars and other planets in the zodiac, followed by more astronomical data indicating the day 30 March 1492 at 10 a.m. The main text of the inscription says that at this time there was an assembly at the future site of the monastery, including the ruler of Chiang Mai, King Yot Chiang Rai (1487–95); his queen, Atapa Devi; and 100 senior monks. The queen formally asked the king for permission to found a monastery, which

---

[2] Rebuilding began in 1971.
[3] As one of the first 'satellite' monasteries to adopt the meditation programme propagated by Wat Mahathat, the monastery in Chiang Mai city was described in detail by Tambiah in 1971 (1984: 172). He reports that at that time there were sixteen regular monks, six 'temporary' monks, forty-three novices, eleven *mae chee* and nineteen temple boys. Each person who wanted to ordain was requested first to complete a seven-day meditation course. The then abbot told Tambiah that Thai and foreign women had taken ordination as *mae chee* at his monastery. He estimated that in the previous year approximately fifty people had attended his *wat* for short meditation retreats, including foreign disciples from Australia, England and other Asian countries. The Abbot had studied insight meditation in Burma for two years with Mahasi Sayadaw and has been one of the principal teachers of this method in northern Thailand (see also Swearer 1995: 144–5).

the king gave. He donated a huge annual income, over 3 million cowries meant for the upkeep of the monastery, derived from field taxes.[4] The inscription closes with the wish: 'May the merit resulting from the foundation of the ... monastery go to the former king of Chiang Mai, to all people, gods, and all creatures so that they may progress until they reach *Nibbāna*.' The monastery lay deserted for years and during the Second World War Japanese armed forces camped very close to the compound. Buddha images, the *stūpa* (reliquary monument), *ubosot* (consecrated assembly hall; Pali: *uposatha*) and *vihāra* (main temple) built in the reign of King Yot Chiang Rai were badly damaged. During this time the main Buddha image was moved to Wat Phra Singh in Chiang Mai city for safekeeping. It was only as part of the Mahanikai sect's evangelical nationwide programme of meditation propagation that the monastery was re-established in the 1970s.

Entering the temple gates, one comes to the *vihāra* in the middle of the monastery. Behind this is the ancient *stūpa*, and behind this is the *sala* (meditation/*dhamma* hall). These buildings in the centre of the compound are the areas in which the whole community comes together regularly for religious services and meditation. To the left of the *vihāra* is the *mae chee* hall (used for meditation and chanting twice a day), two open-air meditation areas, the kitchen and dining room, and the *mae chee*'s *kuṭis* (small houses). To the right of the *vihāra* are the monks' *kuṭis*, a consecrated assembly hall (*ubosot*), a two-storey library containing palm-leaf manuscripts of the Pali Canon, the main office, and the monks' office. It is forbidden for women to go to the second storey of either the Abbot's *kuṭi* or the library that holds the Buddhist Canon. No woman is allowed to enter the relics hall, *ubosot*, used for male ordination, monks' renewal of precepts and confession. The *ubosot* is the only communal building that is not cleaned by women. Outside the walls of the compound is a four-storey building for meditation (in which women are allowed to go to the top floors), a school and the building that houses the water tank. The *kuṭis* are comfortable but basic. Inside each there is a bathroom and a larger room for meditating and sleeping. While *kuṭis* are small, private and at the edges of the monastery, the communal areas of the *vihāra*, the *stūpa* and the *sala* in

---

[4] For instance, 400,000 cowries for the *stūpa*, 500,000 cowries for the main Buddha image in the *vihāra*, and 400,000 cowries for the *ubosot*. One and a half million was to provide food for monks and 200,000 cowries for the service of certain outside lay men. The total of twenty-three households were donated as slaves to the monastery. Among them were ten whose combined debts amounted to 9,700 silver pieces and who had to be redeemed for that sum. The construction of the monastery cost 695,980 silver pieces of which 513,810 where paid by the King and the rest by other sponsors.

Figure 2: The *vihāra*

the centre of the compound are huge by comparison. It is in this area more than any other that monks and *mae chee* come together. Here, huge Buddha images surrounded by other religiously significant images, including portraits of the King and Queen, and in some cases lavish gold decoration, dominate the interiors. Most ritual is performed in this central space and the new building, where men and women come together, while the less ritually significant areas on either side of the compound are strongly gendered and marked by spatial separation between men and women.

Individuals and large groups of Thai laity attend the monastery for periods of three days or longer. Groups usually comprise work colleagues, students or school children, and are not infrequently as large as 200 people. The last few years have seen a dramatic increase in the numbers of Thai and foreign lay people coming to the monastery to learn meditation and the monastery has consequently expanded to accommodate them. The new four-storey building outside the monastery wall is used as a meditation centre in conjunction with the already substantial facilities within the compound. As a fundraising pamphlet for the building put it, the building is intended 'to accommodate the increasing numbers of meditators as well as to maintain Buddhism in the world of globalisation'. Throughout the year the monastery is open to laity, Thai or foreign, who wish to learn meditation and it has its own Thai- and English-language websites and email address.

STRUCTURAL BUREAUCRATIZATION

Not all monasteries, and not all meditation centres, are the same. Indeed, there is variation in spatial organization, community make-up, focus and teachers in both kinds of institutions. Those monasteries that do not teach meditation to laity are designed for a relatively stable monastic community and usually have a limited amount of spare accommodation. In contrast, a meditation monastery is designed to accommodate as large a number of people as possible for temporary periods as well as the permanent community. The meditation monastery requires different facilities in addition to the core monastic buildings, such as administrative offices, sleeping quarters, meditation halls, dining areas, large kitchens, toilets and showers, and so on. Furthermore, the coordination of large numbers of meditation students requires a large administrative organization. The propagation of meditation to the laity has resulted in important structural changes in Wat Bonamron itself and a bureaucratization of monastic duties. I turn now to an examination of the effect that teaching meditation to large numbers of laity has had upon the monastic community and compare this with ethnography from a Burmese meditation centre.

The monastic community in the *wat* is relatively stable. Though large numbers of boys receive novice ordination in April in celebration of the King's birthday, during the rest of the year the numbers of monks, novices and *mae chee* fluctuate very little. The monastery is focused upon the teaching of meditation. Visitors are only welcome to stay if they practise meditation, and strict rules for behaviour are given to all meditation students in Thai or English prior to their entry. The monastery accommodates approximately 317 *yogi* at any one time, but it is possible for this figure to be comfortably increased for up to a week when large groups, such as university students, attend meditation courses. During the rainy season many more monks and novices ordain, and Buddha Day (*Wan Phra* or the Buddhist Sabbath), festival days and school holidays see a rise in attendance. From July to October, during the 'Buddhist Lent' or 'rains retreat' (*Khao Phansa*), monks commit themselves to staying in one monastery, visiting monks return to their own monasteries and many people ordain for the duration of this auspicious period. In 2003, 3,799 *yogi* (meditation students) entered the monastery for meditation. All students receive accommodation and two hot meals a day for free. All work in the monastery, such as cooking, cleaning, teaching, administration and maintenance is performed by the stable community.

Table: Number of people in the wat in 2003

	Jan	Feb	Mar	Apr	May	June	July	Aug	Sept	Oct	Nov	Dec
Resident monk	62	62	58	58	59	54	82	84	85	85	89	89
Visitor monk	17	11	34	35	60	47	0	0	0	0	0	0
Novice	32	32	33	83	45	39	40	40	40	40	40	40
Mae chee	62	62	62	61	61	60	59	59	59	59	59	59
Resident male *yogi*	2	2	2	7	8	17	3	3	3	3	3	3
Resident female *yogi*	18	18	18	18	18	18	18	22	23	23	23	23
Male temporary *yogi*	21	9	40	49	42	40	22	21	22	22	30	34
Female temporary *yogi*	170	121	265	305	287	186	178	141	158	161	187	179
Foreign male *yogi*	30	34	36	36	38	45	51	47	50	57	61	27
Foreign female *yogi*	32	25	28	24	25	23	29	31	31	30	32	24
Resident pious lay men	4	4	4	4	4	4	6	6	6	6	6	6
Resident pious lay women	15	15	15	15	15	15	15	15	15	15	15	15
Temple boys	4	4	4	4	4	4	5	5	5	5	5	5
Drivers	3	3	3	3	3	3	3	3	3	3	3	3
Total	472	402	602	702	669	555	515	478	500	509	553	507

The Abbot is the spiritual and organizational leader of the community. The sangha Supreme Council appoints the Abbot and the organization of the monastery is then divided into different subordinate chairs and committees. The Abbot of the monastery, Phrakru Dhammathon Sila (Ajharn Sila), is supported by a committee of four monks whom he appoints. This monks' committee is in turn a part of the central committee of the monastery, consisting of eighteen people: the Abbot, as committee head, and the four monks appointed by him; a further six monks; two *mae chee*; one *upāsikā* (pious lay woman); two lay women who do not live in the monastery; and two lay men who do not live in the monastery. With the exception of the Abbot and his deputies, members of the committee are elected by vote in a general meeting of the monastery.

It is felt that the central committee, headed by monks, may not easily respond to the needs of female members of the community. Underneath this committee then is the *mae chee* committee, which reports to the central committee on the progress of plans to develop, and problems arising in, the women's section. The *mae chee* committee consists of five *mae chee*, two of whom also sit on the central committee. This committee has a further six *mae chee* who act as consultants and advisors. Decisions taken by the monastery committees are discussed at the weekly meeting to renew precepts, *Wan Gon*, the day before Buddha Day (*Wan Phra*).

There are also several offices in the monastery to shoulder the administration of meditation courses and the stable monastic community. The monks' office takes care of male *yogi*, novices and monks. A man who wishes to ordain as a monk for fewer than forty-five days, become a *yogi* or a temple boy will be approved by the Abbot's assistant in this office, while those who wish to ordain for longer or remain in the monastery as permanent *yogi* are required to pass the basic meditation course and advanced retreat and their profile will then be sent to the Abbot for consideration. The *mae chee*'s office is responsible for the welfare of *mae chee* and female *yogi*, and considers applicants for *mae chee* ordination or a permanent *yogi* position before sending their profiles to the head monk and committee. There is a separate office for foreign meditation students. This office is responsible for the provision of information to foreign visitors, as well as accommodation and initial instruction for meditation students.

In 2002 Wat Bonamron developed a mission statement and constitution (*thammanun*). I am told that it is the first monastery in Thailand to take such a step, and that it did so as a result of the large numbers of laity being taught meditation: because Thailand is a democracy, it is felt that the monastery should act as a democracy also, being fully accountable in its organization and economy. The mission statement declares that the *wat*

acts to provide information about Buddhism, particularly information pertaining to meditation. The monastery provides knowledge about insight development to monks, nuns (*mae chee*), novices, and interested people from around the world. The success of the *wat*'s purpose depends upon living peacefully together and preventing bad observance of the precepts. Observing sections 37 and 38 of the Buddhist monk's commitment instructions, dating 1962 and 1992, which inform the abilities and power of the head monk, the monastery prescribes the rules for control and management of the community.

The constitution sets out each of the roles required in the administration and hierarchy of the monastic community. It makes clear that each individual, committee and office falls under the control of the Abbot or his representatives and that no act ought to go against the order, discipline or the rules of the national sangha Supreme Council. The Abbot therefore heads a network of committees, sub-committees and offices, with potentially over 200 working members, all orchestrated in the running of the monastery, meditation training and accommodating large numbers of people as well as ordaining and disciplining monastics.

Houtman (1990) compares a Burmese monastery not involved in the teaching of meditation and a Burmese monastery which has been given over to teaching *vipassanā* meditation. He argues that the different outlook of meditation centres and monasteries has an important impact upon how they are run. 'Being a special abode dedicated to a special purpose, the meditation centre is founded upon an awareness of the scarcity of time and resources, which is not the case with a conventional monastery' (1990: 129–30). He argues that the decision-making processes about access, day-to-day running and maintenance in the meditation centre have been 'bureaucratized'. Whereas in the conventional monastery organizational structure is the prerogative of a couple of senior monks, in the meditation centre it is the responsibility of lay trusts, committees and sub-committees (1990: 124). An important difference between the meditation centre studied by Houtman and this Thai monastery is that in the Burmese case the committee structure (which is used to define and implement specific goals, and formulate constitutions and regulations) is controlled by the laity (1990: 133). In the Thai monastery, however, the committee structure is made up of monks, *mae chee* and lay representatives, all of whom are appointed by the democratic vote of the community as a whole, with the exception of the head monk and his senior advisors. The meditation centre that Houtman is discussing is much larger, demanding a greater bureaucratization, but we can see a similar structure in Wat Bonamron, a consequence of the focus of the monastery and the organization required to teach and accommodate large numbers of people throughout the year.

DAILY SCHEDULE, MEDITATION AND MONASTIC DUTY

The monastery is a ritual context in which renunciates work towards release from *saṃsāra* through monastic discipline and understanding of the

The monastic community: duty and structure

Figure 3: Mae Chee Im working in the monastery shop

Figure 4: Mae Chee Poy and Mae Chee Suey working in the office

dhamma. It is also a centre for the propagation of meditation to the laity and a place in which the stable community experiences the mundane social interactions and activities that make up daily life. The daily schedule of the monastic community depends in part on the duties of individual monastics. With a few exceptions discussed below everyone in the monastery wakes at 4 a.m., breakfast is at 6 a.m. and lunch is at 10.30 a.m. From noon until 6 a.m. the next day all monastics observe fast. Members of the permanent monastic community attend chanting twice a day for an hour and a half, once at 4 a.m. and once at 5 p.m. This is voluntary and some people choose to meditate in their rooms instead. Before breakfast some, but not all, monks go out to collect alms from laity. They walk up to 4 miles from the monastery. A daily alms round is conducted within the monastery as well, enabling laity staying in the monastery to make merit (see Chapter 7).

Duties are varied and the collective commitment to individual responsibilities ensures the ongoing maintenance of the community. Allocation of duties depends on an individual's abilities and inclination. For example, a *mae chee* who was a property developer before ordination enjoys running the main office and a *mae chee* who was a chef in lay life heads one of the teams who work in the kitchen. *Mae chee* and pious lay women working in the kitchen begin at approximately 3 a.m. to prepare the breakfast for 6 a.m. They work throughout the day, preparing the lunch, prepping food for the next day and buying food from the market before resting in the evening. The monastery shop, selling clothes for *yogi*, toiletries and snacks, opens at 6 a.m., staffed by one *mae chee*, and remains open until 5 p.m. After breakfast there is time for individuals to clean their rooms, sweep the monastery and wash clothes. All the offices in the monastery open at 8 a.m. Shortly afterwards some monks and novices leave the monastery for the day to attend university and school in Chiang Mai. Throughout the day laity come to the monastery to enquire about meditation, begin meditation courses, attend ritual, make donations or speak to monastics.

Both monks and *mae chee* do manual work in the monastery. Monks do all building and maintenance jobs, which are numerous and an important part of the upkeep of the monastery, while *mae chee* and lay women do all domestic chores, and perform administrative roles. One clear area in which they come together is in sweeping the grounds of the monastic compound: this is done throughout the day and involves everyone. At 5 p.m. the evening bell chimes, at which time all people who are staying in the monastery ought to be within the compound. The offices close and evening chanting begins. Once a week at 8 p.m. a ceremony is held in order for novices, *mae chee* and laity to renew their precepts, listen to *dhamma* teaching, chant and meditate together. At this meeting all business, such as plans for new developments, groups of meditation students, expenses and donations, is read out to the assembly. The next evening the ceremony for *Wan Phra* is held in which the monastic community comes together to make offerings to the Buddha and meditate.

Clearly, people in Wat Bonamron lead highly structured lives: waking at 4 a.m. every morning and conditioning themselves to sleep no more than six hours each night; fasting for eighteen hours a day. Days are spent meditating, learning the *dhamma* and working in the monastery, as well as being involved in ritual and teaching meditation. This daily structure is distilled in the strict timetable of the meditation retreat. The sheer volume of hours of meditation to be completed on each day of retreat means that students have little time for anything other than meditation. The daily schedule is hard and singularly focused:

4 a.m.:	Wake up and begin meditating.
6 a.m.:	Breakfast and then meditation.
10.30 a.m.:	Lunch and then meditation.
3–6 p.m.:	Students take a half-hour break from meditation to report to the teacher about their experiences in meditation. After this each returns to meditation.
10 p.m.:	Sleep.

If the schedule is observed strictly there is little time for conversation with other students and students rarely have much interaction with the monastic community: they are prohibited from attending daily chanting and ritual, though they are allowed to attend the weekly Holy Day (*Wan Phra*) and the Renew Precept Ceremony the night before (*Wan Gon*).

In 1970 Tambiah described the daily routine in a village monastery in northeast Thailand:

The daily routine usually consists of prayers in the early morning followed by cleaning the *khuti* and compound, and going into the village to receive food; after breakfast, the learning of chants, attending to personal matters like washing clothes and bathing, and resting in the slack period before and after lunch; evening prayers at about 6 pm, and a further studying of chants before going to bed. Odd jobs connected with maintaining the *wat* and its compound may be done as necessity arises. (1970: 117)

This is similar to the routine described by Spiro of a Burmese monastery (1970: 305). One of the most obvious differences between Spiro's and Tambiah's descriptions and the daily routine of the meditation monastery is that here all free time is ideally spent meditating, and even those people not doing meditation retreat ideally do at least six hours meditation a day. In contrast, Tambiah reports that 'If there is any religious preoccupation, it is not so much with practicing salvation techniques as with learning Pali chants which are necessary on various ritual occasions' (1970: 118). In the Burmese case monks said that they did not have enough time to meditate (Spiro 1970: 307). The accounts of both Tambiah and Spiro focus upon monastic communities comprised solely of men. The contrast between these examples and this contemporary meditation monastery highlights some of the changes in Thai Buddhism since the 1950s that we have been exploring. The extent to which women are incorporated into the monastic community and the monastic focus of the propagation of meditation have created a monastic structure and daily routine which is very different to those recorded by anthropologists in the 1970s and 1980s.

ORDINATION: BECOMING A MONASTIC

Ordination marks entry into the monastic community for all renunciates. However, because of the ambiguity of *mae chee* status, the ordination ceremony differs in some important respects to that of monks. *Mae chee* only adopt eight or ten precepts, in comparison to the 227 of monks. Here, as an entry into the monastic context, I will briefly sketch out the *mae chee* ordination, referring specifically to the events of my own ordination, and highlight the ways in which this is ritually similar to and distinct from the ordination of monks. It is hoped that this will begin to introduce the qualified differences between monks and *mae chee*. My commitment to the monastery and social status within the monastic community were officially marked by my ordination as a *mae chee* and the subsequent meditation retreat that all new ordinands undertake.

On the night before the ordination ceremony for both monks and *mae chee*, offerings of money, white lotus flowers, candles and incense are prepared. These are to be offered by the ordination candidate during the ceremony and are common to all Thai Buddhist ceremonies. The three offerings of lotus, candles and incense represent the Buddhist 'Triple Gem' of *Buddha*, *Dhamma* and *Saṅgha*. Money is commonly given as alms, though the amount given in the ordination ceremony is relatively large. All money is placed in envelopes, which are offered to the quorum of officiating monks, the monastery and to the *mae chee* in attendance once the ceremony has been completed. In this monastery it is common for monks and the monastery to receive offerings of 500 baht (bt) (approx. £9) and *mae chee* to receive 100bt each. The total cost of the ceremony is around 6,000bt (approx. £114). This money is either paid by the ordination candidate or by a lay sponsor.

On the morning of the ordination ceremony the candidate has tufts of his or her hair cut by elder relatives and friends before the head is shaved by a senior monk or *mae chee*, depending upon the sex of the candidate (this may also be performed by a senior lay supporter). I was called from my room at 7 a.m. by a group of *mae chee* who clustered around me as I sat on a chair outside my door. I held a bowl of soapy water as a senior *mae chee* shaved my head with a traditional razor. I was told that it was auspicious to have my head shaved by a *mae chee* with a long ordination and a good heart and that during the shaving I should meditate and send loving-kindness (*mettā*) to my mother and father in England. As the last hair was shaved from my

The monastic community: duty and structure

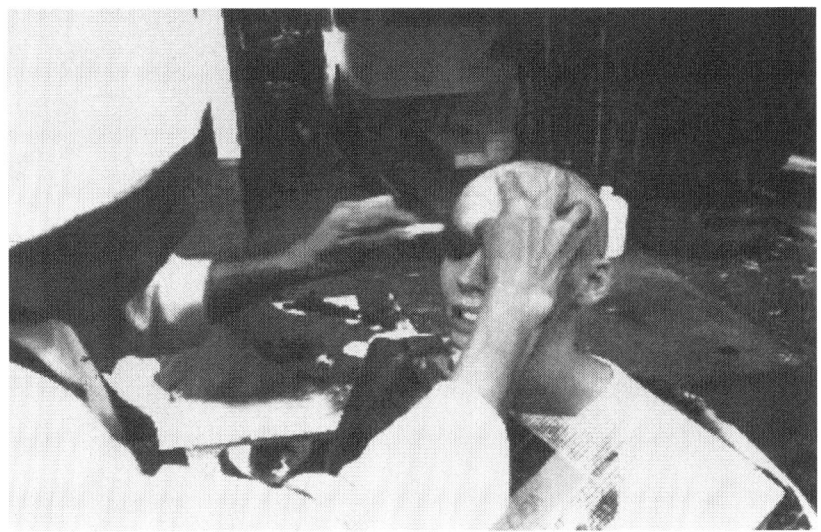

Figure 5: The author having her eyebrows shaved by Mae Chee Suti on the morning of ordination

eyebrows the group of *mae chee* held their hands together in prayer position and proclaimed '*sattu, sattu, sattu*' (Pali: *sādhu*). I translate this as 'thus it is so' and may be understood as equivalent to 'amen'. After the head shaving the candidate changes into white clothes. The female candidate changes into the skirt and shirt of a *mae chee* but wears the loose scarf (*sabai*) of a lay woman across her chest.

In the monastery the ordinations of both monks and *mae chee* begin in the *vihāra*. For male candidates, once the head has been shaved, there is often a procession of family and friends accompanied by drums and dancers prior to ordination. The procession circles the *vihāra*, the main temple at the centre of the monastic compound, three times in a clockwise direction before entering the building. I have never seen this done for *mae chee*.

At my own ordination five monks officiated on the raised platform down one length of the temple and twenty *mae chee* were in attendance. The same number of officiating monks is required for the monk's ordination. Both ceremonies begin with the candidate going to the Triple Gem for refuge by reciting Pali stanzas (see the Appendix), making offerings and prostrating three times to the Buddha image.

The candidate turns away from the Buddha and the quorum of monks and prostrates once at the feet of a senior family member, usually their mother, who gives them the robe of a monastic; I was honoured to be sponsored by a senior *mae chee* who took on this responsibility. Turning back to the quorum of monks the candidate then prostrates three times to their preceptor (*upacha*; Pali: *upajjhāya*), the monk leading the ordination, and offers him flowers, candles, incense and a tray containing the outer robe he or she will wear after ordination. The preceptor returns the robe by laying it over their hands held in prayer position. Holding the robe the noviciate faces the Buddha and seeks refuge in the Triple Gem again, then, turning to the quorum of monks, they request in Pali to be recognized as one who has gone forth by the sangha. For the noviciate *mae chee* this is done by reciting the following stanza three times:

Esāhaṃ bhante, sucira-parinibbutaṃ pi taṃ bhagavantaṃ saraṇaṃ gacchāmi, dhammañ ca bhikkhu-sanghañ ca, pabbajjitaṃ maṃ bhante saṅgho dhāretu, ajjatagge pāṇupetaṃ saraṇaṃ gataṃ.

Venerable Sir, I take refuge in the Blessed One – though he long ago attained liberation – together with the *dhamma* and the *bhikkhu* sangha. May the sangha henceforth regard me as one gone forth, having attained refuge from this day forward.

The noviciate monk must recite an almost identical stanza but the last line is changed plus an additional stanza:

Esāhaṃ bhante, sucira-parinibbutaṃ pi taṃ bhagavantaṃ saraṇaṃ gacchāmi, dhammañ ca bhikkhu-sanghañ ca. Labheyyāhaṃ bhante, tassa bhagavato, dhamma-vinaye pbabbajjaṃ (labheyyaṃ upasampadaṃ).

Venerable Sir, I take refuge in the Blessed One – though he long ago attained liberation – together with the *dhamma* and the *bhikkhu* sangha. Venerable Sir, may I obtain the Going Forth (as a *sāmaṇera*) in the *dhamma-vinaya* of the Lord (may I obtain the Acceptance).

Ahaṃ bhante pabbajjaṃ yācāmi. Imāni kāsāyāni vatthāni gahetvā, pabbājetha maṃ bhante, anukampaṃ upādāya.

Venerable Sir, I request the Going-Forth. Having taken these ochre robes, please give me the Going-Forth out of compassion for me.

The preceptor then gives the noviciate instruction on the Triple Gem, the objects of meditation and the benefits of ordination. At this point in my own ordination my preceptor gave a *dhamma* talk explaining the significance of ordination:

In the time of the Buddha men and women who wished to attain enlightenment became *bhikkhus* or *bhikkhunīs*. Now the *bhikkhunī* lineage has died out but it is possible to become a *mae chee*. Whether ordaining as a monk or *mae chee*, ordination is the opportunity to follow the Buddha's lifestyle and understand the true Buddhist teaching. The robes give the opportunity to be free from many duties and so focus on the duty to free oneself from suffering. So the ordination is of the mind as well as the body. Although *mae chee* have only eight precepts, if they guard these precepts well they can free themselves from suffering in the same way as a monk who guards his precepts well. This means taking the middle way in life so that all of life becomes a path of purification. This is not something that is too hard or involves great sacrifice. Instead, by taking the middle path one needs less and less to be happy so that one is comfortable because one has moderation in all things. The precepts of a *mae chee* are for morality of life but to be a *mae chee* means to meditate so that the moral precepts come from within the heart rather than being imposed from the outside. The benefit of your ordination will be felt by many people, not just yourself. This ordination will enable the world to be a better place and the merit of your actions will be passed to your mother and father. Your life will not be wasted because you will gain insight into the three characteristics of life: impermanence, suffering and non-self. On this path you will be able to reach *nibbāna*.

The under-robe of the candidate monk is then changed in the *vihāra* by his preceptor before he is led out and dressed in the full robe by two senior monks. Similarly, the candidate *mae chee* prostrates three times at this point and is taken out of the *vihāra* by senior *mae chee* who remove the scarf from her chest and dress her in the *mae chee* robe. As a very senior *mae chee*, Jau Mae, dressed me in the robe for the first time she said to me, 'You are my daughter now; I have given birth to you in the *dhamma* family'. They re-enter the *vihāra* and the candidate *mae chee* prostrates three times and requests the eight precepts from her preceptor (see the Appendix) while the candidate monk requests the ten precepts of a novice monk. Both go to the Triple Gem for refuge.

At this point, then, the *mae chee* has taken her eight precepts and her ordination is almost complete. The candidate monk on the other hand is still only ordained as a novice monk (Pali: *sāmaṇera*). He prostrates three times and goes on to receive full ordination, which *mae chee* never do. The novice monk is given an alms bowl by his family and is taken from the *vihāra* to the *ubosot* by the monks, where, in a closed ceremony, he requests dependence on the preceptor. Then the preceptor formally scrutinizes the alms bowl and the robes before the noviciate is questioned in Pali as to his eligibility to be a monk and receives the monk's precepts. This aspect of the ceremony is often a point of great anxiety for the novices, who are fearful of answering incorrectly. The series of questions establishes that the novice does not have any diseases, that he is a human, that he is a man, that he is not in debt and is exempt from government service, that he has his parents' permission, that he is at least 20 years old, and his own name and that of his preceptor.[5]

---

[5] The pattern of having two ordinations is found in Jainism for both monks and nuns, since the latter are 'full renouncers' in the Jain case; see Laidlaw (2006).

Mae chee are not questioned during the ordination ceremony. Interestingly, the questioning that is so central to the monk's ceremony is covered in a declaration, which all *mae chee* must sign prior to ordination. Each woman completes an application form in Thai giving details of her place and date of birth, physical description, education attained, profession and her parents' details. She must proclaim that 'I have faith in Buddhism and am asking to be a *mae chee*. I offer myself to be a student under the leadership of the head monk and committee of this place'. She must then swear that,

I am able to ordain and am in a good condition. I am a female; I am not pregnant; I have no baby; I have good behaviour and health; I am not in debt; I have no addiction; I am not running away from government service or duty; I have not broken any criminal law; I have no fatal or contagious illnesses; I am not old or infirm; I have the ability to follow the lifestyle of a *mae chee*; I have no handicaps; I have received permission from my parents/husband/guardian to ordain. After ordination I will pay respect to the preceptor, teacher, advisor and committee and I will behave following Buddha's teaching and the rules (precepts, *dhamma* and rules). If I break this promise I will acknowledge my mistake and accept the punishment. Please allow me to ordain into Buddhism.

After the questioning in the *ubosot*, the monk returns to the *vihāra*. Back in the *vihāra*, the relatives of the new monk or *mae chee* or the new *mae chee* herself offer flowers, candles, incense and envelopes containing money to each of the monks, who give him or her individual blessings (*mae chee* may make these offerings themselves because they are not fully ordained, while monks may not). Offerings of envelopes are made to each of the *mae chee* present (I have only ever seen this happen in this monastery and it is usually the case that *mae chee* do not have a prominent role in the monk's ordination). As these offerings are being made *mae chee* hold their hands in prayer position; some give the new renouncer individual blessings while others give small presents that will be useful in life as a renouncer, after which the group of *mae chee* chant blessings.

In both the *mae chee*'s and monk's ordination ceremonies, the new renouncer pours water into a small bowl and visualizes the faces of his or her parents in order to dedicate the merit of ordination to them while monks chant blessings (*hai pon*). At my own ordination when I re-entered the *vihāra* as a *mae chee* my preceptor gave a *dhamma* talk on the benefits of ordination:

There are three benefits of ordination: first for yourself because it gives you the chance to guard your mental faculties and train your mind; secondly, for the people around you such as your mother, father and friends, because you now have an opportunity to give back to them; thirdly, for Buddhism to continue because through ordination and meditation you continue the Buddha's lifestyle through practice. To begin with, the change to a life of moderation is difficult because the mind is unstable. Ordaining as a *bhikkhu* (monk), *bhikkhunī* (nun) or *mae chee* is unimportant. One who makes the decision to ordain as a *mae chee* in Buddhism does so through faith. Faith to take up the robe gives the opportunity to get rid of so many things that you are used to as a lay woman. It is hard but you receive the teaching by doing meditation.

As the new monk leaves the *vihāra*, the waiting laity give him alms. I was initially surprised to see people placing coins in the alms bowl on these occasions and I was told by a lay woman that giving to a monk straight after ordination is highly meritorious because he has yet to sin as a monk (alms money and merit will be discussed in detail in Chapter 7). As I was being told this, a very senior monk walked by me, grinning, and joked that this was quite so and that old monks were good for nothing. After the ceremony each new renouncer does a meditation retreat and is appointed at least one guide and mentor. For *mae chee* this person is known as a '*mae chee pi liang*' (lit.: 'elder *mae chee* nurturer'). My own *mae chee pi liang* cared for me as a daughter and showed me how to be a *mae chee* through counsel and example.

DOUBT, FAITH AND THE ONGOING PROCESS OF RENUNCIATION

Monastics constitute a heterogeneous category and in any given community, motivation for monastic commitment and experience of monastic life will be varied. There is huge variance in age, reasons for ordination, educational attainment and social background, for example. Prior to ordination monastics had occupations ranging from civil servants, farmers, hoteliers, office workers, policemen, shopkeepers, or society ladies to labourers. While one *mae chee* had no education and was a construction labourer before she ordained, another was a wealthy Laotian princess.

Reasons for ordination are equally varied. Many monks and *mae chee* felt motivated to ordain after doing a meditation retreat. One monk who had been ordained for twenty years did so after being inspired by the *dhamma* teaching of a monk who encouraged him to meditate. Prior to ordination he had worked on his family's rice farm and ordained because he believed that this was the way to find peace. One *mae chee*, who had been ordained for twenty-eight years, ordained at 18 as a result of her faith in the religion. She recounted crucial points in her adolescence, such as a *dhamma* teaching she attended with her grandmother, the death of a friend at 14, and the example of the hardships of her mother's life, as cementing her faith in meditation and renunciation. Others ordained for a variety of reasons. For example, one *mae chee* had promised that she would ordain for a month if her father recovered from a life-threatening illness. Once in the robes, she decided to stay. One monk from a poor family took ordination in order to receive an education and was confident that he would disrobe once he completed his Master's degree. Another monk took ordination because he had promised his mother that he would. More than one elderly *mae chee* took ordination after her husband had passed away, stating that it was appropriate for them to dedicate their energies to meditation now that they were no longer focused on family life. Mae Chee Bun, who had been ordained for three years and was 44, told me in interview that she came to practise meditation because she felt that she was leading a bad life:

The first time I ever tried meditation I did it because I felt bored. Nothing was good in my life and I felt so bad for myself that I did no good for my family, my friends, or me and it hurt my heart. When I came to practise I cried for a long time. Then I decided to be a *mae chee* because I could do good. I could stop doing bad.

Though the reasons for ordination and duties of monastics in the community were various, renunciation was understood by all as an opportunity to do 'work' by learning to cut attachment to a sense of self. This work was conceived of as challenging and questions of ability to renounce attachment were an ongoing concern. Through articulating my own anxieties about my monastic duties as they arose I was afforded insight into the ways in which others understood the ongoing responsibilities of monasticism. Often, counsel came through illustrative examples from the lives of others and how their understanding of the experience of emotion had changed as a result of further meditation and mindfulness. For example, in response to my concerns about my ability to be physically disciplined, Mae Chee Sati told me that,

When you become a *mae chee* people respect you. Automatically you have to look at yourself to see if you are worthy of respect. So you have to act properly. If you didn't act properly then people would follow. Sometimes I forget to do some things properly. It is forgetting to be mindful, or acknowledge what we are doing. Like when we are working together and someone is joking, at that time you laugh loudly and *mae chee* shouldn't have loud voices. It's not good for another to hear it, but already its forgotten. Mindfulness is knowing exactly what you are doing. Just only sitting, but you will know how about your hand, how about your leg, how about your mind, how about your feelings; you will know.

Periods of doubt are a recognized part of a monastic life. This was made explicit in sermons given by senior monks for which the whole community gathered once a week. During these sermons monastics were encouraged to act as '*dhamma* friends' (Pali: *kalyāṇamittatā*; variously translated as 'good friend', 'virtuous friend', 'noble friend', 'admirable friend') for those experiencing doubts and anxieties. '*Dhamma* friendship' refers to spiritual friendship and support in a Buddhist community: a special relationship either between a teacher and student or within a communal peer group that encourages the development of skilfulness and ethical virtues. As in Mae Chee Sati's response to my doubts above, the responsibilities of a *dhamma* friend are to offer counsel and example when others are experiencing doubts about their abilities to maintain discipline in their lives. It was commonly assumed that younger monks and *mae chee* would have 'struggles' with their ordination because the lure of a worldly life was stronger at a young age. Doubts, as with renunciation, unfolded over time. Recounting periods of doubt after the fact was often a way of illustrating the extent to which mindfulness had developed. Monks and *mae chee* would recount doubtful periods from the past, particularly during the first few years of ordination, as a way of demonstrating how they had overcome doubt through the gradual development of mindfulness.

The way that doubts are dealt with in the monastic community more broadly is to a certain extent self-selecting. Many people who ordained for short periods only ever intended to be in the robes for a limited time, while those people who experienced doubts about their vocation as a monastic and were unable to overcome them, disrobed. For example, one woman disrobed after six years as a *mae chee* because she doubted that ordination was right for her. Over a number of months she discussed these doubts with the Abbot, who encouraged her to undertake several meditation retreats to consider them. Finally she felt that she could not use the doubts as a meditative tool and continue as a *mae chee*. She now lives close to the monastery as a lay woman with a young family. She continues to practise *vipassanā* exclusively and visits the temple on a daily basis.

In the monastery doubt and the dispossession of certainty appear to play a qualified role in relation to the 'power' of the religious experience. In the practice of *vipassanā* emphasis is placed on dealing with the attitude produced by negative feelings such as doubt, rather than in examining the causal chain that has generated such feelings; to consider cause is to be part of this-worldly truth and is identified with maintaining a sense of self. Doubt is not what drives the initiate; as a condition of the mind it is one tool among many used in the cultivation of detachment. I turn now to the meditation technique itself to consider the very specific methods and practices by which monastics intend to change their responses to their internal processes.

CHAPTER 4

Meditation as ethical imperative

> The great principles of insight meditation are the four foundations of mindfulness. Lord Buddha claims that mindfulness is the only path to purification, freedom from suffering, and thus to *nibbāna*. This means there is no other practice to purify the mind, escape suffering and reach *nibbāna* besides the practice of the four foundations of mindfulness.
>
> (Phra Ajharn Yai, founder of Wat Bonamron)

> [A]t any particular stage in the historical development of any particular culture the established patterns of emotion, desire, satisfaction, and preference will only be adequately understood if they are understood as giving expression to some distinctive moral and evaluative position. Psychologies thus understood express and presuppose moralities.
>
> (MacIntyre 1988: 76–7)

In the meditation monastery the primary monastic duties of the community are to practise meditation and facilitate the meditation practice of others. Following the work of Luhrmann (2009), I interpret meditation as a social learning process. In so doing, I shall consider some of the socially taught rules by which the cognitive categories of Buddhism are identified in the experiences of the practising monastic. The practitioner learns to engage with and interpret internal and external sensory phenomena in specific ways. Thus, the development of meditative discipline and monastic identity involves a process of learning to reinterpret subjective experiences and learning to alter subjectivity. The monastic learns to experience thoughts and emotions not as the uninteresting slough of the daily grind but rather as evidence of the fundamental truths of Buddhism: that all phenomena are conditioned by non-self, impermanence and suffering. These three tenets become the context in which all logical analyses and apperceptions of phenomena are carried out. Thus, the renunciate learns to experience her own mental and physical activities as evidence of the importance of the project of renunciation. Mae Chee Sati, a young woman who had been ordained for nine years, explained the significance that meditation holds for her when she said:

I can say to you that meditation is the most important thing in my life and it's what I was born for. I want to practise and I want to improve my mind. Practice gives you more understanding of yourself and of life. You can do good more easily; you can see right or wrong more easily also. And then you're good for other people too. It changes the way that you see yourself; I can see my greed very easily. I look at my greed and I say to myself 'can you cut it?' 'Yes.' I can see my power, if it's strong enough or not; first, understanding and after that, doing. When I cannot cut it, little by little this improves through practice. With other people I have more kindness and more forgiveness; more loving-kindness and less selfishness. Practice is not easy. You go little by little for learning. But it's not too difficult. There's more and more to learn, so that you don't follow your defilements. It's hard, but it's good. When you take medicine it tastes bitter but it's good for you.

Meditation, which we might think of as being a solitary activity, in fact has important social dimensions that are collectively understood and taught. The renunciate who comes to experience his or her subjectivity as congruent with religious tenets has done so through active learning and engaging with specific, socially taught techniques by which subjectivity is intended to be shaped.

It does an injustice to the lives of monastics to understand 'monasticism' only as a set of codes or rules by which one may live one's life and thereby be 'monastic'. This provides us with an understanding of the context of monastic practice, and the supportive framework in which monastic practice takes place, but it helps little in our understanding of the significance of the lived experience of monasticism, or the transformative effect that practices such as meditation have, and are intended to have, upon individual monastics. In this chapter I do not assume that ascetic practice will be the same for all monastics or that asceticism and ethical training will be uncomplicated, or indeed complicated in the same ways, for all members of the community. Rather, I argue that the existence of an ascetic and ethical ideal provides a telos and a technology for cultivating such a reality, which individuals incorporate into their understandings of themselves and by which they constitute themselves as ethical subjects.

The asceticism at the centre of monastic life in Wat Bonamron may be traced back to the practice and tenets of meditation training. As we have seen, the daily routine of those doing meditation retreats is markedly different from the normal monastic routine: during retreat the daily schedule is centred entirely on meditation. It is said that the most highly respected place is the room in which one does intensive meditation. To stay in the meditation room doing intensive practice and be separate from the rest of the community is highly meritorious. Through practising meditation monastics intend ultimately to attain enlightenment – the telos of a religious life.

In this chapter I will examine the practice of *vipassanā* meditation in Wat Bonamron in order to understand what it is that people do when they meditate, why this is an appropriate practice, what is achieved by it, and what changes are effected by it, through which subjects make themselves Buddhist. In this context, meditation practice is intended to bring about a change in perception in the meditator which is consistent with Buddhist ethical principles. In order to understand these principles and their significance for monastics in other areas of monastery life it is necessary to understand the means by which they are actualized in the bodies and minds of monastics themselves. I shall examine meditation as an ethical project, or in Foucault's terms as a 'technology of the self', focusing on the paradox of will and spontaneity in religious attainment and the way this is addressed in meditation practice. Describing the experience of the basic meditation retreat as an introduction to meditation, leading the reader through the meditation as it would be learnt by a novice meditator, I will then focus on the final stages of the retreat and examine their meaning for Buddhist subjects. In the next chapter I will expand on the ways in which meditation becomes a practice through which experienced meditators understand themselves. I hope to show that these specific bodily and mental practices may bring about the experiences of what it means to be religious in this monastery, and so to provide an anthropological analysis of an important Buddhist practice of self.

The founder of Wat Bonamron, and meditation teacher of the present Abbot, has written that it is the duty (*na ti*) of all human beings to free themselves from suffering and that the practice of *vipassanā* is the only means of doing so. Phra Ajharn Yai argues that until this is realized 'our lives will be aimless, like one who walks in darkness, unaware of dangers ahead; like a bird circling over the ocean, unable to find land'. He is unusual in Thai Buddhism for his insistence that it is possible to attain enlightenment in this lifetime (see also Pandita 2002) but in the monastery his written and spoken teachings carry absolute authority and he is revered as one who has attained enlightenment himself. His view is that the central teaching of Buddhism is the purification of the mind, that this is to be actualized by everyone, and that all humans are born to effect spiritual improvement on themselves and reach enlightenment. This view is reflected in the proselytizing project of the monastery in which thousands of people are taught meditation every year.

The connection between meditation practice and epistemology is reflected in the experience of meditation and understanding of the resultant changes that are effected within themselves by individual monastics. As I shall discuss, if it is the case in Buddhist soteriological thought that the non-existence of a 'self' is the way in which individuals ought to understand themselves, the realization of 'non-self' becomes a moral imperative (but for the cognitive distortion of a perceived sense of self one would have a true understanding of the world in which the 'self' is rightly understood as nothing more than an impermanent compound). Paradoxically, one's concern then becomes the ethical project of making of oneself a certain kind of person: a project that is actualized through the self-willed ascetic practice of *vipassanā* in which the will is eradicated and non-self directly realized.

As we shall see, a meditation retreat ideally culminates in the embodiment of the release of consciousness from the shackles of a sense of self. The condition of enlightenment, or momentary transcendence of the self and consequent insight into the impermanent and imperfect nature of the world, is thought to be potentially actualized through a process of continuous physical and mental discipline in which resolution may be achieved between the ideals of Buddhist soteriology and ascetic practice.

THE RETREAT PROCESS

The basic meditation retreat in Wat Bonamron takes twenty-eight days. Those people, lay or monastic, who wish to undertake the retreat do so by contacting one of the admissions offices in the monastery in order to be put on a waiting list. There is no charge for accommodation, food or teaching during the retreat but at the end of their stay meditation students make a donation to the upkeep of the monastery. These donations are themselves meritoriously accumulative.[1] There is no recommended amount for donations, which may vary depending upon means or religious intent. I worked closely with the main office in the monastery, and I knew of no students who had not made a donation at the end of their retreat, with the exception of two foreign lay students who skipped off early. While the vast majority of students are women (see table in Chapter 3), adults of all ages attend the courses throughout the year. Occasionally children attend but this is always with an adult or as part of a group organized by their school.

---

[1] See Chapter 7 for a consideration of merit and alms donations.

On the first day of retreat students are required to bring eleven white lotus flowers, eleven yellow or orange candles and eleven incense sticks. These are customary offerings to be used in the opening ceremony that marks the commencement of the retreat (see below). Students are also required to bring a completed application form detailing their name, occupation, address, emergency details, meditation experience and reasons for practising; two photocopies of their identity cards (foreign students are required to provide copies of a valid passport and visa); a working alarm clock or timer that can be set to five minutes exactly; personal toiletries such as soap and toothpaste. Lay people are required to bring at least two sets of loose, modest, non-transparent white clothing and white underwear; women are also required to bring a white scarf (*sabai*), which is worn under the right arm, around the breasts and pins over the left shoulder. It is understood that monastics attending meditation retreat will continue to wear the respective robes of their ordination lineage throughout.

All students are provided with a bedroll, a blanket and a small pillow, and are allocated a private cell, which contains a wooden bed and a rudimentary bathroom (usually with a tap, a large bucket and a scoop for washing, and a Western-style toilet). Lay students are required to wear their white clothes at all times, including during sleep. They are encouraged to sleep no more than six hours a night. Ablutions are to be performed twice a day, once after breakfast and once at 5 p.m. During the retreat all students will be provided with two meals a day in the monastery canteen: breakfast at 6 a.m. and lunch at 10.30 a.m. Lay meditation students must observe similar precepts to *mae chee*, including to fast from noon until 6 a.m. the next day. The daily food is donated as alms to the monastery and prepared by *mae chee* and *upāsikās* (pious lay women).

Within a short time each student will be doing twelve hours of meditation a day and sleeping for four hours a night. The pressure of fitting the hours required for practice into the day is an ever present consideration for students. People come to the monastery with the intention of doing the meditation retreat and it is felt that anyone who wished to stay in the monastery without practising this type of meditation would be denying someone else the opportunity to improve themselves. During the retreat students are not allowed to talk about meditation practice with anyone except their teacher. They may not mix the practice with other techniques; have physical contact with others; enter other people's rooms; read (this includes Buddhist books); write; listen to music; leave the monastery or have contact with the outside world without the teacher's permission; or sleep during the day. They must keep their rooms clean and tidy and leave them as they found them when they arrived. Once students are settled in their rooms and have changed into their white clothing *mae chee* give them the basic instruction in meditation. The meditation technique will be examined in detail below. Here it is worth noting that while *mae chee* give the basic instruction, senior monks guide the meditation students during the retreat. Monastics from the monastery receive the same opening ceremony each time they undertake retreat and they stay in their own rooms for the retreat period.

On the evening of their first day students attend a formal 'opening ceremony' conducted in Pali in which they go to the Triple Gem (*Buddha, Dhamma, Saṅgha*) for refuge; request the meditation practice from the teacher ('Holy Sir, Teacher, may I humbly offer my body and mind to you for the purpose of practising Insight Meditation[2]'); and ask for forgiveness from the teacher, in case they have done (or will do, during the retreat) anything wrong, intentionally or unintentionally ('Forgive me, Venerable Sir, for all wrongdoing carelessly done to the Reverend One by way of the three doors'[3]). For laity this also involves adopting the eight precepts of *mae chee*; monks and *mae chee* already hold monastic precepts and as such do not need to take new ones.

The retreat comprises a structured series of different practices, 'mindful prostration', walking meditation, sitting meditation and reporting to a teacher (discussed in detail below). These form the daily schedule, with walking and sitting meditation periods increasing in length as the retreat progresses. The meditation teacher decides the amount that a student will meditate and sleep throughout the retreat. Initially the meditation student will begin with alternating fifteen-minute periods of walking and sitting, for a total of six hours a day. These periods usually increase five minutes at a time so that towards the end of the retreat the periods will be an hour in length and total fourteen to eighteen hours a day. As the amount of meditation increases, the amount of time for sleep decreases; towards the end of a retreat the student will be sleeping no more than four hours a night. The final three nights and four days of the retreat are spent without sleep, meditating continuously.

Before walking, the meditator stands with her feet parallel, the hands clasped in front or behind with the right on top of the left. The head is straight and the eyes look at a point on the floor about a metre away. She

---

[2] *Imāhaṃ bhagavā attabhāvaṃ tumhākaṃ pariccajāmi.*
[3] *Ācariye pamādena dvārattayena kataṃ sabbaṃ aparādhaṃ khamatha me bhante.* The three doors are mind, speech and body.

Figure 6: Mae Chee Or giving the basic meditation instruction to new meditation students

mentally notes 'standing, standing, standing' while being aware of the standing posture. The walking meditation builds up from a basic step (for which the meditator acknowledges 'right/left goes thus') to a complicated six-step movement (for which the meditator mentally notes 'heel up – lifting – moving – lowering – touching – pressing'). The meditator walks slowly for a distance of a few metres, stops and turns using the same process of mental noting, mentally repeating each part of the turn three times ('stopping, stopping, stopping, standing, standing, standing, intending to turn, intending to turn, intending to turn, turning, turning, turning, standing, standing, standing, intending to walk, intending to walk, intending to walk').

For sitting meditation a traditional cross-legged sitting posture is adopted, and the torso ought to be straight and the eyes closed. The right hand rests on the left with the tips of both thumbs touching and the two hands resting in the lap. The meditator focuses on the breath as it is manifest in the movement of the abdomen. As the abdomen swells with inhalation the meditator mentally labels the movement 'rising'; as it recedes with exhalation the meditator labels this 'falling'. Any distraction from the focus on the

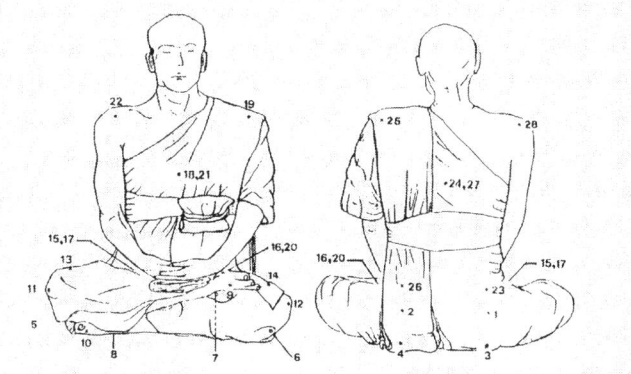

Figure 7: The sitting posture showing the twenty-eight touching points

abdomen is mentally labelled three times (for example, 'thinking, thinking, thinking') and the attention is returned to the breath.

The walking and sitting meditations become more complex over time until the meditator is doing six-step walking meditation and acknowledging and mentally labelling the rise and fall of the abdomen followed by the 'sitting' of the whole body and 'touching', for which the meditator focuses on one of twenty-eight specified areas of the body, each approximately the size of a coin, in sequence. This focus on 'touching' may or may not result in different sensations in the area being focused on, such as the area feeling warm or painful. There are twenty-eight touching points followed in sequence, given in fourteen pairs.

1. Right hip	2. Left hip
3. Right buttock	4. Left buttock
5. Back of right knee	6. Back of left knee
7. Right anklebone	8. Left anklebone
9. Top of right foot	10. Top of left foot
11. Right kneecap	12. Left kneecap
13. Middle-front of right thigh	14. Middle-front of left thigh
15. Right fold of groin	16. Left fold of groin
17. Right fold of groin	18. Solar plexus
19. Left shoulder (front)	20. Left fold of groin
21. Solar plexus	22. Right shoulder (front)
23. Back of right hip	24. Middle of back
25. Left shoulder blade	26. Back of left hip
27. Middle of back	28. Right shoulder blade.[4]

[4] Touching points 17–22 and 23–28 form crosses on the front and back of the body.

Once the meditator has completed the sequence of twenty-eight touching points she begins again at the right hip. Each pair of points is associated with a different mental condition. For example, it is expected that when a meditator is using only the first ten points (to the top of the feet) he or she feels restless and will want to run away. The effect of the complete sequence, including the front and back cross, is to give the meditator a sense of wholeness and equanimity.

Laidlaw describes the *puja* worship of Shvetambar Jain idols in which the idol is washed, decorated, rubbed with oil and coated with sheets of silver (1995: 249). As part of the rite the idol is daubed with sandalwood paste, anointing nine body parts in turn: toes, knees, forearms, shoulders, the crown of the head, the forehead, the throat, the centre of the chest, and the navel. In so doing, worshippers read spiritual qualities directly onto the physical form of the idol. A Khartar Gacch nun described the significance of each point to Laidlaw. For example, 'When we put sandalwood paste on the feet, we think that this big toe of God is so pure and holy. May its holiness come to me' (Laidlaw 1995: 250). The Jain worshipper is encouraged to measure herself against the ideal of the Jina's (one who has over come all spiritual obstacles) attainments. It is through such self-contemplation and mimesis that the worshipper attains insight into the uniform essence of all souls (cf. Humphrey and Laidlaw 1994: 248–50). In contrast, the body of the meditator is used as a focus of mindfulness through which the meditator ideally develops the apperception that there is no self. Focusing on the points of the body is intended to actualize specific bodily, mental and emotional conditions in the development of mindfulness. As we shall see below, these conditions must be experienced in order that the meditator may transcend them.

After the initial instruction on the technique all meditation students meditate alone, using a timer to begin and end each meditation period, and meet the meditation teacher once a day in a one to one interview. Mindful prostration and walking and sitting meditation are practised continually and cyclically for the period of time prescribed by the meditation teacher. When taking a break the meditator should try to maintain the same level of mindfulness in all activity, such as going to the toilet, eating or washing. Such a level of mindfulness is relatively easy to attain and will be experienced by most meditators towards the end of their retreat and by more experienced meditators in subsequent retreats. To be able to continue the process of mental noting in all activity requires the meditator to slow their actions down and never perform any physical action unthinkingly. For example, during retreat I would mentally note 'chewing' and 'swallowing' while eating, as well as 'lifting' as I brought the spoon of food to my mouth. Before gulping I would note 'intending to gulp' and 'gulping'. Other activities such as going to the toilet or washing up were also broken down into their constitutive physical movements and labelled. When lying down for sleep the same process of mental noting is used as the meditator acknowledges 'lying' and 'rising, falling' until they fall asleep. Advanced meditators are able to remain in a state of mindful awareness constantly; even during sleep a process of mental noting occurs. In my own experience of intensive retreat I would sleep for four hours a night during which my sleep would feel like an extension of my waking meditation and I would feel as if I remained conscious of the rise and fall of my abdomen throughout. The ability to maintain this level of mindfulness confirms for meditators that they are progressing in the meditation and that they have the capacity to progress further still. This experience of the achievement of mindfulness as a psychological state corresponds to what the meditator is encouraged to experience by the teacher. This acts as an important validation of both the meditator's faith *in* the practice and the meditator's compatibility *with* that practice.

The meditation teacher encourages the student not to become involved in thoughts or physical or emotional sensations but rather to note mentally their occurrence and maintain a continuous meditative focus (for example, in walking meditation the focus is the feet, and in sitting meditation the focus is the abdomen, the whole body and the successive points on the body). This can be an exhausting process for those new to meditation. Often, sitting without moving is physically painful and may give rise to strong emotional states. For both new students and seasoned practitioners the first few days of a meditation retreat are often very hard and there is a strong urge to give up. Eventually the mind settles down and it becomes easier to remain focused. An illustration of this change in mental focus may be seen in the daily meeting between the Abbot and a lay meditation student who had been practising for four days:

STUDENT: I'm tired; mentally tired. I only did eight hours but I did 30:30 minutes (30 minutes walking; 30 minutes sitting). I spent so much time thinking, that it's mentally worn me out. It wasn't until the last half an hour that it changed and I felt pretty good.
AJHARN: Today, focus on 'acknowledging' more; bring your bare attention to it. The same as if you were watching a movie, you're just seeing. As if you were the award committee, acknowledge detail. Pay attention.
STUDENT: I had doubt then everything became effortless. I was still observing but it was so much easier... only in the last half an hour though.
AJHARN: Good. Continue. Do five minutes more walking and sitting and at least nine hours.

A balance must be struck between mindful awareness and intensive concentration. A student who is not sufficiently focused will become lazy and find it hard to complete each meditation period. If concentration is too high the meditator will become restless or may enter low-level trance states in which awareness of the meditation objects (such as 'rising/falling') becomes impossible. In such states the meditator will have experiences of unusual feelings, visions and movements of the body.

Meditational experiences may be accompanied by moments of profound physical and mental bliss, clarity and resolution. At such a point it is easy for a student to become stuck in or attached to these experiences. This is known as '*vipassanā kilesa*' or *vipassanā* defilement. Defilements in Theravāda Buddhism are understood to taint or contaminate the minds of all beings. These defilements are attachments leading to craving, greed, hatred or anger, ignorance, pride, envy, jealousy, delusion and so forth (Silananda 1990: 18). *Vipassanā* is intended to purify the mind of these attachments. However, strong experiences in meditation are often attached to by the new meditator (and the old) and become a source of pride, fear and craving (the fear that the meditative state will finish and the desire to attain such a state again). This leads new students to believe delusionally that they are very close to enlightenment when in fact their attachment to such states is antithetical to the retreat process. The role of the teacher in such cases is to encourage the student to acknowledge and let go of these experiences just as they would with pain or discomfort. Nonetheless, such positive experiences may be a heartening fillip for the hardworking student. The final days of the retreat, prior to the period without sleep, are usually characterized by feelings of profound clarity, peacefulness and self-acceptance, and this is reflected in a marked difference in the posture and facial expression of students. Going without very much sleep is no longer a struggle and the student finds it easy to remain focused in meditation. Until the meditation teacher thinks that the student has reached this state they will not be allowed to enter the intensive sleepless period. Some students are kept at the point prior to the sleepless period for as long as five days because they are having trouble maintaining only four hours sleep, are unable to do a minimum of twelve hours practice a day or have not attained the equanimity necessary to do the more intensive sleepless practice.

It should be noted here that while meditation may engender profound and transformative experiences for some practitioners it does not do so for everyone. I have known students to complain of lack of attainment or ability and either drop out of the retreat early or complete it with a minimum of meditation. One lay woman explained her motivation for completing the retreat to me by saying, 'If I can climb a mountain in platform shoes, I can do this!' Furthermore, the quality of the meditation of seasoned practitioners varies and it is usual that periods of 'good' meditation will be tempered with periods when it is a struggle to keep one's eyes closed, let alone maintain mindful concentration on the breath.

THE ROLE OF THE MEDITATION TEACHER

The teacher has a high-profile role throughout the retreat. Four senior monks in the monastery act as meditation teachers. The Abbot, Phra Ajharn Sila, is the meditation teacher for foreign students, with the assistance of the Deputy Head *mae chee*, Mae Chee Sati. If Phra Ajharn is away Mae Chee Sati will assume the duty of teaching meditation; this duty is never given to other *mae chee* and is in part a consequence of Mae Chee Sati's English-language skills and in part her phenomenal ability as a meditation teacher. Thai students are divided between three senior monks and the main office assigns them quite arbitrarily, depending upon which teacher has the fewest students.

Though some senior monks and nuns who have been practising for many years may choose to do retreat without the guidance of a teacher, common consensus holds that the teacher is necessary if one is to have a successful retreat. As the primary meditation teacher in the monastery, and the person recognized by others as having the most spiritual attainment, the Abbot plays an important part in guiding the meditation practice of almost all monastics. The level of devotion to the Abbot is instrumental in the system of meditation retreats and 'selfless' practice and is used as a tool for apprehending ultimate truth. In interview a very senior *mae chee*, Jau Mae, was keen to talk about her relationship with the Abbot. Originally from Laos, Jau Mae came to Thailand fifty-seven years previously. At the time of interview she was 91 years old and had been ordained for twenty-five years. When I questioned her about her relationship with Ajharn she looked me in the face and said, 'If I thought it would help him to see, I would give him my eyes'.[5]

---

[5] It is possible that Jau Mae is likening her own devotion to that found in the narrative structure of *The Therīgāthā*, a collection of verses ascribed to the earliest female followers of the Buddha (see Blackstone 1998). *The Therīgāthā* is a canonical text attributed to female authorship and focusing entirely on women's religious experiences. Blackstone understands these texts as 'liberation manuals' offering a functional model for the successful quest for liberation and argues that therefore it is possible to interpret them as 'symbols that reflect communal values and preoccupations' (1998: 6). In one poem, a would-be suitor accosts the nun Subha in a mango grove. As a demonstration of her detachment from

Once a day each student reports to the meditation teacher about the conditions of their practice in a one to one interview. This meeting is called in Thai '*Sop Arom*', or 'Examination of Feeling/Emotion'. Students enter and leave the teacher's room on their knees. Before and after the meeting they must prostrate three times to the Buddha image and three times to the teacher. During the meeting they must kneel with the hands in prayer position in front of the chest. Students reflect on the day of practice and judge whether they have been successful in acknowledging and letting go of emotional and mental conditions. They are then given advice and instruction for the next day.

An example of the daily meeting is set out in an English-language information pamphlet given to new foreign students:

'You told me to do the first walking step acknowledging "right goes thus, left goes thus" for twenty minutes. I was asked to do twenty minutes sitting too, observing and acknowledging the rising and falling of the belly as "rising and falling". In total, I was told to do seven hours. I did eight hours.

The practice is both easy and difficult. Walking is easier than sitting, and pain is a problem, with cramped legs when thinking. I never imagined that twenty minutes sitting could be so long. I have had doubt, anger, impatience and I was always looking at the timer. Sometimes I felt a little bit tired, sometimes the thinking became like a movie.'

If the teacher wants to know more, then he will ask you. Give short answers. So, no story about the pain, anger, or thinking is necessary. You do not have to find excuses as to why you are not perfect. You must just learn to understand your imperfection. Be patient with yourself.

With prohibitions on speech, reading, writing and contact with anyone outside the monastery this meeting becomes the only contact that the student has with anyone else (new students do talk to each other, but this is minimal and decreases when their meditation becomes more intensive; monastics spend the retreat period in total silence apart from their daily meeting with the teacher). The relationship with the teacher is therefore pivotal to the retreat experience: his advice is central to the student's understanding of meditative experiences, and confidence in the teacher is paramount for the students to commit themselves to such an extreme level of self-discipline. A large part of the incentive to maintain such physical discipline is this daily meeting in which the hours of meditation achieved and whether the student was able to abstain from sleep are recorded. A

---

physical beauty and sexual desire she gouges out one of her eyes, and presents it to him. This act of selflessness quells the passions of the libertine. In Jau Mae's narrative, eye donation indicates both her non-attachment to her physical form and her devotion to the Abbot.

student may push herself to go without sleep for three days even though her organs hurt inside her, by and large because of her faith in the teacher and because he told her to.

There may also be an element of confession to this meeting, as thoughts of shame, guilt and remorse are spoken of as well as the need for atonement. However, it is not the teacher's duty to impose penance. In each case, the teacher encourages the student to observe such feelings and desires without acting upon them or becoming involved in them. Foucault suggests that the practice of Christian confession is able to assume a hermeneutic role because it is modelled on the renunciation of one's will and one's self. He argues that in Christianity each person has the duty to know himself and to disclose that knowledge to others, thereby bearing both public and private witness against himself and linking truth obligations of faith and self (2000d: 242). Self-knowledge is therefore a necessary precondition to spiritual purification: and that self must be disclosed in order that it might be renounced (Foucault 2000d: 249). As Foucault has it, 'By telling himself not only his thoughts but also the smallest movements of consciousness, his intentions, the monk stands in a hermeneutic relation not only to the master but to himself' (2000d: 248).

This appears at first blush similar to the process of 'confession' during the retreat but they are differently weighted in importance and in the effect they have. I suggest that this is in part because understanding of the 'self' that is being confessed in the Thai case is very differently constituted. As we shall see, in the retreat process the meditator's relation to herself becomes at once similar and different to her relationship with the meditation teacher. Whereas in the Christian example discussed by Foucault, self-examination is subordinate to obedience (Foucault 2000d: 248), here the total obedience the meditator has to the teacher is a means of maintaining a perpetual process of self-examination. The role of the teacher is not to give forgiveness but rather to encourage the student to witness experiences as transient conditions. There is no doubt, however, that a happy consequence of speaking to the teacher about meditative experiences is cathartic release.

Luhrmann discusses a similar relationship between the psychoanalyst and the patient in American psychiatry (2000: 181–202). She argues that the analyst listens to the patient in order to understand, rather than to judge. The analyst is attempting to reveal intentions, both conscious and unconscious, and the way in which these intentions lead to action. The analysts see 'action as in service to the self, and what fascinates them is not what people do but why – what self those actions serve' (Luhrmann 2000: 182). Interestingly, the analyst believes that the 'why' of action is inherently unknowable: 'aspects of one's own psyche are always hidden and an observer can never see clearly because his own unconscious intentions distort his vision' (Luhrmann 2000: 182). This suggests a power dynamic between the analyst and the patient in which the patient can never really know her own mind as well as the analyst can and must submit herself to the examination of the analyst in order that she might come to know more than she did, even if she can never know everything. For the analyst then, the ethos is one of honesty in the way that she tries to know and of caring in the way that she tries to help another person to know. This seems similar to the dynamic between the meditation teacher and student. The crucial difference is that through meditation the truth of reality, the insight into the three characteristics of life, is potentially revealed completely through the practice and through submitting to the guidance of the teacher. These are general truths, in the sense of not being specific to the individual, and most people will have some knowledge of them in advance of the retreat.

The meditator uses a process of mental noting to observe and detach from the normal processes of the body and mind, such as grief, sleep, pain, doubt, restlessness or desire. In order to do this it is necessary to see all mental and physical phenomena as neutral, responding to them with neither desire nor aversion but rather developing a position of equanimity and balance. However, it is believed that the student herself is so ensnared in mundane truth and a perceived sense of self that she cannot detach herself sufficiently in such an intense process. The teacher, having a clearer insight into supra-mundane truth, is in a position to know what is best for the student. As the Abbot told me, 'Just acknowledge "knowing", not good or bad. Don't explain the meaning. This supports the mind having less attachment with conventional truth. More important is absolute truth, which you realize by doing now [being mindfully attentive in the present moment], just noting'.

In psychoanalysis the patient is required to reveal his most private thoughts and emotions, while the analyst is expected not to reveal herself nor respond with normal emotions. Similarly, in reporting meditation experiences the student reveals the often very powerful emotional experiences she has had during the day but this is not met with either reciprocity or interest in the reasons for the emotions, but rather with technical instructions for further meditation (such as, 'acknowledge "fear, fear, fear" when a sense of fear arises'). In each instance the relationship is one of emotional deprivation. Luhrmann writes of the psychoanalytic relationship that it,

does not allow the other listener to respond with his face, with a touch, nor even much with his words. It does not allow him to reciprocate or respond in kind. At the same time, the analytic relationship permits the analysand an extraordinary degree of freedom. Here, for the first time, he is encouraged to say anything – everything – that enters his mind, without worrying whom he might offend or what social mores he might violate. It permits him to say everything and places him in a passive, dependent, exposed position from which to do so. (2000: 188)

In contrast, the relationship between the meditation student and teacher is structured around confessional honesty about the student's emotional, physical and mental experiences, while the student is simultaneously prohibited from discussing the *reasons* for such experiences. The meditation teacher is inhibited from revealing any interest in the student's reasoning because this would not enable the student to cut attachment to her experiences and thereby realize non-self. Nonetheless, the student is placed within a passive and dependent position, no longer having her own explanations of her experiences for comfort but rather depending entirely upon the guidance of the teacher. During a reporting session with meditation students, the Abbot told me that when people come to meditate they become stronger, but in order to do this they must first become more vulnerable: 'like a snake shedding its skin to grow, when it first loses its old skin it is defenceless against attack'.

Luhrmann argues that psychoanalysis may be understood as 'a powerful expression of the modern age's belief in authenticity' (2000: 200). It is through understanding who we 'really' are that we are able to become ourselves; salvation therefore lies in self-discovery: 'Our uniqueness lies in part in our limitation. To live without lying to ourselves about those limitations is to be ourselves – and to be free' (Luhrmann 2000: 200). This need for self-discovery in psychoanalysis sharply contrasts with the dissolution of the self in meditation practice in the same way as architecture may be contrasted with archaeology: one is a building up; the other is a stripping away.[6]

IMAGINATIVE IMMATERIALITY

Within the retreat process this mental discipline slowly extends to a conscious awareness in minute detail of what one is doing both bodily and mentally in each moment. Any thinking about the past or the future is contemplated as a thinking process in the present. By observing the conditions of the body and the mind in this way individuals detach themselves

---

[6] It should be noted that other common practices in psychotherapy are based on the dissolution, not discovery, of the self. Certain schools of therapy, such as narrative therapy, have adopted post-modern social constructionist models which negate the idea of a 'real self'. While this is in no way equivalent to the experiential realization of non-self in *vipassanā*, it is not based on the idea that there is a 'real' self that needs discovering.

from their involvement with these conditions sufficiently to be able to *look at* them rather than *look through* them. The individual is no longer exclusively identified with these conditions and this creates a psychological 'space' or perspective, from which change is effected in the conditions of the body and the mind. It is precisely this shift in subjectivity that is emphasized in monastics' understandings of themselves. The subjectivity of the ascetic self contains an ambiguity between the intention to eradicate the will, the expression of will through ascetic practice and the experience of the dissolution of the will as a result of that practice. In Buddhist practice this involves the *experience* of non-self by the individual as a result of the assertion of the self in willed ascetic practice.[7]

Similarly, Foucault identifies the 'battle for chastity' in the works of fourth-century Latin writer John Cassian as concerned not with the outward performance of sexual abstinence, but rather as an internal struggle in which the signs of impurity are reduced one by one through ascetic practice (2000a: 189–90). Foucault understands Cassian's advance towards chastity as a challenge of dissociation: as one progresses towards chastity one's progress is charted by the dis-involvement of the will (2000a: 191) until, as a result of constant mental vigilance, even involuntary 'nocturnal pollutions' cease. The ascetic effort comes in the form of unceasingly analysing all thoughts, through techniques of self-analysis (*technologies de soi*) characteristic of monastic life and the spiritual battle (2000a: 194). Foucault argues that these techniques of self-analysis are not concerned with observing 'a code of permitted or forbidden actions' or a 'sexual ethic based on physical self-control' but rather a process of 'subjectification' involving the constant analysis and diagnosis of thoughts and the 'objectivization of the self by the self' in a quest for truth (2000a: 195). This endless task creates the subject in relation to himself and also, through the act of confession, to others; confession, submission and obedience to one's superiors are essential in the process of purification. In this instance obedience means the sacrifice of the subject's own will, and complete control of behaviour by the master as a technology of the self (Foucault 2000d: 246).

---

[7] Such a cultivation of religious subjectivity has been the subject of recent ethnographic analyses of Christian contexts. In an ethnographic study of a Roman Catholic convent in Mexico, Lester (2005) examines the ways in which the force of 'the call' of novice nuns shifts their understanding from initial uncertainty about their own motivations to an experience of their decision to ordain as reflecting a personal calling. She argues that through engagement with specific daily practices in convent life, novice nuns experience a shift in perceptions, interpretations and dispositions and that they understand this transformation as an increasingly clarified revelation of their true vocation (Lester 2005). Each postulant learns to read the sensations and inclinations of the body as indicators of her progressive success in managing a relationship between worldly and spiritual demands.

Foucault's understanding of ethics and freedom underlying his discussion of chastity provides us with a significant insight into the nature of ascetic practice. He examines what he terms 'technologies of the self', 'which permit individuals to effect by their own means, or with the help of others, a certain number of operations on their own bodies and souls, thoughts, conduct, and way of being, so as to transform themselves in order to attain a certain state of happiness, purity, wisdom, perfection, or immortality' (Foucault 2000d: 225). His interest lies in the training of individuals as they acquire not only certain skills but also certain attitudes.

Returning to his discussion of Cassian, Foucault reveals obedience and vigilance to be indicative of a supreme good, and as such it is the obligation of the monk to concern himself with the course of his present thoughts. 'Thought' in Foucault's understanding is

> what allows one to step back from this way of acting or reacting, to represent it to oneself as an object of thought and to question it as to its meaning, its conditions, and its goals. Thought is freedom in relation to what one does, the motion by which one detaches oneself from it, establishes it as an object, and reflects on it as a problem. (2000c: 117)

The actualization of a very different kind of religious ideology is revealed through the disciplined and mindful bodies of *vipassanā* practitioners. In the practice of *vipassanā*, the permanent mental articulation of all bodily and mental processes and sensations, the constant self-examination, creates for the meditator a hermeneutic relation with herself. Through her own mindful awareness the meditator experiences her physical and mental processes as discrete, impermanent and observable phenomena. By telling herself that the process of thinking is occurring, as well as noting all the smallest ripples of bodily sensation, movement, desires and emotions, indeed bearing witness to every act of conscious volition and movement, the meditator develops a relational stance to herself which is at once attentive and detached. In the retreat process vigilance becomes an ethical imperative: any lapse of mindfulness, any moment of mental laxity, is a moment of self-identification, of being lost in the self rather than observing the self, and is therefore a perpetuation of the cycle of rebirth.

ATTAINMENT

An important distinction between the Thai case and that of Foucault's battle for chastity is that in the practice of *vipassanā* the cessation of sexual drives is not the primary goal or consequence of ascetic practice. Rather, the result of practice is finally the extinguishing of *all* volitional activity, and cessation of sexual drives is a happy consequence of this. In contrast, the goal and consequence of practising *vipassanā* is to attain a level of physical and emotional equanimity and selflessness. As we shall see, practising meditation and doing one's duties, such as teaching meditation and sitting through very long ceremonies without moving, all develop the 'power of patience' (*kanti barami*; Pali: *khanti pāramī*). As practice deepens the individual no longer desires 'selfish' or pleasurable experiences; instead she is able to work tirelessly and selflessly for others.[8] Through the practice of *vipassanā* meditation and the cultivation of mindfulness in daily life monastics aim to reduce their emotionality and maintain a 'cool heart' (*jai yen*). One of the primary characteristics of the Buddha and *arahants* is their equanimity, to which monks and *mae chee* aspire. The ability to work tirelessly without emotion, to remain composed in the face of large demands are experiences and concerns treated as an important index of spiritual attainment and success. As Mae Chee Poy told me, our emotional state would be one of continuous equanimity if we were enlightened:

We'd still sweep the monastery, still have hunger, thirst, get tummy ache. We'd still have to be hot or cold in the same way as we do now but we wouldn't have emotion attached to any of this. If we have happiness then we also have anger, but a great teacher is still able to teach, it's not that they just stay doing nothing at all but that they have equanimity and so will not have happiness or sadness developing. They have loving-kindness to give and so have to smile but don't laugh like when we joke about. There is no like and dislike, no preference.

Mae Chee Poy was 55 and had been ordained for seventeen years at the time of fieldwork. Prior to ordination she had battled with addiction and had ordained with the intention of being a *mae chee* for a short time. One of the primary *dhamma* teachers for lay practitioners in the monastery, Mae Chee Poy is fervent in her conviction that meditation and being a *mae chee* have transformed her life. As I shall discuss in detail in Chapter 6, this inner state of equanimity, discussed by Mae Chee Poy, is outwardly demonstrated through controlled movements and minimal bodily activity. It is thought that the body of an enlightened person is radiant in appearance and smells sweetly. Controlling the body and bodily purity are understood to be consequences of ascetic practice and leading a moral life.

During intensive meditation periods the meditation student remains in her room and goes without sleep for several days. During this time she is not

---

[8] We will examine monastic duty in detail in Chapter 6.

allowed to wash. Purification of the mind through meditation takes over from purification of the body and it is said that if one has good meditation the body will smell sweetly, if at all.[9] Not washing also enables the meditator to cut attachment to the body, which is no longer tended to in the same way, and helps her remain focused on the challenges of sleeplessness in the meditation rather than avoiding them by splashing herself to stay awake. With the development of ascetic practice the practitioner gains increasing control over her body, mind and emotions and as attachment to the body is reduced both the body and the mind undergo change.[10] Indeed, it is considered to be good luck to die meditating because the mind is in a 'pure' state and this results in rebirth in heaven. As Mae Chee Suey told me, 'If at the time of death one is mindful one will be reborn into a heaven realm. This is why we ought to be mindful all the time, not just once or twice a day during practice'. Furthermore, this mental purity is believed to act as a protective power and those who meditate have no need of external protections such as the amulets or tattoos blessed by monks (cf. Tambiah 1984; Cook 2008a). The ultimate goal of *vipassanā* is enlightenment, a state of final purity reached through the development of meditative discipline. The purchase of self-identity on the meditator is reduced and, ultimately, extinguished entirely. This is thought to be attainable during the final hours of the retreat, during 'determination' (*attitan*; Pali: *adhiṭṭhāna*), when the meditator has spent days without sleep.

DETERMINATION AND SPONTANEITY

The final four days and three nights of the initial 28-day course are spent without sleep. During this period the meditator has her meals brought to her room; she is not allowed to leave the room except to meet with the meditation teacher; she is not allowed to wash, change her clothes, lie down, meditate leaning against anything, or talk to anyone. She remains alone in her room in silence, focusing upon the meditation, using her own self-discipline to ensure that she does not sleep for the 72-hour period. As the meditation progresses the effects of the sleep deprivation make the meditation increasingly challenging.

---

[9] In my own experience I found this to be true, but it is hard to judge because during periods of meditation without sleep I had no contact with anyone but the meditation teacher and he was very polite.

[10] As we shall explore further in Chapter 8, it is thought that one aspect of this change is that the body becomes less gendered as a result of ascetic practice.

While there is no change to recognition memory, sleep deprivation affects free recall. Levels of concentration decrease and subjective levels of sleepiness increase. It has been shown that sleep deprivation for twenty-four hours is equivalent to a blood alcohol level of 0.10 per cent, which is above the legal driving limit in the UK (Taffinder *et al.* 1998: 1, 191).[11] The brain is able to compensate for the effects of sleep deprivation while maintaining at least partially intact performance. Interestingly, Drummond *et al.* suggest that following sleep deprivation, performance is often initially intact and then declines with increasing time-on-task, which suggests that individuals can compensate for the effects of lack of sleep (Drummond *et al.* 2000). This illustrates the brain's plasticity and its attempts to compensate for the failure of normal neural systems. Pilcher and Huffcutt found that mood is more affected by sleep deprivation than either cognitive or motor performance and that partial sleep deprivation has a more profound effect on functioning than either long-term or short-term sleep deprivation (Pilcher and Huffcutt 1996). The negative effects of sleep deprivation on alertness and cognitive performance suggest decreases in brain activity and function, hindering alertness, attention and higher-order cognitive processes (Thomas *et al.* 2000). Remaining focused upon one repetitive task, such as mindful awareness of the meditation subject, will become increasingly challenging the more deprived of sleep the meditator becomes. She will have periods of lucidity and concentration that will rapidly alternate with periods of subjective sleepiness and physical exhaustion. Furthermore, those mental and emotional conditions which are to be detached from during meditation will become more pronounced with sleep deprivation and the meditator will find it increasingly hard to focus attention on the process of mental labelling concomitant with mindful awareness. The ability to remain mindful during sleepy or hallucinatory periods is understood as evidence of progression in meditation. The challenges of such periods, no matter how unsuccessfully met, are understood as an opportunity to cut attachment to a sense of self.

On the first and third night the meditator alternates walking and sitting for one-hour periods to complete twenty-four hours without sleep. However, the sitting meditation changes each night. Before sitting on the first night the meditator resolves 'May gross perceptions of the Three Characteristics of Phenomena cease, and may more subtle realizations of the Three Characteristics be attained within twenty-four hours.' On the second night the meditator is given a schedule, which varies the number of minutes

---

[11] It is worth noting that none of the experiments that I discuss here were carried out on people who had deliberately set out to accustom themselves to sleep deprivation.

walking and sitting, and a string of prayer beads. Before sitting the meditator resolves 'During ... minutes sitting period may the Phenomenon of Arising and Ceasing appear as often as possible.' The phenomenon of arising and ceasing feels similar to nodding off, and while this would be understandable at this stage of sleep deprivation, the feeling of arising and ceasing is closer to that of a rush of adrenaline when something unexpected happens. It leaves the body momentarily energized and tingling. The meditator uses the beads to count the number of times the condition occurs and makes a note of it on the schedule after each sitting period.

On the final night walking and sitting is returned to one hour. Before sitting meditation the meditator resolves 'May I find bliss; may all sentient beings find bliss. If any sentient beings have thoughts of revenge against me, I forgive them. If I have thoughts of revenge against any sentient beings, may they forgive me. Within this hour let me experience the state of meditative attainment [*phalasamāpatti*] for five minutes.' If the meditator feels that she is successful she increases the time for a further 5, 10, 15, 20, 30 minutes and one hour successively.

Phalasamāpatti is a Pali word describing an experience of '*dap*': to lose consciousness for a given period of time, much like a blackout in which one has no consciousness of phenomena from the six external sense bases.[12] Arising from this state one feels an acute sense of clarity and alertness. It is said that one's consciousness has deepened and attachment to conventional truth has been reduced. The experience of *dap* at the end of retreat is explicitly linked to the experience of the first and subsequent stages of enlightenment.

In Buddhist soteriology there are four levels of enlightenment: Stream-winner, Once-returner, Non-returner and Perfected One. These are levels of insight that the founder of Wat Bonamron identifies as being the result of *vipassanā* practice. He writes,

In practice for the first level of insight, the meditator, aiming for meditative attainment, makes a determination to have momentary yet complete extinction of consciousness and does indeed succeed. When the meditator (now also a stream-winner) makes another determination for the attainment of the second level of

---

[12] In Buddhist psychology there are six internal sense bases: the eyes; the ears; the nose; the tongue; the body; and the mind. They are 'the place of consciousness and of some mental factors' (Silananda 1990: 119). 'Mental factors' are considered to be one of the six external sense bases, along with visible objects, sounds, smells, tastes, and tangible objects (Silananda 1990: 119). Consciousness is dependent on a connection between an internal sense base and its corresponding external sense base. The mind sense base (*jai*) is located in the chest and is closer to the Western understanding of the heart (see next chapter).

insight, the mind's complete extinction will not occur. What happens instead is the knowledge of contemplation on arising and cessation; i.e. perceiving the rising/falling of the abdomen, as it occurs in the practice for the first level of insight. While the stream-winner keeps alternatively walking for one hour and sitting for one hour, different stages of knowledge will come to mind: knowledge of contemplation on dissolution followed by other stages up to knowledge of equanimity regarding all formations.

Crucially, new meditators do not know what *phalasamāpatti* means. It is said that this enables meditators to continue practice without desire for attainment. In order to experience *dap* one must be entirely present and mindfully aware in the present moment. The desire for attainment itself is a hindrance to meditation because desire conditions the mental state of the practitioner. When *dap* does occur it does so spontaneously, and for new meditators it would be harder for this to occur if it were rationally understood beforehand. I shall discuss the use of language, and the connection between word and experience for more practised meditators in the retreat context in more detail in the next chapter. Here it is important to note that the condition the student unwittingly asks for, in which she loses consciousness, going into a deep absorption (that is said to transcend rational thought), is explicitly linked to the process of enlightenment. The spontaneous experience of *dap* is not willed by the practitioner beyond the initial stated intention: it is an act without reference to or constrained by a self-identified subject.

In a discussion of the Jain religious practice of fasting to death (*samadhimaran*) Laidlaw demonstrates that in Jain mytho-history the deaths of saints through fasting are seen as the natural end result of the state of detached equanimity they have achieved through their spiritual practice and their consequent indifference to worldly pleasure and pain (2005: 186). *Samadhimaran* is a positive aspiration for Jains, and one that shapes the life lived prior to it. While few Jains actually undertake the fast, most accept that this is the most fitting end to a Jain life (2005: 186). In Jain practice, as in Buddhist practice, progress towards enlightenment involves reducing desire and emotion until finally the volition which was necessary for the practice to be undertaken in the first place is itself extinguished. A fast which is undertaken with the intention of effecting change in the world, even change in the internal state of the faster, will be counter-productive in terms of progress towards enlightenment because it is an expression of attachment and desire (Laidlaw 2005: 190–1). Laidlaw writes, 'If the Jain fast is to be thought of as an exercise of "agency", which in some respects surely it must, this is a circumstance where being an agent equates with an absence of desire, and is possible in what seems from the outside to be a state of extreme passivity' (2005: 193).

The problem being addressed differently through spontaneous *dap* and the Jain fast is one of intention: it is counterproductive to strive for enlightenment, to desire equanimity. Laidlaw argues that the end-point of a fast to death makes sense of the idea of agency without action, of agency as potential energy (2005: 194). In a discussion of Jain ethics and freedom Laidlaw argues that in Jainism the ideal of human perfection is a systematic negation of actual human life which is achieved through extreme self-denial and, finally, death (2002). The practices through which such an ideal is realized are therefore a matter of enlightened self-interest: 'where the "self" whose interest is at stake is not that of the living person but the imagined future purified soul one could become after enlightenment and death' (Laidlaw 2002: 321).

This highlights a crucial difference between Jain and Theravāda Buddhist soteriology: in Jainism there is no denial of the reality of the 'self'; the Jain self that really exists is the soul, which is what remains after the illusory self has been stripped away through ascetic practice. In contrast Buddhist practice is intended to reveal the illusory nature of any sense of self; the soul does not exist. Whereas Jain self-renunciation reveals the uniform essence of all souls, in Buddhist soteriology the notion of 'soul' is identified with 'self' and, as such, it too must be renounced through ascetic practice. Nonetheless, in Laidlaw's account of Jainism we may identify a similar dynamic between ascetic practice and ethical imperative. As Laidlaw writes of Jain ethical practice:

Someone for whom the idea of a pure and liberated soul was present, not just as a believed-in ideal, but as the 'I' that stands at the centre of his sense of self, such a person's body, identity, thoughts, acts, and character – his *karma* – would be debts he owed to himself and, indistinguishably, to God. For such a person Jain asceticism would be … a matter of moral obligation. (2002: 321)

The spontaneous experience of enlightenment as the ideal final result of meditation retreat is an embodiment of the ideal telos of Buddhist practice. While it is unlikely that it will be experienced by the majority of meditators, it is ultimately what it means to be religious in this context. The individual no longer has any will, though it is through their willed discipline and effort that such a state has come about. In Foucault's discussion of Cassian the internal battle for chastity is waged by the individual but the final stage of complete cessation of the sin of fornication is a blessing of grace and not an attainment of effort. Final purity is a supranatural phenomenon and as such may only ever be conferred by a supranatural power (Foucault 2000a: 193). The will is differently understood in the Jain *samadhi-maran*, which is, in Laidlaw's own words, 'a form of action that leads to a state of non-action, a distillation of agency by means of resolute non-execution, and a state of coexistence with the rest of the world achieved by means to the extinction of one's own embodied life' (2005: 195). In each of these examples the possibility of the cessation of self-control is implicit in the ideal telos of the religious life. Each practice is shaped by the cosmology and ethical project of its tradition. In each, spontaneity plays a crucial role in very different ways. In Cassian's writings, the final battle for chastity is won not through the willed fight of the individual but through the grace of God. In the Jain fast, death and release from the sin of *himsa* (violence) are attained through the absence of desire indicative of a pure soul. Through the practice of *vipassanā*, both the destruction of the will and realization of non-self (and no soul) are attained through detachment. Such a state could never be attained through will alone, as this would necessitate recognition of a delusional sense of self. *Dap* must be the spontaneous extinction of volition; attaining it through will would be impossible.

CONCLUSION

As we shall examine in detail in Chapter 6, in this monastery the religious precepts, monastic regime, physical appearance and framework of the monastic community are all significant ways through which monastic identity may be produced. But the ethical ideals of monasticism in this monastery are actualized through the practice of meditation. The extent to which meditation is employed varies and is dependent on the practitioner, but that it is the means by which one may become ethically perfected makes the practice significant for the community. In meditation practice the human body, mind and emotions are made mediums for religious action in the constitution of the religious self. The bodily and mental disciplines of meditation are both self-imposed and institutionally prescribed: they are self-imposed in the fundamental sense of something being done to the self by the self, and they are institutionally prescribed in the sense of being guided by a teacher, to whom the meditator is completely obedient, and located within clear hierarchical structures. They are also voluntary in that the individual chooses when and how often they do retreat. Through intensive meditation and submission to a teacher both monks and *mae chee* attempt to go beyond the intellectual cognition of reality and gain an experiential understanding of ultimate truth; as we shall see in Chapter 5 this involves an emic understanding of knowledge and wisdom. Within gendered hierarchical relations monastics attempt to go beyond the limits of cognition, that is, by behaving as selflessly as possible and submitting to the will of another in a process that is not always understood by the practitioner one employs practices specifically in order to transcend the rational, seemingly autonomous, mind and gain insight into ultimate truth.

As the discipline required to concentrate the mind develops the individual both observes and experiences the changing nature of the mind and body. The process of mental labelling enables the meditator to look at the conditions of the body and the mind rather than viewing the world through them. They are no longer a means through which one comes to understand the world, and thus one is no longer exclusively identified with them. The way in which the meditator perceives herself has changed. The meditation practised in the monastery is extreme and complicated. It generates a special kind of constitutive knowledge of the self. As the means to eradicate inner desires, meditation is the spiritual training by which these monastics make of themselves ethical subjects. It is the way in which people in the monastery make themselves Buddhist and, critically for my argument, the way in which monks and *mae chee* make themselves monastic. This self-forming (*pratique de soi*) is a practice in ethical freedom.

CHAPTER 5

Language and meditation

In the last chapter we considered meditation as a practice in ethical self-formation. In this chapter I want to examine in more detail the cognitive impact of meditative and ritual experiences and the way in which they are understood in Wat Bonamron. I will do this by examining the use of Pali language in both the retreat process and in ritual. As we have seen, Pali is used to induce the spontaneous experience of *dap* during intensive meditation. Here I explore how this might be understood and the effects that Pali language is thought to have upon individuals. I examine understandings about language in the monastery more broadly to highlight the significance of the use of Pali. I argue that the effects of Pali language reveal that beliefs or belief systems may not always be accorded causal primacy in religious experience. We have examined the method by which the meditation technique is taught to beginners. I will now focus upon the structure of the advanced retreat, a structure that is repeated on each consecutive retreat. All people in this monastery follow the retreat structure that I present here each time that they do retreat, be they laity, novices, *mae chee* or monks. Though it is not necessary for Pali to be understood for it to have an effect on the practitioner, the perceptive capacity that the practitioner progressively seeks to cultivate through successive retreats also incorporates their repetitive use of specific Pali words of which the practitioner usually has some understanding. With this in mind, I return to the meditation practice to examine the extreme or profound experiences that it sometimes engenders. Though meditation is guided by a teacher the practice itself is an intensely solitary activity. People undertaking the advanced retreat not only time their own meditation sittings but are also encouraged to meditate alone in their rooms. Private meditative experience is taken as compelling evidence of changes in and by the meditator, changes that are first and foremost within the private person. Pali language, the language of the Theravāda Buddhist Canon, is understood to induce experiential, phenomenological changes in ritual practitioners. I consider this in the context of broader understandings of language and experience, wisdom and knowledge, in the monastery.

PALI AND *PĪTI* IN RITUAL

During rituals Pali language is chanted aloud by monks with the intention that it be heard but not necessarily understood by the congregation. Upon hearing the chants the congregation gains merit and shares in a meritorious act, as well as receiving the blessings and protection of the chants. Whether or not the congregation or even the officiants understand the words being recited does not affect the efficacy of the ritual or the effects it produces in the condition of the worshippers. Buddhist lay people know that the chants contain power. That they may not understand them does not make them nonsensical. Nonetheless, liturgical texts have become much more accessible to all in recent years with the development of print and communications media. Each person in the monastery may either buy or borrow a chanting book to help during chanting. The chanting book used in the monastery is *Monpithi plae samrap Phra Phiksusamanen lae Buddhasasanikachon tua bai*, compiled by Phra Khru Arunthammarangsri (1999). It is available in pocket-size and shelf-size editions and monastics often have the pocket-size edition about their person. This includes chants for specific occasions, such as funerals, taking the five precepts and extinguishing candles. As well as specific protective liturgies (*jet tamnan*) and praise of the Buddha, it includes '*Tham Wat Chao*' and '*Tham Wat Yen*' (Morning and Evening Liturgies) at the beginning of the volume. These include common chants like '*Krap Phra*', '*Bot Namo*' and '*Itipiso*', and less common chants such as '*Gata Phra Moggallana Dap Fai Narok*' and '*Tankhanikapaccavekkhanvithi*'. McDaniel (2006b: 132–3) reports that it includes 174 chants in addition to the chants found in other volumes. These 'request' chants are modelled on the '*anisong*' blessing collections in Pali and Thai that praise acts of merit such as giving food, books and images to the sangha. Some chants are in Pali while some combine Pali and Thai.[1]

---

[1] Pali is also used in the weekly sermons given to the entire community by either the Abbot or another senior monk. On these occasions the sermonizer holds a palm-leaf manuscript with both hands in his seated lap. He reads out a word, line or short passage from the text and then expounds upon the meaning of the words in a sermon that draws in recent community events and national news. The intention is to create a sermon that is based on the text but which is relevant to the social and spiritual concerns of the community. On this liturgical practice of 'lifting' (*yok sab*) a word of line from text see McDaniel (2008).

In a discussion of the magical power of words Tambiah examines Buddhist ritual and asks one of the questions I hope to explore in this chapter: 'If sacred words are thought to possess a special kind of power not normally associated with ordinary language, to what extent is this due to the fact that the sacred language as such may be exclusive and different from the secular and profane language?' (1968b: 179). Tambiah demonstrates that the ritual use of Pali language is not intended as a vehicle for linguistic communication. In contemporary Thailand, Pali language is thought to possess a special power distinct from ordinary language and this is evidenced in the physical and psychological effects of its use.

The bodily effects of Pali were illustrated for me in the daily chanting performed by monks and *mae chee*. Monks and nuns spoke casually of experiencing the well-documented Buddhist phenomenon of 'manifest joy' (*pīti*) during chanting.[2] There are different levels of *pīti*, but during chanting it may feel like goose bumps and shivers, or waves of coolness throughout the body. The distinguished monk Silananda reports that seven of the eleven practices that lead to the arising of *pīti* involve the recitation done during chanting (Silananda 1990: 134–5). In many cases *pīti* occurred during chanting without the chants being understood. It is not necessary for the chanted words to be translated for experiences of ecstatic joy to occur.

While the use of Pali in religious contexts may be understood as a poetic expression of feelings, it is understood by religious participants to have direct and unmediated effects upon those who chant it and hear it, whether that be the transference of merit or protection, or a phenomenological transformation of the physical and emotional state of the subject. Monks and *mae chee* understood this to be because of inherent qualities in the Pali language itself that distinguishes it from other languages. For this reason it was understood as an appropriate language for the Theravāda textual tradition. The *suttas* (sermons of Buddha) were themselves understood to contain the wisdom of the Buddha but in a very real sense the original language of the texts, Pali, was thought to be a repository of this power and this was not commensurable with the power of other languages into which the *suttas* might be translated.

This is similar to the use of Sanskrit in the Śāstra textual tradition.[3] The śāstras are written at the dictation of the gods in their language. The precise

---

[2] *Pīti* is commonly also used to mean 'ritual'. In the instances I am describing here it is used to refer to specific psychological and physical experiences brought about through chanting and meditation.
[3] The śāstra texts provide soteriological knowledge leading out of the world and keys to the mastery of the world while within it. They provide practical instruction for the attainment of fabulous power.

reproduction of the correct phonetic sounds is of more importance than the retention of the meaning of the sounds. Parry tells us, 'The words in themselves have power once they are vocalized. For this power to become manifest they must be pronounced with precision and exactly the right inflection' (1985: 209). Textual knowledge is bound up with the transformative power of the words, the metaphysical truth that their oral transmission reveals, and the downplaying of individual innovation. Authentic knowledge is to be found within them, and is to be *recovered* from them, rather than *discovered*: 'The absolute truth has already been revealed and is there for man to appropriate if only he can penetrate their meaning. Sanskrit thus provides an essential handle on eternally valid knowledge' (Parry 1985: 205–6). The śāstra texts must be faithfully reproduced, rather than innovated and changed.[4] This is closely bound up with hierarchy because only those with the authority to do so may transmit and interpret the texts.[5] The connection that the guru creates with the past in this way affirms his authority and discounts any scepticism about his teaching.[6]

The repositories of Buddhist wisdom remain the Pali *suttas* written on palm-leaf manuscripts, irrespective of the translation and availability of their content in Thai.[7] For example, in the monastery there are two libraries. One contains hundreds of Buddhist volumes written in Thai and English. It is on the periphery of the monastic compound and is not accorded ritual

---

Though this would appear to privilege written as against oral culture the power of the texts in fact lies in the spoken word. The written text is a guide to ancient wisdom which should be directly transmitted from teacher to pupil through oral repetition and the exact replication of the correct sounds.

[4] 'Knowledge progressively degenerates with time, and is therefore something to be recovered from the sages of the past, whose wisdom cannot be surpassed in the present' (Parry 1985: 220). What matters is complete memorization rather than complete understanding.

[5] As Parry writes,

The implication here is clearly that the 'text' is not conceptualized as a purely literary document. Its 'authentic version' is rather an original and sacred revelation, the recovery of which may require recourse to *both* written and oral sources (the authenticity of the latter – if not also the former – being validated only by the prestige and authority of its Brahman repositories). (Parry 1985: 213)

[6] Parry uses this to argue against the causal role that literacy is often accorded in transformations of mental life tending towards a 'rational' secular scientific outlook. While literacy is a prerequisite of the kind of rationality characteristic of modern science he does not think it necessarily provides a positive thrust towards it. For Parry the dichotomy between 'oral' and 'literate' cultures is too simple an opposition to account for the complexity of the situation he is describing. He argues that it is necessary to take into account politico-economic conditions and metaphysics when accounting for the development of rationalities. In Parry's pithy terms the occurrence of literacy 'reveals as much about the specific conditions under which ['rational empiricism'] is likely to occur as the Neolithic Revolution reveals about the conditions likely to produce Stevenson's "Rocket"' (Parry 1985: 221).

[7] In an analysis of Thai poetry, Morris argues that in Thailand poetic language is thought to be 'marked by the world', in that one word or language may be substituted for another. In contrast, the use of Pali retains its autonomy from substitution (Morris 2000: 24).

significance. The second is a grand two-storey marble building (*phra-trai pi dok*) to the right of the *vihāra* (main temple). The central area of the building is used for meditation and the walls are lined with elaborately decorated cabinets containing sections of the Buddhist Canon written in Pali on long, narrow, palm-leaf manuscripts. This building was opened officially by Her Royal Highness Princess Maha Chakri Sirindhorn, Crown Princess of Thailand. The veneration of the manuscripts reveals that although the knowledge in the texts is translated and widely available in Thailand, the palm-leaf manuscripts themselves remain highly sacred.

Like Sanskrit, or Khmer in some cases, Pali is a language with transformative power. The experience of truth through Pali language in this context is understood as distinct from the rationality or irrationality of beliefs in that truth (cf. Sperber 1982). As we have seen, the spontaneous experience of *dap* in retreat, in which the meditator loses consciousness and transcends a sense of self, is invoked through the use of Pali and remains independent of the intention of the meditator. The use of Pali remains independent of what Benjamin called 'over-naming' in his analysis of language in the Christian creation (1997 [1916]: 122). Benjamin's argument is entirely distinct from Buddhist understandings of creative language because it rests upon the Judaic notion of a creator God. Benjamin argues that the language of God, active in the creation of the world, is both creative and finished creation. For Benjamin then, man is the knower in the same language in which God is creator: 'The absolute relation of name to knowledge exists only in God, only there is name, because it is inwardly identical with the creative word, the pure medium of knowledge. That means: God made things knowable in their names. Man, however, names them according to knowledge' (1997 [1916]: 115). Human language remains a reflection of the word in name, a translation of the creative infinity of the divine word. Things properly named are called into being by God in His creative word, while in the language of man they are always over-named. Over-naming is for Benjamin the 'deepest linguistic reason for all melancholy and (from the point of view of the thing) of all deliberate muteness' (1997 [1916]: 122). In Benjamin's argument, the language of God is creative while the agency of creation rests with God. In contrast, the use of Pali is creative in that it creates an altered experience of reality but the agency of that creation rests not with God but with the person using the language. In the ritual and retreat contexts Pali language is creative in its revelation of truth as experience.

PALI IN THE MEDITATION RETREAT

As we have seen, Pali language is an integral part of the basic meditation practice; it provides a spontaneous religious experience for the new meditator. During the advanced retreat, which follows a similar pattern to the basic course but only lasts ten days, Pali language is used for every seated meditation period. Before each sitting the meditator asks for a psychological condition to arise during the meditation by either verbally or mentally determining it using a Pali word. Each day a different word is used and the mental conditions that subsequently occur follow in sequence:

Day 1: *Udayabbayañāṇa* – knowledge of arising and passing away of name (*nāma*) and form (*rūpa*)
Day 2: *Bhaṅgañāṇa* – knowledge of dissolution
Day 3: *Bhayañāṇa* – knowledge of fearfulness
Day 4: *Ādinavañāṇa* – knowledge of misery
Day 5: *Nibbidañāṇa* – knowledge of disgust (boredom)
Day 6: *Muñchitukamyatāñāṇa* – knowledge of desire for deliverance from the name (*nāma*) and form (*rūpa*) (restlessness)
Day 7: *Paṭisaṅkhāñāṇa* – knowledge of re-observation
Day 8: *Saṅkhārupekkhāñāṇa* – knowledge of equanimity about formations.

It is implied from the practice that words have power in and of themselves. Each day the teacher gives a new word to the meditator on a piece of paper. Before her sitting meditation the meditator repeats to herself: 'I resolve that *Paṭisaṅkhāñāṇa* [for example] will occur within this hour'. The meditation then proceeds as normal but is influenced by the requested word. Clearly, many of the conditions being requested are quite unpleasant. The effect of some words is even physical; for example, *muñchitukamyatāñāṇa* (restlessness) can feel like ants running over the skin. Ideally the meditation will be conditioned by fear, misery, boredom, restlessness, and so on and this will provide the meditator with the opportunity to cut her attachment to such conditions, and thereby maintain a continual state of mindfulness. It is not necessary to understand the semantic meaning of the words summoned in the retreat process. Second-guessing what one 'should' be feeling is said to be a waste of time.

It is said that the words will impact upon the meditator whether or not she understands them. However, the structure of the retreat is repeated in all subsequent retreats. Experienced meditators have a clear understanding of the meaning of the Pali words and the kinds of experiences that they can expect each day. Commonly, monastics looked forward to day eight (*saṅkhārupekkhañāṇa*) because this is usually characterized by pleasant meditative experiences. The use of Pali in meditation is understood as a method for self-improvement. It is through experiencing the conditions that the Pali words are said to body-forth that the practitioner has the opportunity to cut attachment to a sense of self. Though it is not necessary for the practitioner to understand the Pali words for them to have an effect on the meditation, each time the practitioner repeats the retreat he or she gains more understanding about the nature of each of the states being called for. Being able to cultivate a position of detached observation is thought to bring one closer to an equanimous experience of the truth, a truth that until it is fully cultivated is most accessible for the practitioner in the words themselves as the repositories of Buddhist wisdom. The equanimity attained through the cultivation of mindfulness in meditation – the detachment from the peaks and troughs of emotional disquietude – is understood as involving the entirety of the person. It is a moral state, one that fits comfortably with the principles of Buddhism but that is experienced as the ongoing cultivation of forms of percept rather than understanding of concept. The words are at once the technique and the telos, perfectly realized after much discipline. 'Understanding' of the words is not exclusively conceptual but rather it entails the somatic, phenomenological and perspectival capacity to 'know' them.

Use of Pali in the retreat process is understood as an aspect of the formation of the capacities by which people come to perceive religious truths in their bodies, senses and emotions; that is, in the capacities that enable a particular kind of Buddhist reality that is consonant with religious tenets. Pali, as the original language of the *suttas*, is understood to be a repository of wisdom. It is thought to enact an unmediated effect upon the listener and in this sense it may be understood as 'magical' (Tambiah 1968b) but its use is also the context in which the practitioner cultivates ethical virtues. Through striving to experience such wisdom for themselves practitioners intend to move progressively towards perfection by realizing the truths of which the words themselves are immaculate embodiments. It is as a part of the techniques through which people intend to cultivate a specific religious perception that the effects of the words are readily experienced. The words are understood to have a power in and of themselves but the response to the effect of the words requires a very particular subjective response from the practitioner – for example, if one feels as though ants are running over the skin, the proper response is to acknowledge such sensations without attachment. While challenging, such a response is understood to be progressively more attainable as the discipline of mindfulness develops until the practitioner has gained insight into the ultimate nature of the word (in this case, 'restlessness') and no longer suffers as a result of the condition. This is thought to be the result of attaining experiential insight into non-self, impermanence and imperfection. This appropriate response is understood as hard, but something that can be cultivated. It is understood to be a condition for 'understanding' the Pali words while also deepening the practitioner's capacity *for* understanding. We can see that in the disciplining of the meditative body, the very real sensations, of say ants running over the skin, are understood as a site for moral development: it is through the correct response to bodily, mental and emotional conditions that the moral body is formed. The degree to which one can 'understand' the conditions brought about through the use of Pali in meditation is proportional to the depth of insight attained by the practitioner. Put another way, the capacity for moral sensibility that the practitioner has cultivated will be equivalent to his or her correct 'understanding' of the truths of the Pali words.

The meditation technique and the use of Pali are understood as techniques by which monastics and laity might cultivate the virtues of enlightenment and achieve insight into the three characteristics. Through repetitive and cyclical retreat and through repeating the series of Pali words as an integral structure of the retreat, practitioners are ideally able to cut attachment to a sense of self and live more moral and ethical lives, avoiding increasingly subtle and fine-grained moral transgressions that only become visible through the cultivation of ethical sensibilities that make witnessing such transgressions possible.

It is through repeated employment of the Pali meditation technique, with intention and mindful concentration, that the character of the subject is intentionally transformed and experiential insight is deepened. The Pali conditions evoke particular ethical responses that are elaborated in Buddhist doctrine but in the context of practice they become dispositions rather than doctrinal codes and it is with such dispositions that the renunciate cultivates the capacities of moral discrimination.

LEARNING TO LISTEN

One evening a lay woman offered drinks to myself and Mae Chee Sati at her home close to the monastery. She said that she enjoys the sermon (*tet*) on Buddha Day (*Wan Phra*) because it is in Thai but that she feels frustrated and uncomfortable listening to sermons or chanting in Pali because she cannot understand it. Mae Chee Sati told her that when the proceedings were conducted in Pali she ought to sit in meditation and open her heart/mind (*jai*) to it: 'You know that the words are good and the mind [*jai*] understands them and takes them within itself, they don't have to be understood by the brain [*samong*].' As noted above in Buddhist philosophy there are six internal and six external sense bases, through which consciousness becomes manifest. The mind/heart (*jai*) is the sixth internal sense base and is located in the chest. In an interview with Mae Chee Suat, who had been ordained for twelve years and leads the daily chanting for *mae chee*, she told me that chanting is very important because during chanting one understands from the heart/mind (*jai*) not from the head and that this is the reason why manifest joy (*pīti*) occurs:

> It is because the sound comes from your chest; this is where Buddha is too. *Devatā* come and listen to the chanting, definitely. And if you are pure of heart and have the same feelings as the *deva* then you can communicate together (by mind, not by mouth) and go along together and be friends. The *deva* will be able to speak through you. It's as though you can do-and-do without being tired because you're being given the power from the *deva*. But you can't talk to just anyone about this, only people who practise meditation.

In these two examples it is through the cultivation of mindful attention that the practitioner comes to 'hear' the wisdom of the Pali words – a form of understanding that is not exclusively executed through conceptual clarity. This can be seen in Mae Chee Sati's exhortation that the lay woman open her 'heart/mind' (*jai*) when listening to Pali sermons. She is suggesting that through the cultivation of such a state of awareness this woman will be able to 'hear' the wisdom of the words without understanding them. The utterance and audition of such words is not limited to the capacities of vocal, aural and cognitive competence but requires much more of a person. To 'hear' properly requires the cultivation of the '*jai*' and the moral capacities to 'understand' the experiences of the words themselves. In Mae Chee Suat's description of the experiences of chanting and the power of *devas* she asserts that only people who practise meditation will understand. It is only through the cultivation of the ethical self that such knowledge becomes possible. What makes Pali suitable for such practices of ethical self-formation is its capacity to act on the 'heart/mind' and it is through correct attention to the effects of Pali language that the sensibilities of the ethical subject are formed. This conception of 'understanding' is played out through the distinctions drawn between heart/mind and brain and between wisdom and knowledge in the monastery.

The wisdom attained through the practice of meditation is contrasted with the intellectual knowledge attained through thinking and reasoning. As Khun Jeng, a 55-year-old lay woman who has been volunteering at Wat Bonamron on and off for six years, told me, 'Wisdom is the same everywhere. It's just with thinking that people get into trouble.' Wisdom is said to come through the heart/mind while thinking comes through the head.

For example, reading about meditation and *dhamma* study are viewed as a support for the meditation practice because one recognizes one's own experiences in the words, but it is never believed to be a substitute for practice itself. All monastics in Wat Bonamron are expected to learn the *Abhidhamma* (schematic classifications of Buddhist psychology and philosophy) but the reasons that they give for the importance of this knowledge are varied. *Abhidhamma* classes are held in the monastery and monks and *mae chee* attend collectively. Monks are encouraged to learn *dhamma* as a monastic vocation and may further their studies at the monks' university in Chiang Mai. Despite the incentives of royally supported financial achievement and award for passing higher exams, no *mae chee* from this monastery attend the university and the number who have attained higher levels of *dhamma* studies is relatively low (but see Collins and McDaniel 2010).[8]

Mae chee in Wat Bonamron state that they study *dhamma* in order to enhance their meditative insight. While they view education as useful for advancing the careers of monks, these *mae chee* understand their engagement with both religious and secular education in different ways. Both monks and *mae chee* study the *Abhidhamma* in classes and listen to sermons expounding on passages from the *Abhidhamma* regularly. However, it was stressed to me by both monks and *mae chee* that this is not the only way to attain such knowledge: *Abhidhamma* knowledge will come automatically to those who meditate. The founder of Wat Bonamron is held as an example of one who has complete understanding of the complex *Abhidhamma* and yet has never studied it. Furthermore, it was stressed to me that just reciting the *Abhidhamma* is not of great value; it must be employed in meditation practice. As Mae Chee Sati told me,

---

[8] In this important article Collins and McDaniel present an account of *mae chee* teaching Pali language and *Abhidhamma* in the Bangkok area. The large and increasing numbers of *mae chee* in Thailand who have passed the higher level Pali examinations or who hold advanced degrees in Buddhist studies are celebrated in this work. Through interviews with highly educated *mae chee*, Collins and McDaniel reveal that there are many opportunities for women to study and teach the subjects considered to be the most difficult and prestigious in Thailand. In a consideration of the ways in which these women understand their roles and statuses they reveal some of the sociological complexities that are hidden by a simple binary opposition between laity and the sangha.

If there is a monk who practises there is no need to teach him *Abhidhamma*, he knows by himself, so that the precepts are not hard for him to guard. His *dhamma* is very clear and pure and he has good power to do for people, more than the one who has just started but doesn't practise. Buddha described this as 'the empty Bible' – the one who has only just started and doesn't practise, like a cowboy who has never drunk milk from a cow.

Clearly, there is a difference between knowing *dhamma* and having *dhamma*. Several *mae chee* told me that it is very hard for people of a high level of learning to do meditation practice because they *think* they know. Those who habitually conceptualize their goals in normal life may have a tendency to conceptualize enlightenment and spiritual attainment in the same way when they come to meditate. As one pious lay woman told me 'Education and status are unimportant because the *arahants* of Buddha's time got enlightened and they didn't go to university. It is about how good your mind/heart [*jai*] is and you don't need education for that'. Paradoxically, however, other *mae chee* told me that people of high-level learning are the easiest to teach. I was told that the first people Buddha taught after he attained enlightenment were from high society and that this was because they were more able to receive the *dhamma* than those of lower status and education.[9] However, in discussion *mae chee* drew a distinction between the education of former days, in which the heart/mind was educated, and the modern 'Western-style' education taught in schools today, which is focused entirely on the head.

Hirschkind provides a detailed comparative ethnographic study of cassette-sermon audition in Egypt (Hirschkind 2001, see also 2006). The cassette-sermons that he is examining have become one of the most widely consumed media forms among lower-middle- and middle-class Egyptians since the 1970s. Cassette-sermon audition is usually a self-regulated activity that is thought to enable the strengthening of the will of the listener to resist the Devil and, with repetitive and attentive listening, to enable the listener to change his ways. Hirschkind demonstrates that cassette-sermon audition may be usefully understood as a one-disciplinary practice through which contemporary Egyptian Muslims hone an ethically responsive sensorium: it is through this very specific discipline that they cultivate the sensibilities that enable them to live as devout Muslims.

Hirschkind (2001) argues that the practice of listening to cassette-sermons among contemporary Muslims in Egypt is integral to the formation of the capacities that enable a particular form of Muslim piety to which

---

[9] This reveals an intrinsic hierarchy similar to that of Brahmanic tradition.

practitioners aspire. It is through this cultural practice that perceptual capacities are honed and through which the models of moral personhood, grounded in the textual tradition, are rendered perceptible (2001: 623–4). The people with whom Hirschkind worked described correct sermon audition as 'hearing with the heart' – an activity that is not strictly cognitive or auditory, but requires the entire body as a 'complex synthesis of moral reflexes' (Hirschkind 2001: 624). This means that the listener must engage those sensory capacities that are honed through audition. Hirschkind describes this as the formation of a sensorium: 'the visceral orientations enabling of the particular form of life to which those who undertake the practice aspire' (2001: 640). Such perceptual abilities are intentionally inculcated through self-reflexive practices.

Hirschkind's argument is, in part, that in describing emotions, capacities of aesthetic appreciation and moral attunement as they are intentionally cultivated we can appreciate the ways in which sensory experiences come to be structured. Such an approach is useful for thinking about the ways the perception of religious tenets may be progressively cultivated through intentional practice. Furthermore, it suggests that percept and the means of perception are fundamentally interdependent. In the case of the teaching of the *jai* rather than the brain we see a similarly complex understanding of types of knowledge and the different forms of bodily involvement required in 'knowing'.

In a discussion about spirits and channelling with a group of *mae chee* I was told that 'the meditation and the teaching of Ajharn [the Abbot] is pure wisdom, the pure teaching of the Buddha, but some people need something to believe in'. The distinction drawn between belief and confidence as a result of wisdom implies again that belief *in* something is secondary to wisdom. This points to two very different forms of knowledge organization that correspond to different corporeal prerequisites for knowing. One is conceived of as cognitive while the other is cultivated through Buddhist disciplinary practices that are related to the heart/mind (*jai*). Thus, to speak of understanding the meaning of the words in Pali through conceptual knowledge is insufficient for practitioners' understanding of the significance of this as a knowledge system. Knowing is not understood as primarily conceptual but is rather that which is made possible through the cultivation of the perceptual capacity for mindfulness. This reflects a series of historically grounded concepts of knowing, embedded in cultural practices that give form to particular kinds of experiences.

Jordt (2007a) argues that in the Burmese context of the mass *vipassanā* movement, people who acquire meditation-derived knowledge, in contrast to traditional forms of Buddhist knowledge, come to constitute a community of knowers. Such community membership is not predicated on prior social or religious categories but is based on an individual's achievements towards realizing the soteriological telos of meditation practice. Through the practice of meditation, knowledge is constituted, justified and shared (on this mass meditation movement see also Jordt 2007b). Identity is constituted through new ways of knowing and verifying knowledge in a method that conforms to traditional cosmological truths. She argues that knowledge created through meditation can be known only through internal verification. This produces 'knowing agents' and is combined with more traditional repositories of religious knowledge and authentication. Jordt argues: 'belief as true knowledge includes the sense that a person realizes through practice the conditions that verify truth'. In such a way meditators undergo 'an epistemic reconstruction', a kind of knowledge formation that is understood to be unintelligible to the non-meditator, and distinguishing between kinds of knowledge is one means by which the results of meditation come to be constructed as facts (Jordt 2007a).

In Buddhist meditation it is intended that the practitioner retrains his or her relationship to the senses. It is in so doing that the practitioner cultivates the ability to perceive the fundamental religious tenets in his or her self-identity. The knowledge community that developed out of the meditation movement that Jordt examines was predicated on a particular epistemic outlook that was verified at individual and social levels. She demonstrates that in the Burmese context social and institutional processes support such knowing agents and a consensus is maintained over legitimate belief-forming techniques and legitimating practices.

An empirical problem for both the analyst and the community of practitioners is that narrative accounts of experiences are far removed from the experiences themselves. Practitioners are concerned to discern the extent to which words and actions accurately reflect the experiences of others. 'Knowledge sharing in this context institutionalizes social forms of knowledge production that support inner moral discipline and practice, while maintaining an agnosticism over how one might definitively identify enlightened persons. In other words, the goal of the meditation knowledge community is to produce enlightened persons in the transcendent sense but not explicitly in the social sense' (Jordt 2007a). She argues that, whereas prior to the advent of the mass meditation movement religious professionalism was connoted by role and responsibility, today the meditation knowledge community is constructed through the knowledge individually cultivated through meditation.

THE VALUE OF SPEECH

In the monastery, the distinction between knowledge and wisdom is reflected in the value placed on speech and action. Conduct and speech are believed to be indicative of one's state of mind but it is said in the monastery that in order to know the truth about someone it is necessary to observe what they do, not what they say. Some of the dangers of speech are explicitly conceptualized. The local concept of a 'sweet mouth' (*pak wan*) is used to describe people whose speech is not supported by their behaviour. Speaking with a 'sweet mouth' may include false flattery, speaking to get something that one wants, or protestations of piety that are demonstrably false. This concept is complemented by another, that of having a 'dog mouth' (*pak ma*), which suggests speaking without thinking about what one is saying or the effect that the words have on others. To describe someone as a 'dog mouth' is a great insult, especially in a monastic context, because it suggests that they have no mindfulness, control in speech or action, nor awareness of their own mental state. Someone with a dog mouth may 'bite behind someone's back' though I was told that those who say bad things about others are hurting themselves first and foremost. One lay woman who gossiped maliciously about many of the *mae chee* in the monastery was likened to someone doing a striptease: each time she spoke she would reveal another part of her body until finally she would leave herself naked and humiliated in the eyes of others. This prediction came true and the woman in question was made to feel so unwelcome in the monastery that finally she left. It was said that her defilements had been revealed through her words and actions until finally she had 'burnt herself up'. She had been suggesting that two *mae chee* were having sexual or romantic relations with the Abbot, a ridiculous allegation that was offensive to the people in question and the community more broadly. One *mae chee* described her as '*pak man*' (combining the ideas of 'sweet mouth' and 'dog mouth') because she was manipulative in her praise of some while being malicious in her slander of others.

Much like bodily practice in the monastery it is *misplaced* words that are bad, rather than the words themselves: words and their meaning or 'rightness' are context sensitive. Interestingly, the monastic precept to 'refrain from incorrect speech' does not necessarily constitute a prohibition on lying. I was told that there were times when it was more skilful to bend the truth, remain silent or lie than tell the truth; particularly when the truth would cause great suffering or generate a negative or unwholesome mind state in the listener. This understanding of correct and incorrect speech reflects a pragmatic approach to knowledge in which that which is of benefit is prioritized over that which is strictly true (Jackson 2003: 45). What is of most significance is not the truth of the words but their benefit to the listener.

Returning to a consideration of the meditation practice taught and learnt by monastics, the verbal teaching of non-linguistic knowledge necessitates a double transformation in its transmission. For non-linguistic knowledge to be transformed into language it must change its character, as Bloch writes, 'from implicit to linguistically explicit knowledge made by the teacher and from linguistically explicit to implicit knowledge made by the learner' (1998: 8). Bloch argues against the assumptions that culture is ultimately 'language like' and that it is transmitted primarily through language. Rather, he suggests that much knowledge is non-linguistic and involves networks of meaning formed through experience and practice in the external world. He suggests that where this is the case it may have less to do with a culture of education than with a feature of the kind of knowledge underlying such tasks, which necessitates it being non-linguistic (1998: 7–8). For these reasons he suggests that what people say is a poor guide to what they know and think. His theory appears to be confirmed by the minor role language plays in the transmission of knowledge in learning meditation. Although the verbal instructions are quite explicit and detailed the ability to meditate is developed through imitation, repetition and participation, rather than socratic or linear linguistic forms.[10]

Guidance and instruction are given to students verbally during the meditation retreat. Besides the practical nuts-and-bolts instructions of *how* to meditate, guidance during a meditation retreat is often given through metaphor. For example, the meditation teacher gave voice and description to the way a visiting monk felt at a specific and well-charted stage in his meditation when he said it was 'like a tiger trapped in a cage,

---

[10] Bloch presents a case for a connectionist mind-brain model in which people access knowledge from simultaneous mental processing units. These simultaneous parallel processors are connected through already existing networks and it is in this way that complex understanding and operations may be accounted for. Thus connectionism as a theory may account for practical-theoretical thinking, the time it takes to become an expert at a particular task, why knowledge does not need to be put into words to be transmitted, and why, while language is important, culture cannot be 'language like': 'Making the culture efficient requires the construction of connected domain-relevant networks, which by their very nature cannot be stored or accessed through sentential logical forms such as govern natural language' (Bloch 1998: 13–14). His argument is that learning entails constructing apparatuses for efficiently coping with domains of knowledge and practice; one learns how to *learn* a specific kind of information, which may be unpacked and handled *in an instant*. Such apparatuses are necessarily non-linguistic, because of the speed with which they must be manipulated in order to be efficient.

you walk round and round but no matter where you look there is no way out from this cage. Nothing that you have found solace in before can comfort you. Like fish caught in a net you are desperate for escape'. This is invocation of something other than the meditation in order for the meditation to be communicable between teacher and student. One object is being made to stand for another but the words are ultimately nothing to the meditation. By remaining ephemeral and metaphorical, instruction in meditation is able to come close enough to the concrete to be conceptually transmitted from one person to another, while remaining sufficiently aloof to retain the power that meditation holds as an experiential phenomenon.

The interaction between the discursive meetings with the meditation teacher, the use of Pali and the experiences of the individual while meditating may produce a powerful reality in which forms of rationalization and experience become mutually supporting. An important element of our understanding of meditation must be the potential force and distinctiveness of the subjective meditative experiences of the practitioner if we are to account for the use and significance of meditation in any context. To miss this would be perverse. This is not mere speculation about the subjective experiences of others, nor solipsistic hubris. The powerful and overwhelming experiences of meditation, sometimes ecstatic, sometimes painful, provide a dramatic reality for the practitioner. The extremity and/or profundity of meditative experiences are revealed in the accounts that people give to the meditation teacher.[11] Here I will give brief accounts from three meditators to illustrate some of the variety and impact of meditative experiences. Each of the three accounts was given by a monk to the meditation teacher as he reported on his experiences during the third night of sleeplessness on the basic course:

1. Phra Kata (36) had been ordained for two years and had been practising *vipassanā* for seven years: 'The meditation was good and bad. I had white light on my left side and I felt a cool breeze but the fan wasn't on. During the bad meditation I couldn't find my breath. In the morning my breath and lots of the touching points disappeared. I started to see waves of smoke, then lights, fires and intense colours. Blue. I thought the blue was the most beautiful, then red exploded to compete. It was really beautiful! My body was moving around a lot; lots of motion.'
2. Phra Somsurn (26) had been ordained for thirteen years and had been practising *vipassanā* for four years: 'Big tears growing inside me. Ajharn

---

[11] It should be noted that mindfulness and meditation are not always accompanied by extreme experiences; indeed they are often their own reward.

teaches me how to come to a neutral stage so I can stop it, but I can feel it coming more and more. I don't know what it is. In the past two weeks I have felt old pains, souvenirs, but this, I don't know what it is. I want to let it out. Maybe I'll have a big crash if I go in this direction, maybe I'll break down. Big problems all round. I'm smiling now but I wasn't during the day. I was crying and I don't know why.'

3. Phra Sawat (52) had been ordained for twenty-six years and had been practising meditation on and off for seventeen years: 'Sometimes it was very good. Sometimes I was so close to sleep and then sometimes very clear, clean, very awake. Nothing disturbed me and everything was focused on the points. The time felt very short but when I looked at the clock it was a long time. I don't know if I lost consciousness but it was like a power pushing me to do this thing and I could continue all night. It gave me power from inside. It wakes me up, like from deep sleep; sharp.'

In each of these cases the meditator had considerable experience of meditation prior to this retreat. The meditation involved both pleasant and unpleasant experiences. Reports of extrasensory or hallucinatory phenomena, such as those of Phra Kata, were a common occurrence during the sleepless period. The movement of the body is also a common phenomenon and usually understood as a symptom of *pīti* (discussed earlier in this chapter). In some cases the torso will jerk or move periodically; in more extreme cases the body will move continuously throughout the meditation period. In some instances the practitioner may find this frightening, in others exhilarating. The meditation student is guided to understand this as a manifest example of non-self and uncontrollability. The experiences of strong and seemingly unfounded or past emotions reported by Phra Somsurn are understood in the context of the retreat as the arising of past *gam* (Pali: *kamma*). In such instances it is believed that the meditator is being presented with an opportunity to 'cut' the negative *kamma* of past actions by cultivating mindful detachment to the strong emotional experiences that such *kamma* generates. The experiences of loss of time and the power to meditate throughout the night reported by Phra Sawat sound much less dramatic than the extrasensorial experiences of Phra Kata but suggest a very different and ongoing experiential state during meditation.

In an ethnography of witchcraft in 1980s London, Luhrmann accounts for the persuasiveness of magic, in part, as a result of the intensity of meditative experience: 'The process of coming to terms with the vivid phenomenological experience of magical practice may help to make magical ideas seem natural, unsurprising, unquestionable' (Luhrmann 1989: 202).

Language and meditation

Thus, the beliefs that people associate with their magical practice ar rationalization of an imaginative and emotional involvement, rather t..... ... logical series of consciously held and consistently claimed commitments (Luhrmann 1989: 353). Beliefs are related to the interdependence of concept and experience. Luhrmann argues that the interaction between meditative experience, linguistic styles and vivid symbolism worked together in a process she terms 'interpretive drift': 'the slow shift in someone's manner of interpreting events, making sense of experiences, and responding to the world ... a slow, mutual evolution of interpretation and experience, rationalized in a manner which allows the practitioner to practise' (Luhrmann 1989: 12). She argues that the imaginative rhetoric used to describe magic may be instrumental in engendering the practitioner's confidence in the practice because the rhetoric has a special truth status with referential ambiguity. In the Thai case the teacher guides the meditation but the subjective experiences of individuals are varied: from the outside all meditators look as though they are doing the same thing. Nonetheless, the variation of experience and rationalization are made sense of by the meditator as the practice is made meaningful.

It is possible that the ideas that are associated with meditation practice are convincing because they are themselves interpretations of powerful emotional and phenomenological experiences. It is not necessarily always the case that people act in a particular way because of their beliefs; in some instances people may hold beliefs as a result of their actions. Thus, to put a causal primacy upon either belief *or* experience would be a mistake. That the experiences engendered by use of Pali in chanting and meditation are not dependent upon understanding the meaning of the words confirms their authenticity for monastics. This in turn is further supported by the belief that wisdom and experiential knowing occur in the heart/mind while thinking and understanding occur in the head.

CONCLUSION

To all intents and purposes 'magical language' (Tambiah 1968b) may be understood as practical action in this context. Progress in the meditation technique links the authoritative language of the *suttas* with the development of the capacities of the heart/mind (*jai*), understood to be achieved through attentive and intentional cultivation of particular sensibilities. The appropriately performed act of listening to Pali in ritual or using Pali in meditation is enacted with certain standards of performance and reasons for acting in mind. The listener or practitioner must assume the attitudes that correspond to the understanding attained through correct attention to the words. The attitudinal drift that made such understanding possible becomes the context and the purpose of the practice. Without the cultivation of mindfulness the practitioner will not be able to adopt the attitudes of observation and detachment which are necessary for the successful appreciation of the conditions arising through use of Pali. The meditator evidences the results of her actions in transformations in her physical and psychological condition. Language use in the monastery reflects the emphasis placed on non-verbal and non-conceptual knowing. On the one hand, then, meditation is learnt and becomes important through the solitary practice of the individual and in this sense language is insufficient as a pedagogic aid. On the other hand, Pali provides the meditator with an unmediated experiential access to ultimate truth. This highlights a stark two-track view of language, which is further illustrated in understandings of wisdom and knowledge, language and behaviour, in daily life.

The use of Pali in ritual allows participants to distinguish their activities as different and removed from everyday action. The action in ritual or religion is itself a 'real event', it may refer to something else but it is always a 'technical act', in and of itself. It is this which gives it significance. In meditation, words and practices have an immediate impact upon the practitioner which is powerful, unmediated, embodied and, consequently, hard to put into words. The meditation and use of Pali are techniques for the training of perception and bodily expressions and responses. In this analysis I have not examined the rich semantic content of Pali in the textual tradition. Rather, I have focused on the ways in which practitioners train themselves to 'know' Pali words – that is, to perform these ethical modes of perception and experience. The condition of their full experience is the actualization of mindfulness. The responses and reactions to stimuli of the practitioner become patterned in accord with the religious principles that underscore the practice. Thus, the experience of emotion, movement or sensation is grounded in the sensory capacities of the body as, in Hirschkind's words, ' a complex of culturally honed perceptual capacities' (2001: 629). The capacities of the ethical sensibilities have been shaped through the shared cultural discipline of the meditation technique.

The experiences of meditation can be described and identified; they are vivid and emotive and must be made sense of by the experiencer as she makes sense of herself and the changes that she effects, and intends to effect, through practice. The use of Pali in meditation engenders confidence in the significance and validity of the practice giving it a special truth status. But the significance of Pali language in the ritual context is its incommensurability with other languages rather than its rhetorical flexibility. The styles and techniques employed by contemporary Buddhist meditators are shaped by social and religious modernity, by institutional structures, religious movements and discursive conventions. The contemporary organization and practices central to life in this Buddhist monastery are grounded on authoritative discourses and traditions (such as canonical *suttas*) but this represents a new innovation through which practitioners attempt to cultivate the perceptual conditions for the experience of the truths at the heart of the tradition. As we shall see in the next chapter, the affective gestures of the appropriate performance of mindfulness become the duty of the monastic practitioner. Renouncing the world and cutting attachment to it through meditative practices are understood by monastics to be ongoing processes, rather than a one-off act. It is possible that a whole lifetime may be spent trying to achieve a state of comparative spiritual excellence without ever actually achieving it. Being a monastic in this sense is taken as a process of becoming and the continuing 'work' that monastics do on themselves through meditation is believed to take lifetime after lifetime to complete. As wisdom is deepened through meditation so an individual comes closer to the goal of enlightenment, thereby putting her beyond paltry individual or group identity. This is a practical way of understanding the world in which introspection and isolation constitute dominant social norms used in the construction and realization of the Buddhist self and community.

CHAPTER 6

Monastic duty, mindfulness and cognitive space

As we saw in Chapters 4 and 5, the powerful experiences engendered in meditation effect, and are intended to effect, a change in the meditator. In this chapter I will begin to explore the way in which these changes are articulated and embodied by monastics in the wider context of intersubjective relationships. Thai monastic life is replete with compelling moral and personal concerns. The performance of religious identity is one means by which the moral self is formed and communicated. This occurs amidst considerations of vested interests, self-esteem and duty. Through ascetic practice monastics intend to detach from a sense of self. They further have a duty to behave appropriately for the laity. In this chapter I shall examine why this is, and how it can be that behaviour may be an actualization of the Buddhist principle of non-self *and* a duty to others, as well as a question of social hierarchy and judgment. If in embodying 'non-self' monastics no longer count for themselves then what would it matter how they behaved or how they were judged in terms of social roles and statuses? If the self does not matter then why labour to mould it? As a monastic why does one have a duty to behave in a certain way? And, why concern oneself with the moral state and idiosyncratic matters of other people, if their selves do not matter either?

MINDFUL PRACTICE: MONKS AND *MAE CHEE*

Mae chee in Wat Bonamron do not have as central a role in ritual performance as do monks. Their role in ritual is often confined to that of witness. For example, it is common practice for monastics throughout Thailand to receive alms in the home of a lay supporter. The roles of monks and *mae chee* in this context are importantly distinct. On one occasion five monks and three *mae chee* from the *wat* were invited to a spa resort near Chiang Mai so that the owners could make merit to mark their son's birthday. We arrived and were seated in an open-air gazebo in the gardens. The whole group sat silently with our hands in prayer position as the most senior monk gave a *dhamma* talk and the assembled resort owners and workers took the five precepts. The group of monks and *mae chee* chanted in unison for fifteen minutes before being offered an exquisite breakfast, which was eaten in mindful silence. We recited another brief chant and meditated for five minutes with the laity, who then wished to offer alms before we left. Up to this point monks and *mae chee* had acted as one group in enabling the lay supporters to make merit, the only person whose behaviour had been different from the rest was the senior monk who had given the precepts and the talk.

In the courtyard of the resort the monks lined up with their alms bowls, with their heads bowed and proceeded barefoot and in silence to receive alms, showing no recognition of or gratitude to individual donors. As we saw in Chapter 1 and will consider further in Chapter 7, *mae chee* in the *wat* are not able to receive alms during the alms round[1]. The group of *mae chee* stood to one side with shoes off, hands held in a respectful *wai* and heads bowed in recognition of the meritorious act. Once the alms had been completed the monks gave a blessing and the owners turned to the group of *mae chee* and gave offerings of lotus flowers, candles, incense and envelopes containing a substantial amount of money to each *mae chee*. Offerings of these objects are made during most rituals to either monks or *mae chee*. For example, as we saw in the discussion of ordination in Chapter 1, flowers, candles, incense and envelopes are offered to both the monks presiding over the ceremony and the image of the Buddha after the noviciate has prostrated three times to the Buddha and three times to the monks. It was explained to me that the lotus, candles and incense represent the Buddhist 'Triple Gem' of Buddha, *Dhamma* and Saṅgha. In making these offerings laity and noviciates venerate monastics as icons of morality and good behaviour. This is analogous to the role of the religious icons of the Buddha as visual presentations of moral excellence. In both instances the donor's attitude is one of veneration: religious purity is revealed through the physical comportment and presentation of each. As we shall see below, the mindful comportment of monastics reveals their spiritual perfections for the laity in the same way as the perfection of the Buddha is revealed through the radiance of the iconic image. The offerings of lotus, candles, incense and envelopes are not determined by gender, but the way in which they are offered *is* highly gendered. As we have seen, monks receive alms

---

[1] For an account of *mae chee* who do participate in the alms round see Lindberg Falk (2002).

during the alms round, from which *mae chee* are debarred.² Yet, *mae chee*'s performance of mindfulness presents the laity with an opportunity to make merit nonetheless and this is understood to be an equivalent to the alms received by the monks. The offerings are received without smiles and on this occasion the laity knelt as the group of *mae chee* chanted blessings for them.

In his discussion of the body in Theravāda Buddhist monasticism Collins argues that for monks and nuns correct physical decorum is a requirement of public life (1997: 198). Their social position within a community requires what he knowingly terms 'a spotless performance'. Collins suggests that the reputation of individual monastics is gained and maintained through composed comportment and through social interactions in which they are treated as superiors. The monastic body thus provides the laity with access to Buddhist wisdom and morality: 'the composed, pure, and autonomous body of the monk or nun presented in social life instantiates for lay supporters the immediate existence of that sacred, immaterial, and underlying Truth which their own bodily concerns make impossibly distant from them, and with which they can thus be connected by their material support of its human embodiments' (Collins 1997: 203).

The *Visuddhimagga*³ gives considerable attention to the good conduct of a monk:

A *Bhikkhu*, is respectful, deferential, possessed of conscience and modesty, wears his inner robe properly, wears his upper robe properly, his manner inspires confidence whether in moving forwards or backwards, looking ahead or aside, bending or stretching, his eyes are downcast, he has [good] deportment, he guards the doors of his sense faculties, knows the right measure in eating, is devoted to wakefulness, possesses mindfulness and full-awareness, wants little, is contented, is strenuous, is a careful observer of good behaviour, and treats the teachers with great respect. (VM. I. 48)

This image of the style of deportment appropriate for monks is well established in Thailand and is reflected in the ethnographic example just cited. Carrithers comments on the same image of monks in Sinhalese Buddhist society as typified by slow, low-range movements: 'Perhaps our nearest equivalent is the deportment of a well-brought-up lady: the voice is

---

² See Chapter 7 for a consideration of the qualified ways in which *mae chee* do participate in alms donations.
³ The *Visuddhimagga*, meaning 'Path of Purification', was written in Sri Lanka in the early fifth century AD by the scholar monk Buddhaghosa. It has long been and remains the most authoritative text in Theravāda Buddhism apart from the *Tipiṭaka* itself.

gentle, the knees kept together, the arms held close to the body. The glance in public is controlled' (1983: 57). Carrithers suggests that training in deportment has the social function of inspiring confidence in lay supporters and creating smooth relations within the sangha.

The level of this emphasis on physical control and demure comportment was reflected in my education as a *mae chee*. Learning to be a *mae chee* I followed the example of more experienced *mae chee*, usually by copying everything that they did. Occasionally my behaviour would be addressed directly by another *mae chee*; for example, I was told by Mae Chee Bun, 'You shouldn't sit with your legs crossed, it makes you look like you think you're something.' Every action was to be done slowly and mindfully. One way I was encouraged to appraise my own behaviour was to consider whether my actions were silent: if my robe swished around my ankles when I walked then I was walking too fast; if the dishes chinked in the sink as I did the washing up this was because I was not being sufficiently mindful.[4] *Mae chee* who sat silently with their knees and ankles together and back straight, who spoke quietly with little bodily gesticulation were pointed out to me as '*riap roi*' and suitable people to emulate. *Mae chee* who sat with their legs apart, who spoke loudly or were emotionally expressive explained to me themselves that this was the result of their lack of education, but that they could nonetheless use their behaviour as a means for improving their mental control of themselves, and that they had already seen a marked improvement in their behaviour and emotionality since ordaining. Monastics around me were in some cases teachers and in others embodiments of full participation in the monastery to which I, as a young *mae chee* and relatively inexperienced meditator, could aspire.

As we have seen *vipassanā* meditation involves a process of detaching from a sense of self. Such detachment is evidenced through the level of sartorial neatness exhibited by the monastic practitioner. The 'mindful awareness' (*sati*) developed in meditation is evidenced in '*riap roi*' behaviour. Someone who is physically and emotionally neat, tidy, composed and controlled is described as '*riap roi*'. *Riap roi* is also used when a business has been settled or completed, such as eating or washing up; everything is in order and as it should be. To be *riap roi* is also to be emotionally tidy and in control so that one is not rippled by strong emotions and may therefore conduct oneself properly. A *riap roi* person is also obedient, not controlled

---

[4] See Samuels (2004) on the role of 'doing' and 'performing' in learning to be a monastic for Sri Lankan Buddhist novices. Samuels terms this 'action-oriented pedagogy' in which activities such as eating, walking and sweeping are ritualized and become the context for learning how to be a monastic.

by a strong sense of self but able to demonstrate suitable respect and deference with an even temper. Opposed traits are bragging, greed, self-importance, uncleanness, overly expressive emotions and disrespect for others. To say that someone is not mindful or *riap roi* is to say that they have no understanding of what they are doing. Ideally, *riap roi* should arise from one's inner state, sense of self having been reduced as a result of meditation practice. *Riap roi* and mindfulness should result in harmonious interaction, with a correct observance of hierarchy.

Lave and Wenger (1991) develop the theory of 'legitimate peripheral participation' to account for learning ways of being as a dimension of social practice. For them, learning involves increasing levels of participation in communities of practice, rather than the acquisition of knowledge alone: 'A person's intentions to learn are engaged and the meaning of learning is configured through the process of becoming a full participant in a sociocultural practice' (1991: 29). They give examples of apprenticeships in midwifery, tailoring and quartermastery in which learning involves moving towards full participation in a community of practice (1991: 79). In order to be a tailor it is necessary to sit, stand and talk like a tailor; it is more than the knowledge of a job. 'Activities, tasks, functions, and understandings do not exist in isolation; they are part of broader systems of relations in which they have meaning. These systems of relations arise out of and are reproduced and developed within social communities, which are in part systems of relations among persons' (1991: 53).

The role of masters in the examples given by Lave and Wenger is not always as teachers but as embodiments of full participation, as examples of identities of mastery: 'Becoming a "member such as those" is an embodied telos too complex to be discussed in the narrower and simpler language of goals, tasks, and knowledge acquisition' (Lave and Wenger 1991: 85). In this approach to learning the focus is not on observable teaching, which is minimal, but rather on the phenomenon of learning by which learners make cultural practices their own. For Lave and Wenger, therefore, the person is a practitioner and a member of a community of practice. This provides us with a useful tool for understanding the development of meditation and mindful practice in the monastery. The identity that is formed and the membership that is created are tied up with the motivation for action. 'If the person is both member of a community and agent of activity, the concept of the person closely links meaning and action in the world' (Lave and Wenger 1991: 122).

On the return journey to the monastery from the spa resort Mae Chee Sati told me that our behaviour had helped develop faith among the laity.

She said that it would not have been right for *mae chee* to 'run for alms' because this would have been motivated by ego, would have upset the laity and would not have been meritorious. I will discuss the duty monastics have to act as 'fields of merit' below. It is worth flagging here that, in this *mae chee*'s reasoning, 'running for alms' would have been demeritorious because it would have been motivated by ego and would have been upsetting, not because it is demeritorious to give alms to a *mae chee*, per se. Though *mae chee* from this monastery do not receive alms on the alms round, they are involved in the ritual process through bearing witness as they embody correct deportment and morality.[5] I was told, and it was evidenced in behaviour, that the lack of formal rules for *mae chee* means that their behaviour becomes the site in which their spiritual progress is demonstrated, in a way that differs from monks. Monks and *mae chee* share the common duty to behave 'mindfully'. However, the lack of ritual duty coupled with the ambiguity surrounding *mae chee* ordination status means that their scope for action is confined more than monks to the capacities of their bodies. Furthermore, those bodies are more subject to the judgmental eye of others.

SOCIAL MERIT

In Thai Buddhism each person may acquire merit of his or her own volition, for example through participating in a religious ceremony or offering alms. This merit may be passed on to others, living or dead, through its stated dedication. This is illustrated through the dedication of merit chanted in Pali during rituals:

May all beings – without limit, without end – have a share in the merit just now made, and in whatever other merit I have made. Those who are dear and kind to me – beginning with my mother and father – whom I have seen or never seen; and others, neutral and hostile; beings in the cosmos – the three realms, the four modes of birth, with five, one, or four aggregates – wandering on from realm to realm: If they know of my dedication of merit, may they themselves rejoice, and if they do not know, may the *devas* inform them. By reason of their rejoicing in my gift of merit, may all beings always live happily, may they attain the serene state, and their radiant hopes be fulfilled.

Intending to transfer merit to another is itself meritorious and both persons thereby acquire merit. Sharing merit with another augments the original amount of merit created through a meritorious act; the more

---

[5] See Chapter 7 on *mae chee* giving and receiving alms and Chapter 8 on the gendered hierarchy of monastic duty.

people share in a meritorious act, the more merit is created. Merit sharing is an important motivation in many Thai rituals. For example, Thai men and women enter the monastery for a limited period in order to transfer merit to their parents or deceased relatives; the *Abhidhamma* is chanted at wakes in order to pass merit on to the deceased; lustral water and string are used as specific tools for the physical transference of merit in most rituals. Transferring merit to others is done through specific verses and acts, while sharing in the merit of another may be as simple as bearing witness to the act. In this sense the role of witness *mae chee* performed in the private alms round created more merit for both themselves and the laity involved. As a *mae chee* I was often asked to attend ceremonies so that I might share in the merit of the sponsor and thereby produce more merit. It was a question of my individual merit that I had the opportunity to attend such ceremonies and my attending them thereby produced more merit for myself and others. On completion of a meritorious act (such as listening to a *dhamma* talk, receiving alms from another, attending a ritual) those involved and witnessing it hold their hands in prayer position and say '*Sattu*' ('Thus it is so'), three times. This acquires even further merit for the one who sincerely proclaims it.

Writing of a similar situation Spiro argues that in Burma the pronouncement of '*tha-dhu*' confers merit on the one who utters it because it is of their own volition or intention that they acquire merit, rather than merit being conferred on them by another, which Spiro holds is impossible (1970: 126). Spiro argues that the intention to share merit is meritorious but that merit cannot itself be transferred (1970: 25). In Spiro's understanding the transfer of merit is logically incompatible with the 'inexorability of karmic doctrine' (1970: 127). He argues that such a transgression in correct Buddhist practice is a result of the faithful (and here I take him to mean all who believe that merit can be transferred) being unable to follow karma to its logical conclusion; they *need* a way to avoid karmic retribution for sin (Spiro 1970: 127): 'The psychological necessity for such an escape hatch from the stern consequence of the doctrine of karma need not be argued on theoretical ground only, but may be inferred from the fact that, despite its inconsistency with the entire structure of Buddhism, merit sharing entered Theravāda Buddhism very early in its history' (Spiro 1970: 127). Gombrich too argues that the transfer of merit is a rationalization of practice which 'affords some psychological relief from the oppressive doctrine of man's total responsibility for his own fate' (1971: 284). For Gombrich, the theory of karma thus remains cognitively intact, while affectively its rigours are avoided. Furthermore, there is much evidence to suggest that the logic of karma is avoided without the doctrine being challenged (see Keyes 1983).

It remains the case that most Thai Buddhists believe that merit may be shared, passed on to others, and that both the donor and the recipient of the merit benefit from this. However, merit is not 'given' in exchange for actions or participation. Rather, the situation provides participants with the opportunity to act meritoriously. While I am questioning of Spiro's analytical approach, his excellent ethnography reveals that the alms offered to monks in the Burmese context are understood to be meritorious in proportion to the spiritual quality of the recipient and it is for this reason that laity emphasize the importance of the piety of monks (Spiro 1970: 107). Regrettably, he does not examine the implicit sharing of merit between monastic and laity in this context: that the monk must already have a high degree of merit in order to behave in such a way as to constitute a fertile 'field of merit' for the laity. I suggest that the significance of the spiritual level of monks for lay merit making reveals that in the Burmese context, as in Thailand, merit making is not a question of individual intent alone.[6]

All action and interaction in the Thai monastic context is more or less meritoriously accumulative: for the monastic this includes doing one's monastic duty, whether that be working in the monastery or providing a living exemplar of Buddhist ethics for the laity. For example, a *mae chee* who was an expert gardener was reluctant to landscape the flowerbeds in the monastery because she felt that this work was not sufficiently meritorious. She confined herself to creating the elaborate floral displays offered to the *stūpa* by senior monks on *Wan Phra*. This was highly meritorious work because it facilitated the religious offerings of the most meritoriously potent people in the community. Klima views merit making in Thai ritual as being simultaneously shared and generated by individuals, groups and 'those that embody the highest spiritual values' (Klima 2004: 451). He writes that, 'the enhancement of one's spiritual condition is afforded, oftentimes, not only through one's individual concentration and effort, but through the communal presence of others sharing in the power of the rituals themselves as well as the degree to which the recipient already embodies a refined and meritorious character' (Klima 2004: 450).

The mindful deportment of monastics was explained to me as being a meritoriously accumulative spectacle for others and the result of the morality (*sīla*) of the monastic. The appearance of the body of the monastic

---

[6] See Walters (2003) on the ways in which intention is thought to bring about 'sociokarmic' effects among Sri Lankan Buddhists.

reveals an inner state of moral attainment: others bear witness to moral qualities and virtues in monastic physical performance. Sitting up straight, speaking quietly, eating slowly, and so on, therefore become a question of morality for the monastic. It was further explained that having the opportunity to witness such a spectacle was itself the result of past merit. Importantly, the obverse of this is also true: it is demeritorious to witness a monastic behaving badly *and* it is the result of demerit in the past. It is one's own merit that determines whether one sees such a spectacle and it also increases one's demerit to do so.

For the laity, seeking out monastics renowned for their discipline becomes a positive duty. For the monastic this translates into a duty to others to behave in an appropriate way. As Mae Chee Poy told me,

> When we behave and carry ourselves with morality others can observe us and this is about our morality and it is about their merit. They have merit to be able to see one doing good in this way. We do good for ourselves but others can benefit too. When they meet a *mae chee* who is pretty and well behaved then they have merit to see something so beautiful. This we do for ourselves but it also has effect for those around us. For ourselves first, even if we weren't going to see anyone else we would still wash. If you stay on your own and don't wash you stink yourself. If you stay by yourself and eat *mama* noodles in your room in the evenings, no one else will know and they will think that you have good morality but we cause problems for ourselves. We have to be careful for ourselves. If you stay alone be careful of your thoughts, if you stay with others be careful of your speech. This is what it means to be ordained.

Monastics have a duty to behave well for the benefit of others because this induces faith/confidence (*saddhā*) in the laity. Ideally the physical control involved in this comes as an automatic result of ascetic practice (see Chapter 4). Yet, by refining behavioural characteristics and holding them up as indicative of a virtuous state of mind, one's behaviour becomes not only a question of individual morality but also social responsibility. As such the correct behaviour of monastics does not always result from an attitude of detachment. As Phra Sop, a 35-year-old monk who ordained as a novice when he was a child, told me, 'Sometimes in ourselves we know that we are not doing good but we want to keep it to ourselves so that it is only our own demerit and no one else has to share it.'

HIERARCHY AND SELF-PLACEMENT

In the monastery one's identity is constituted in a hierarchical relationship with others depending on relative age, status and length of ordination.

This is further illustrated through linguistic first-person reference. Speakers of Thai are faced with a multiplicity of words to use for first-person reference, each with particular resonance and connotations of deference. The process of linguistic self-placement in reference to other social actors, called in Thai *kan wang tuam*, can be quite self-conscious and productive of anxiety: it can lead to practical problems or even a complete communicative breakdown (see Chirasombutti and Diller 1999: 132). This may be evidenced in the relative kin terms used between all *mae chee*: one is either '*pi*' or '*nong*' (elder or junior) to the person being spoken to, but one may also be grandmother, mother, elder or younger sister, child or little one (*noo*).[7] By referring to each other through relational kin terms *mae chee* locate themselves hierarchically. This hierarchical placement may be the result of age difference but it is often determined by relative lengths of ordination. For example, a woman who was a few years older than me but who had been ordained for less time referred to me as 'elder sister'. On occasion one's name is used but this is always prefixed with 'Mae Chee' and usually only occurs between *mae chee* who do not know each other. One way to show respect to a *mae chee* is to place oneself linguistically below her, thereby showing deference. When speaking with a monk a *mae chee* will never use his name without prefixing it with 'Phra' (the closest English equivalent would be 'Brother') and he will use the prefix 'Mae Chee' before her name; he will always be placed linguistically above the *mae chee*. For example, it is appropriate for a *mae chee* to refer to a monk as 'respected grandfather', 'respected father' or 'respected elder brother' ('*luang po*', '*luang pau*' or '*luang pi*'), but no matter how many years junior a monk may be to a *mae chee* he may not be referred to as respected younger brother ('*luang nong*'). Only novices may be referred to as younger ('*nong*') but this is always accompanied by their title as 'novice' ('*nong naen*').

Addressing a mixed group of people one may hold varying relational positions at the same time depending on respective ages and lengths of ordination. For example, a *mae chee* in her thirties may be 'little one', 'child', 'elder sister' and 'younger sister' in relation to the different people present. Self-reference then becomes a challenge, which is avoided through the use of '*mae chee*' instead. *Mae chee* never use the common female first-person

---

[7] In the Royal Institute System this would be transliterated as '*nu*'. I have chosen to transliterate it here as '*noo*' to emphasize the long vowel sound. Self-reference is made using these relational terms. So, for example, I would refer to myself as '*nong*' when speaking with someone who referred to themselves as '*pi*'.

pronouns of '*dichan*' or '*chan*', I was told that this would be completely inappropriate. When speaking to laity one refers to oneself as '*mae chee*' in the first-person singular in contrast to '*yoam*' ('householder'). This constructs the monastic self as a generalized 'other' in relation to the generalized 'other' of 'laity'. This emphasizes the monastic identity of *mae chee* and maintains social distinction within the relationship. In a discussion of self-placement Herdt argues that 'When people identify with a category, they endow it with a meaning beyond themselves. Thus, to say, "I am berdache", is to suggest an "I" (subject) in active identification with "berdache" (categorical object); and again that the subject and categorical object are in a stable formation across time' (1994: 61). *Mae chee*'s use of the categorical object as the subject when talking to laity constructs a stable and privileged place from which to speak, one that not only depersonalizes them but also locates them firmly within the monastic hierarchy.

The monastic is grounded in, and defined by, the relationships and institutions of which they are a part. For the laity the implicit moral expectations and constraints of monastic behaviour are defined in terms of quite absolute standards of behaviour and ethics. Interestingly, this is not the case *between monastics* where, as we shall see, expectations and constraints of behaviour are defined relationally and moral judgments are influenced by social role and position.

MERIT AND THE CONTROL OF EMOTION

The display and concealment of emotion in the monastery thus takes on an important role for monastics. Before examining the significance of physical and emotional control in the monastery I wish to emphasize that the focus of my enquiry is not 'emotions' themselves. Concern with the social and cultural construction of emotion in anthropology has been an expanding field of enquiry since the early 1980s (see, Bailey 1983; Boellstorff and Lindquist 2004; Geertz 1973; Karim 1990; Lutz 1988; Lutz and White 1986; Peletz 1996; Rosaldo 1980; Rosaldo 1984). I employ an analysis of the use of emotion as a way of understanding monastic duty and behaviour. However, while my ethnography reveals local understandings of rationality and emotion that differ from prevalent Western understandings (on this see Parkin 1985), I do not want to confine my examination of monastic duty and mindful deportment by aligning it to either side of an individual/social dichotomy. On the one hand, the inner bodily experiences of mindful awareness are consistent with highly individuated concepts of personhood, while, on the other hand, the communicative aspects of monastic deportment may be interpreted as a public performance that can be traded in social exchange. Interpreting my ethnography as either 'individual' or 'social' risks leading to an impoverished understanding of the significance of monastic duty and ascetic practice. Instead, my focus is on the ways in which such ideals are valued and negotiated by people in the context of intersubjective relationships.

As we have seen, to witness a *mae chee* behaving 'emotionally' is demeritorious. The emotions that count as 'emotional' are disruptive and overtly expressed, such as anger or grief. When a *mae chee* behaves in an emotional way, for whatever reason, she is avoided until she has regained her composure. On the one hand, this encourages the individual not to attach to their emotional state, on the other, it reduces the amount of demerit incurred by those around her, and reduces the impact of her acting while controlled by her defilements and so creating more demerit for herself and others. For example, after my mother had been to visit I saw her off at the airport and was close to tears as she went through the departure gate. The monks and *mae chee* with me made no mention of this and spoke about other matters rather than discuss her departure. In the car on the way back to the monastery none of them would look at me and the usual tactile hand holding of *mae chee* was withdrawn to try to help me stop behaving emotionally. The next day a man who had not been present said that he had heard I was crying at the airport and openly laughed at me and encouraged me to laugh at myself. My emotional display had been ignored by others and yet had been discussed within the monastery. Behaviour that contravenes social codes is not merely aesthetically offensive: it is reflective of one's spiritual impurity and demerit.

The smooth and polite presentation of the self may mask the conflicting emotions experienced in the person. The monastic community may be understood as a hierarchical society in which relationships are nuanced by a complex nested power system characterized by emotional control and gracefulness. In order to behave appropriately and to second-guess the emotions of others one must be enormously attentive to one's own and others' behaviour. These are complex power relations in which the most appropriate course is often to leave everything unstated.

Wikan argues that in Bali sanctions against showing anger or offence and the injunction to smile despite displeasurable feelings must be contextually located in complex concerns of morality, social control, health and sorcery. She argues for the Balinese conception of 'grace' as 'embedded in *particular* webs of significance that they [Balinese] have spun regarding persons, morality, emotionality, and health. It bespeaks, moreover, a shared, interpersonal perception of others – what we might call the agents of "culture" – as demanding and judgemental beyond what one can at times endure' (Wikan 1990: 22, emphasis in original). Wikan locates people's emotional actions in a world of effort: 'What Westerners have perceived as an innate aesthetic mood, an ingrained disposition to be graceful and poised, I found instead to reflect a deliberate attitude, a willed response of "not caring," "forgetting" the bad that has come to pass, and "letting bygones be bygones" if one is to thrive, or even to survive' (1990: xvi). Wikan writes that the effort recognized in social life necessarily involves private matters because the private experience is an important part of the context in which salient cultural symbols derive their significance. 'From their perspective, it is the *effort* (*usaha*) required in bridging, and moving across, thresholds and domains that gives meaning to a host of interpersonal signs' (1990: 17). In the Balinese case people are perpetually concerned to decipher each other's 'hidden hearts' because the consequences of anger are extreme and magic may be instigated by sentiments that are never openly expressed (Wikan 1990: 43).

In the monastery, on those occasions when people have misinterpreted each other's hidden feelings and engaged in open conflict, the rift has been hard to heal. For example, one of the most senior *mae chee* in the monastery was good friends with an *upāsikā* (pious lay woman) who volunteered in the main office. They are both highly educated women who had been as close as sisters for many years. One day, acting on behalf of the Abbot the *mae chee* referred the head of the local village down to the office with a note requesting the office to give him funds for a project. The *upāsikā* became very angry and screwed the note up refusing to give the money out, indignant at the thought of this *mae chee* feeling that she could tell her what to do. When the *mae chee* heard about the *upāsikā*'s reaction she felt insulted that she would have such arrogance attributed to her. Neither of the two women ever spoke to each other directly about the incident. Though they are civil to each other now they spent many years not speaking and it is clear that they can never be intimate in the way that they once were. I was told that it was not the Thai way to speak directly (*phut drong drong*); sacrificing the friendship was preferable to openly discussing the misunderstanding. The concern to decipher the intention of each woman had led to misinterpretation and emotional display. Consequently, it was not possible for them to regain smooth relations without further acknowledging the mistake that had been made. They saw no alternative but to break all contact.

NEGOTIATING HIERARCHY AND MINDFULNESS

Monastics may be restricted in their emotional expression by cultural conventions prescribing appropriate behaviour but the extent to which these restrictions impose upon people and the points at which one may choose to express emotion depend upon personal placement and negotiation. People in the monastery are differently positioned with respect to ordination status, rank, age, length of ordination, life experience, education, wealth and emotional state, to name a few culturally relevant distinctions. These influence one's perspective on oneself and the world, and their negotiation diversifies the monastic community.[8]

It is true that it is inappropriate to be overtly emotional as a monastic, for example it was inappropriate for me to cry at the airport, but this does not hold true in the same way in all circumstances and for all people. At the end of fieldwork the Abbot and three *mae chee* with whom I was particularly close took me to the airport. Before going through the departure gate I knelt on the floor and prostrated at the feet of the Abbot and then at the feet of my *mae chee pi liang*. As I rose I was surprised and touched to see Phra Ajharn wiping away a tear. Ajharn had been like a father to me during my ordination, he ordained me and was my meditation teacher, and we worked closely on an almost daily basis translating his meditation teaching. I had been ordained for over a year and as such his duty to provide an example of equanimous deportment was not as great when faced with me as it would have been with someone completely identified as lay. Furthermore, whereas my tears at my mother's departure revealed one *mae chee*'s attachment to the world, his worldly detachment was not called into question by this fleeting display of emotion witnessed by a handful of other monastics and myself. His monastic role was much more than one impermanent emotional expression. Wikan notes a similar inequality in the negotiation of emotional expression in Bali: 'Highly positioned, powerful men will even say, "Oh no, people will not laugh if they see you sad!" And they are right. No one would – at them' (Wikan 1990: 24).

Understanding the personal experience of private lives provides us with an important dimension of public and interpersonal performance. The lack of confrontation in the monastery in some instances leads to feelings of frustration. The lay woman mentioned in the last chapter who behaved

---

[8] This will be examined in more detail in Chapter 8.

inappropriately was never confronted about her behaviour. She was made to feel unwelcome but this was done through subtle behaviour and subtext, rather than any explicit comment on her actions. However, it took a period of weeks of her gossiping about *mae chee* before she finally left. She was encouraged to leave by other people volunteering to do the work she was there to do, rather than openly criticizing her for her behaviour. In this way no one could be overtly offended, but the monastery is a small community and everyone was aware of the situation. However, among other things, she had been suggesting that two *mae chee* had inappropriate feelings for the Abbot, a suggestion that was deeply offensive to the women involved. This slander continued for a number of months until the lay woman finally left. One of these *mae chee* was hurt that the Abbot had allowed this behaviour to continue for so long. She told me privately, 'She is a chicken; she comes into the monastery and runs around squawking. Why be angry at a chicken for behaving like a chicken? No, I am hurt by the one who has the power to coop the chicken and does nothing.' In public, however, she appeared as happy and mindful as always. After the lay woman had left the monastery this *mae chee* drafted a letter of resignation from all of her official duties in the monastery. She gave a signed copy of the letter to each office in the monastery and one to the Abbot himself. She then removed herself from monastery life by embarking upon intensive silent retreat. It was three months before she returned to work.

Through mindful performance the individuality of a particular monastic is not disguised – on the contrary, the performance of selfless mindful action, even in the face of great trials and accusations, speaks volumes about a person's status, morality and kammic attainment. This *mae chee* was able to express her dissatisfaction without revealing her feelings to her accuser. She used a form of mindful performance, formally detaching herself from all community interaction and going into silent retreat, to communicate her dissatisfaction in a non-emotional way, which was forcefully felt nonetheless. This also gave her the opportunity to regain her composure and offered her a needed break from the pressures of monastery life; by withdrawing from the monastery she was able to calm her emotions and act skilfully. The ideological significance of the practice of mindfulness as a means of cutting attachment to a sense of self underlies the development of monastic identity. What 'mindfulness' means to people depends on the many permutations of context and circumstance. To understand the significance of 'mindful awareness' and composure for monastics it is necessary to examine the way in which different people, differently positioned, make use of such cultural terms, to what ends, and in what ways in interpersonal experience, practical concerns and interactions.

THE PARADOX OF MONASTIC DUTY AND NON-SELF

Monastics are 'on show' to the laity for much of the time. They must therefore provide a constant example *for* the laity. The role of monastics as ritual specialists and embodiments of a monastic ideal is conceptualized in terms of selfless giving and non-reciprocity. The monastic body becomes a spectacle of religious perfection for the laity, and as such it is never appropriate to see a monastic body misbehaving or in the wrong place. If the monastic appearance communicates how the monastic is to be treated *by* the laity then it also communicates how the monastic is to behave *for* the laity. The appearance of the monastic both physically and performatively acts as a buffer zone between the social world and the bounded self. It is the space in which lay impressions of renunciates are realized, and where renunciates communicate themselves to others in the light of the religious ideal. The body may speak to others about one's personhood but by being ordained one's body becomes part of the public domain – one has a moral duty to behave in an appropriate way, something which is understood as the ultimate gift of the monastic. Sitting in a public area of the monastery on opposite sides of a large stone table I interviewed a monk of a similar age to me. Phra Jit had been ordained for ten years. He speaks good English, is studying for a degree at Suan Dok University and is responsible for the maintenance of the monastery computers. He told me:

We have to think about society because many of them come and stay here. So we must be careful in order to give them faith in Buddhism. Suppose they think that *phra* and *mae chee* sitting like this is no good then we'll have been the cause of them losing faith in Buddhism. If we stay in the monastery we can relax a bit because we know that there is no danger, but if a lay person is watching we must be careful because of them. Supposing we're sitting here and we feel pure of heart but another doesn't know what we're talking about. We don't want someone else to think we're doing a bad thing, but looking at ourselves when we're lay people and we see monks talk like this we don't think anything about it. We have to behave properly even if the truth isn't like that. Sometimes people from outside see monks have to be *riap roi*, have no fun, have to be brilliant 100 per cent perfect. But our life is not like that; life has happiness, heart, desire, feelings, the same as people outside. They see us as very high, we've come to this point. But sometimes this behaviour doesn't come from our heart, it's for society because of what they expect of us.

As a monastic one is related to by the laity as one who has renounced a sense of self but there is necessarily a discrepancy between this and one's own awareness of the ongoing process of renunciation: between oneself as a spectacle of asceticism and the reality of one's own imperfection. As a monastic there are times when there is a difference between one's self-presentation and what one feels. One's morality presents a paradox as a process of self-aware reflection, on the one hand, and, on the other, absence of self in the performance of one's moral duty to the laity as an act of non-reciprocal giving by a religious specialist.

Of course, being mindful is not merely a monastic injunction upon public emotionality; it is valued in and of itself. It is indicative of a deepening level of wisdom as a result of ascetic practice and bespeaks a level of spiritual attainment. While it may be performed as a duty rather than as a genuine reflection of equanimity, the value of mindfulness is ideologically sustained. The empirical evidence for the state of virtue is to be read from a monastic's conduct – by themselves as much as by others. By doing one's duty selflessly and performing the role of the ideal renunciate, one hopes to 'fill the robe from the inside' as the precepts 'settle in the heart'. The full weight of others' moral expectation lies on one's personal morality as it is expressed through the body; the external world impinges on the internal through the robe. As Benson (2000: 252) writes of Euro-American tattooing practices, so I understand renunciation partially as 'a consequence of engagement, imagined as detachment' because in the context of the monastery self-willed practice is enhanced by the moral expectation and elicitation of others.

Collins demonstrates that in the Buddhist textual tradition purity and impurity are said to occur through body, speech and mind. The rules of morality (*sīla*) and the monastic code (*vinaya*) govern speech and body, while mental life cannot be disciplined by external rules. However, when this tripartite system is used in the texts, virtue and vice are understood to operate in the three places together. 'Thus the usual assumption is that the internal mental condition of a monk or nun can be inferred from his or her physical and verbal behaviour, since it is the latter which express the former' (Collins 1997: 199). Collins argues that the expected public body image of one who practises meditation is a form of private self-control and self-supervision. He juxtaposes the deconstruction and rejection of the body of the monk or nun in certain meditative practices with the construction of it in social behaviour as a 'unified and valued public object' (Collins 1997: 199). He argues that this creates the cognitive 'space' in the Buddhist monastic practitioner for individualized analysis.[9] 'In this private zone of operations the desexualized, and thus in one sense desocialized individual can embody in imagination the immateriality posited in the doctrines of Buddhism, and in this way 'touch the deathless with the body' (Collins 1997: 200).

Thus, Collins suggests that the Buddhist monastic practitioner is in one sense radically individualized but that this necessitates the complicity of the laity and the monastic community. For the laity, the monastic body provides access to Buddhist wisdom and morality. For monastics, the social position of a monk or nun means that they may be constructed by themselves and others as independent and autonomous agents: 'the orientation towards a purely personal and immaterial goal both differentiates them from the laity, bound up in networks of material concern, and creates the actual behavioural space in which the "subjectivized" interiority inculcated by meditative practices can take place' (Collins 1997: 202). Given this brilliant insight, the paradox of monastic performance becomes the vehicle by which monastics actualize the monastic ideal: through monastic duty monks and *mae chee* intend to come to a position of detachment but even at this point they continue to be socially engaged.

CONCLUSION

Though meditation is a solitary pursuit, the self that the monastic progressively produces through meditation is firmly located within a community of practice. The idea that monastics have a moral duty to be 'brilliant 100 per cent perfect' for the laity is, in Wat Bonamron, a self-evident cultural proposition, but it must be located within the dilemmas and conflicting interests of monks and *mae chee* as they negotiate their lives. Such a cultural tenet may be noted by the anthropologist but she must also make sense of the experience of emotionality as it is negotiated, negated or employed by the person as a lived experience. The control of the body is the means to and result of detachment from a sense of self, yet 'mindfulness', in some instances, may intensify personal concern rather than depersonalize behaviour. In order to understand this it has been necessary to examine what the continual practice of asceticism means for the monastic as an *ongoing* project of self-formation. Those emotions and impulses that do not conform to Buddhist soteriology are at issue in interpersonal relations: if everyone exerts effort to mask their feelings, they also exert effort to unmask the feelings of others. Thus, 'mindful

---

[9] We will return to a consideration of the meaning of individuality in Chapter 9.

awareness' emerges as a moral injunction: a way of establishing who one is in the moral landscape of intersubjective relationships.

In order to cut attachment to a sense of self it is necessary to adopt the markers of selflessness associated with cultivating this state of mind. At the same time, the level to which an individual is able to attain this ideal state is read through his or her behaviour: thus to remain emotionally detached in every situation is indicative of one's level of wisdom, attained through meditative practice. In a community typified by sartorial neatness and physical control, striving for an ideal of non-self, the ultimate act of giving is of oneself and it is *through* renunciation of the body that renunciation *becomes* embodied. Sartorial neatness is understood to result from moral purity and is a monastic duty. The duty to behave in accord with such an ideal creates the cognitive space required to actualize spiritual development and it is through such a performance that people become members of a community of practice. Ascetic life in the *wat* is not merely about conforming either to the precepts or to monastic practice, and to think of it as such would be an inadequate conception of the relation between values and practice. As Laidlaw argues of Jain asceticism, a gap between hope/intention and reality does not necessarily suggest a deviation from the religious system or a dysfunction of social organization: it is in that dynamic tension between precept and practice that asceticism is really lived (Laidlaw 1995: 7).

CHAPTER 7

Money, mae chee *and reciprocity*

In this chapter I examine the part that women, in the ambiguous role of Buddhist nun (*mae chee*), are now taking in the emblematic Buddhist practice of alms donations.[1] As we have seen, the monastic office of '*mae chee*' is complicated. It is conveyed through the ritual adoption of religious vows and is usually undertaken for life. However, *mae chee* ordination is only partial and its status is far below that of monks.[2] Because of this ambiguity *mae chee* are able to employ both the ascetic practices of renouncers (such as accepting alms) and those of lay women (such as offering alms). *Mae chee*, while debarred from the alms round in this monastery,[3] both receive alms from the laity and donate alms to monks. Furthermore, *mae chee* receive monetary alms from the laity on behalf of the monastic community as a whole. In this chapter, I argue that by handling money given to the monastic community *mae chee* mediate in a relationship of generalized reciprocity between the monastic community and lay society. By *donating* alms to monks *mae chee* appear to be reaffirming their status of partial ordination, yet in order for them to be able to *receive* alms donations from the laity they must see themselves, and be recognized by the laity, as an integral part of the monastic community. A nuanced understanding of these economic, religious and gendered roles is crucial to our understanding of the incorporation of women into the monastic community and the ways in which gift practices are related to interpersonal and group dynamics in the context of modern Thai monasticism. As I shall show below, the performance of monastic identity is also crucial to our understanding of both monks and *mae chee* receiving alms.

---

[1] Some of the information here also appears in Cook (2008b).
[2] The status of *mae chee* will be considered in detail in the next chapter.
[3] See Lindberg Falk (2002) for an account of Thai *mae chee* who do daily alms rounds.

GIFT GIVING AND THAI BUDDHIST MONASTICISM

All Thai Buddhist monks and *mae chee* are celibate renouncers. They observe fast for eighteen hours a day, receiving and eating food only between the hours of 6 a.m. and noon. The strict observance of fast is intended to reduce attachment to desire. The food eaten is enough to maintain the body for meditation rather than for pleasure or fun. Lay people donate all the food eaten in the monastery. The laity either offer small amounts of food to monks when they go for alms or they donate larger amounts (such as sacks of rice or crates of vegetables) to the main office in the monastic compound. While monastics usually have a limited number of personal possessions, monasteries are often very wealthy as a result of lay support. This is reflected in the grand gilded temple buildings found in most Thai monasteries. Furthermore, the food in monasteries is often of a very high standard and large amounts of food are donated to the monastery on a daily basis.

In the *wat* the monks' community performs two alms rounds simultaneously every morning. The first is in the surrounding area outside the monastic compound. The second is conducted within the monastery. Monks slowly walk the alms route barefoot, with their eyes downcast and alms bowl covered. During the alms round the monk does not ask for food. As he is walking lay people who wish to offer alms will come and kneel at the side of the street holding their donations up to their foreheads. Without smiling or looking at the lay person the monk stops and moves the lid of his alms bowl to one side so that the lay person can place the food inside. Without any sign of gratitude for the donation the monk replaces the lid of his bowl, chants a short optional blessing for the lay person and moves on (see Carrithers 1983: 57).

Making merit is one of the primary motivations for donating alms to monastics (see Spiro 1970: 105) and the daily alms round is just one means by which this is achieved. The monastic economy is based entirely on alms donations. Alms donations of food, money and objects, such as electric fans or water heaters, are made to the main office, staffed by *mae chee*, on a daily basis. The name of the donor and the amount donated, received by *mae chee*, are recorded and read aloud each week on the eve of *Wan Phra* (Buddha Day). On this occasion novices, *mae chee* and laity also publicly renew their commitment to the monastery and receive a *dhamma* teaching (*tet*). Any unusual expenditure by the monastery as a whole, for example for computer parts and so on, is also made explicit. These finances are then posted on a notice board outside the main office for the rest of the week. The donation and public recognition of alms are both highly meritorious acts. Some people donate relatively small amounts and economic resources are not an obstacle to being recognized in this way. Nonetheless, the public recognition of alms amounts implies that there are those that give, and those that give more: the announcement necessitates an audience other than those who are named as well as those who receive donations. By reading out the amounts donated by individuals the merit of their acts may be measured by others, and is given public recognition by the monastic community as a whole. Crucially, however, reading the amounts of alms donations is itself a meritorious act that is shared by the whole community.

Mae chee do not go for alms but instead donate alms to monks. In donating alms *mae chee* are performing the religious role of the laity. However, on different occasions *mae chee* also have the duty to receive alms from laity on behalf of the monastery and as individual monastics, thereby giving lay devotees the opportunity to make merit.

UNDERSTANDING THE GIFT

As we have seen the behaviour of both donors and receivers of alms is highly prescribed. I will argue that this behaviour enables merit making precisely because it de-emphasizes social reciprocity. Selfless giving, or *dāna*, is rewarded with merit, but only if it is unreciprocated. Were the receiver of alms to reciprocate with gratitude or recognition of the gift, it would not be selfless and as such it would not be meritorious. In order to understand the gift as 'free', that is, free from all reciprocity or socially binding activity, it is necessary to reject understandings of gift exchange as the opposite of commodity exchange (see Gregory 1982). In such a formulation commodity exchange is assumed to stand squarely in the economic realm, influenced by disinterested rationality and commercial gain, typified by alienability and non-reciprocal relationships. Gift exchange, by contrast, is assumed to carry with it moral obligation and the social concerns of the non-economic realm; as such, it is essentialized as reciprocal and socially binding. In such a formulation the gift, including the gift of alms, could never be 'free' because it always entails the obligation to be reciprocated in some way.

Examining Buddhist alms giving Carrithers (1984) suggests that relationships between the sangha (monastic community) and alms givers are created through a process of positive reciprocity because failing to meet the exacting standards of the ideology of selfless giving for the alms giver is 'as natural as falling off a high wire' (1984: 322). Alms giving is understood by Carrithers as 'gift exchange' – reciprocal exchange between the laity and the sangha – because in daily life there is almost always recognition of a personal relationship between sangha and laity. However, it is difficult to see how this relationship can be understood as personal given that 'laity' and 'sangha' are defined as generalized entities (cf. Laidlaw 2000: 625–6). As we have seen, the personal relationships that can exist between individuals are purposefully de-emphasized by the rules for comportment during alms donations as well as the verbal reference to categories of persons ('laity' and 'sangha') during ritual donations. Contra Carrithers, Strenski (1983: 472) states that the *bhikkhu* (monk) is an ideological paradigm of non-reciprocity. As he points out (1983: fn. 4), it is impossible for the sangha to 'give' merit in return for alms donations because to have gained merit is 'simply to have acted in a karmically good way'. The sangha provides the occasion for people to act in a karmically good way but cannot give merit for *dāna* 'any more than it can give someone virtue for having been virtuous' (1983). Strenski suggests that *dāna* is precisely a rejection of the idea of reciprocity between particular laity and particular monks. Instead the ritual services provided by monks and the *dāna* given by laity constitute a system of generalized exchange, which has naturally evolved into the 'domestication' of the sangha, as 'regular patterns of social relationships grow along with regular patterns of giving' (Strenski 1983: 470). Generalized exchange 'seeks an unbalanced condition between exchange partners, which requires repayment at some unspecified time, typically by another group or person than the original receiver of the first gift' (Strenski 1983: 471). In Strenski's evocative terms, this is 'a model of society moving in spiralling circles of generosity and sympathetic joy' (1983: 476). The laity performs *dāna*, and the sangha performs rituals and teaching, but neither is in direct reciprocation of the other. Alms donations may therefore be understood ideologically as 'free' gifts: that is, a voluntary donation made without expectation of this-worldly return (see Bloch and Parry 1989: 66).

Parry (1986) suggests that it is a distortion of Mauss's (1966) seminal work on the gift to assume that self-interest is the necessary opposite of altruism, or that Mauss was concerned to reveal the self-interest inherent in all gift exchange. The assumption in such readings is that the gift for which an equivalent return is expected is a '*non*-ideological verity that nobody does anything for nothing' in contrast to the notion of a 'pure gift' as 'mere ideological obfuscation' (Parry 1986: 455). Parry argues that the ideology of the 'pure' gift emerges parallel to the ideology of self-interested pursuit of utility; the total social fact of Mauss's gift exchange is fractured. This is Mauss's comment upon modern society: that it represents something different to archaic society. Individual pursuit becomes the guiding principle of modern economic life, and it is this that Mauss wistfully contrasts with a primitive past in which interest and disinterest are combined (Parry 1986: 458). Parry argues, therefore, that while Mauss is often read as revealing why the gift can never be free, he is in fact revealing how a theory that this should be the case has developed. Interested exchange and disinterested gift appear as two sides of the same coin: 'Given a profound dislike of the first, mistrust of the second is only logical' (Parry 1986: 458).[4]

While it has been argued that this may be taken to mean that Mauss's use of the term 'gift' does not imply altruism (see Kelty 2002: 34), I suggest that the ideological significance of self-interest is no less present in our theorizing of the gift than is the notion of the 'pure gift' as ideology. For Mauss, the implication of the possibility of both self-interest and altruism as mutually constitutive is the reason why the gift may be understood as 'total social fact'. Laidlaw argues that in fact the idea of the 'free' gift is central to Mauss's argument. He writes that,

> Mauss can only really make the argument because the idea of what a real free gift would be is left unexamined. The reader's understanding of it is tacitly invoked. Because the invocation is implicit, and because the idea of the gift is, as Derrida has shown us, anyway unstable and paradoxical, it can be made to work in two quite contrary ways at once. (2000: 627)

Laidlaw makes the astute point that what gives the gift its capacity to create the moral basis of society in Mauss's theory is the everyday understanding of what a pure gift would be. In Laidlaw's words, 'Gifts evoke obligations and create reciprocity, but they can do this because they might not: what creates the obligation is the gesture or moment which alienates the given thing and asks for no reciprocation' (2000: 628).

Laidlaw argues that alms giving to Shvetambar Jain renouncers is an institutionalized elaboration of the idea of the free gift (*dān*). Jain alms giving may – in terms set out by Derrida (1992) – be understood as a free gift because renouncers are forbidden to express gratitude or reciprocate for food given in any way; the gift is not recognized because the small gifts of many are merged and thereby depersonalized; the beneficiary of the gift is

---

[4] See Copeman (2005) for an interesting discussion of the entanglement of altruism and commodity logic in blood donation practices.

not recognized as such (though the donor is understood to have given); and finally, in language and in action the idea that something is given is undermined. That the donor is recognized as having given something is important in both the Jain and the Buddhist context because in each it is believed that giving alms is beneficial. It would appear that in Derrida's four-part definition it is only in this area that the gift fails to be free:

> The recipient is spared the obligations that arise from receiving, but the givers have still given. Making a *dan* is meritorious, an act of *punya* or good karma. As such, it is expected, by an entirely impersonal process over which no one has any influence, to bring its own reward, although one cannot know when or in what manner the resulting good fortune will come. (Laidlaw 2000: 624)

In Jainism, as in Theravāda Buddhism, what is given should be an expression of a positive sentiment and should create no social relation between donor and recipient. Thai monks and *mae chee*, when not performing *dāna*, do have personal relationships with each other, with history, feeling and emotion. It would not be possible for people to live in such a community and not interface in terms of social interaction at some point. It is interesting, therefore, that when there is a disagreement between a monk and a *mae chee* it is often settled by one party suggesting that they engage in the alms donation. Either the *mae chee* will request to donate alms to the monk or the monk will suggest that he receive alms from the *mae chee*. Though suggesting that they engage in alms donation and receipt reaffirms that two individuals are involved, the act of the alms donation returns the relationship to one of generalized exchange rather than the relatively lower level of social interaction that made a dispute possible. The act is understood as a resolution of the disagreement. The practice of alms donation de-emphasizes the personal relationship and creates a new reality wherein they may face each other as if they were detached givers and receivers not caught in relationships characterized by reciprocity.

Thai Buddhist alms donations are meritoriously accumulative and often earning religious merit is the motivation for giving, but this is understood as leading to spiritual attainment and insight. The merit attained through selfless giving is both generated by and leads to understandings of the Buddhist tenets of impermanence, suffering and non-self (*anicca, dukkha, anattā*). *Dāna* as an aspect of mindful practice is used to cultivate the qualities of generosity, mindfulness and joy. In Buddhist philosophy *dāna* is understood as one of each of the following: the ten Perfections or *pāramī* (Thai: *baramī*), the three kinds of meritorious deeds, the ten qualities of a virtuous king and the four forms of hospitality. In *dhamma* talks in Wat Bonamron it was repeatedly described as one of the first steps for the cultivation of a virtuous state of mind. The quality of generosity was understood to begin with acts, such as donating alms, time or services. Such acts are understood to be an aid for the cultivation of the 'power of generosity' (*dānapāramī*) and an aspect of the process by which one cuts attachment to a sense of self. As well as an important human value that is meritoriously accumulative and promotes social harmony, *dāna* is a quality of generosity that, through repeated and intended acts, comes to imbue all activity as the power of generosity deepens. Such a quality of mind is understood as a support for the meditation and the cultivation of mindfulness. To give generously is understood as the ability to cut attachment to such negative emotions as fear, greed and hate and to cultivate the heart/mind (*jai*). The more attached to something one is, the more merit there is in renouncing it. It is not that each giver must take a speculative risk, but rather that understanding of the nature of the world is reached as a result of selfless giving, which simultaneously leads to the creation of religious merit. The sangha facilitate the merit making of laity and *mae chee* but this cannot be understood in terms of commodity logic. If the 'free' gift of alms donation becomes the price of salvation, culminating in the calculation of merit accrued by acts of donation (see Spiro 1970), this is the case because the correlation of the ideology of merit with donation is consistent with the soteriological ideology of purely disinterested action.

Parry (1986: 468) argues that in ethicized salvation religions, such as Theravāda Buddhism, the gift is completely alienated from the giver and the ideal goals of social action are orientated towards a future existence. For this reason gifts made to Buddhist monks are never reciprocated: they become a denial of the profane self and a means to salvation. 'The more radical the opposition between this world and a world free from suffering to come, the more inevitable is the development of a *contemptus mundi* which culminates in the institution of renunciation, but of which the charitable gift – as a kind of lay exercise in asceticism – is also often an expression' (Parry 1986: 468). In the Thai context we see that not only is the gift necessarily alienable and non-reciprocated but also that the ideology of the free gift as embedded in the alms donation may be understood as the same process of ascetic renunciation which is seen in the meritorious performance of monastic identity by monks and *mae chee*. It is precisely because alms gifts *do not* create obligations that they are socially important and, as I shall argue below, it is through the embodiment of detachment and cultivation of non-self through giving and receiving alms that the social position of *mae chee* is changing. Were the giving and receiving of alms to entail the social binding and personal reciprocity that once made the gift the logical opposite of commodity exchange (see Gregory 1982) then this could not be the case.

The alms gift is ideally given without desire for merit on the part of the donor. *Dānapāramī*, or 'the power of giving', is cited as one of the virtues of enlightenment that is to be cultivated through focusing upon one's state of mind during alms donations. The prescribed behaviour of donors and receivers of alms de-emphasizes social reciprocity and the reason for this lies in Buddhist soteriology: it is impossible to transcend the cycle of rebirth through the act of giving or receiving alms if the very act itself ensnares one further into the morass of social debts and attachments. Thus, giving alms is instrumental as both a means of escape from the wheel of rebirth through cultivating detachment to a sense of self and acting without desire, as well as a method for securing a better rebirth through acquiring merit; in both instances the gift must be free.

MAE CHEE RECEIVING ALMS AND MEDIATING GENERALIZED EXCHANGE

Though *mae chee* may not do the alms round they, like monks, receive alms in the form of money, food, clothes and toiletries from laity who come to the monastery to donate. This is often done as a part of rituals such as wakes or funerals. Individual donations from laity to *mae chee* occur on a daily basis, as do donations to monks. Often, such donations are the result of lay faith in a particular monastic's meritorious discipline. As we saw in the last chapter, laity are concerned to offer alms to those monastics who offer the most fertile 'field of merit'. Alms donations are understood to be meritorious in proportion to the spiritual qualities of the recipient. While this has traditionally been understood to be monks because they hold the highest number of religious precepts and are officially recognized as members of the sangha, *mae chee* are increasingly sought out as appropriate recipients of alms donations. In the meditation monastery the meritorious worth of individual monastics is measured by the extent to which they are understood to have gained insight through meditative discipline and the extent to which this is revealed through their embodiment of mindfulness.

In 2003 I interviewed Jau Mae, a highly respected *mae chee* in the *wat*. Originally from Laos, Jau Mae came to Thailand fifty-seven years previously and was 91 years old at the time of interview. She passed away in

2004. I asked her to tell me about her reasons for ordination and her life as a *mae chee* and she was keen to tell me about the massive amounts of alms donations she had been able to raise through the support of lay donors:

I became a *mae chee* because I want to be released from suffering. I have seen the suffering of birth and illness and life and death. I don't want to have that suffering again. So I do practice through meditation and do goodness: never stop working for the temple. I made the road that leads to the *wat* from the main road, and the bridge too. Before it was only wood. I bought the land the school is on, the land where the centre is built, the small temple in front of the school, the prayer room, my *kuṭi* and the air conditioning in the office. Everyone gives money to me and then I give it to the monastery. Every year I am given donations of about 1 million baht [£19,000]. And if I have something then you too will have it. All money from the people who respect me I give to the temple. In the kitchen I gave 3,000 baht. I am the main sponsor for the monastery. Also I make candles to sell to raise money for the monastery. If I weren't a *mae chee* I would not be able to do this. I also gave 400,000 baht for repairs in the school. I do this to offer it to the religion then I feel very good. I have this chance to support the religion, and when we do this the right way it helps our mind to be clear and happy. I am happy.

Meditation is very important because the Lord Buddha taught that there were two ways to get merit. One is to give to the religion and the other is to practice. When we worship to the Lord Buddha each time we must ask ourselves two things, we have given to the religion or not, money or alms, if you can't do that you can do meditation as worship with the mind. I do both. It is good to do merit because it releases you from suffering. I cannot answer about enlightenment because only you can know that. You have success enough you know yourself, you cannot explain to another one. You cannot explain the taste of food to another.

Mae chee are also frequently donated to in large public ceremonies. The donations on such occasions commonly take the form of an envelope of money, toiletries and material for making new robes. Such donations echo the structure of donations made to monks on such occasions and are built into the organization of the ritual itself.

Interestingly, when monetary alms are donated to an individual monk or *mae chee* the money is always concealed in an envelope. I have found this to be the case throughout Thailand. Money in this instance is not denied or negated but the amount itself is concealed. The emphasis is placed on the act of giving, facilitated by the renouncer's willingness to receive, because the amount donated is given no significance. By concealing the amount in an envelope the renouncer receives all monetary donations in the same way, and performs the same blessing. Putting money in envelopes distinguishes it from more mundane transactions and adds a temporal dimension

Figure 8: *Mae chee* offering alms to monks on the morning alms round

to generalized reciprocity. Much of the activity in Wat Bonamron and the interaction with the laity takes the form of teaching *dhamma* and meditation, after which money is often given in envelopes. Money given in this way to 'a monastic' (rather than 'a particular monastic') and the blessing received afterwards maintain an opposition between the world and its renunciation. In contrast, when giving to the monastery, rather than individual monastics, there is no risk of the donation being misinterpreted as a personal exchange because the recipient is in no way individuated and it is therefore not necessary to mask the amount. As such, the amount may be celebrated because it demonstrates the meritorious worth of an individual's action.

This contrast between masked donations to individual monks and *mae chee* and the public recognition of donations to the monastery was highlighted during the celebrations for the Abbot's birthday in 2002. The Abbot stressed that this year his birthday gifts should take the form of offerings towards the building of a meditation centre, thereby making it possible for more people to practise meditation. The day before his birthday a stage covered in colourful material went up at the back of the large meeting hall (*sala*) and on it were presented ten beautiful money trees (*pha pa*; see Figure 9). These are trunks with decorated sticks coming out of them. On each stick is a bank note, with larger ones at the top and smaller amounts at the bottom. They stand about 6 feet (1.8 metres) tall and will usually have at least 10,000 bt (approx. £190) on each tree; some may be as large as 100,000 bt. Displays of monetary donations are commented on in terms of aesthetic display and meritorious worth and donations are celebrated by all. (I have never seen a tree with less than 10,000 bt on it and I was told that this was because a tree with less money would not look good.) Each tree is conspicuously labelled with the name of the individual or group who donated it. On this occasion a large ceremony was conducted to bless the trees, after which many people wanted to have their photograph taken with the largest.

After all the ceremonies were completed, during which people had donated yet more money, I helped to count the money from the trees with a group of *mae chee*. A senior monk watched us as we did this and with a wry smile told me a parable of the Buddha:

Buddha and his disciples were going along and as they passed someone digging in the field Buddha prophesied that a poisonous snake would bite him. Now, the digger unearthed a treasure and as he did so some robbers who were passing by set upon him, killed him and took the treasure. Buddha observed that money would kill you as surely as a bite from a poisonous snake.

Given the quantity of hard currency on the floor in front of us this highlighted the paradoxical association between massive meritorious alms donations and the teachings of Buddhism. The grand total was 633,265 bt (approx. £12,000), which is a sizeable snake! However, the monk was in no way suggesting that the money was inappropriately given or that it ought to be given back.

The monetary donations that form the basis of the monastic economy are put in the monastery's collective bank account and the donor is given a certificate in recognition of his or her good work. The monastery's accounts are organized through the main office, run by *mae chee* in conjunction with monks. Money paid into or taken out of the bank is overseen by monks, while *mae chee* organize its collection and distribution. A lay accountant also checks the accounts. *Mae chee* organize the amounts required for 'household' expenses, such as food cooked in the kitchens and so on. Much of the alms food eaten in the monastery is donated in the form of money; because the food is bought using alms money it is considered to be as morally pure as food donated directly. Wat Bonamron's monetary resources, though entering the monastery as *dāna*, must leave the monastery as commodity when paying bills or shopping at

Figure 9: A money tree (*pha pa*) before it is offered to the monastery

the market. Therefore there must be a point at which the generalized exchange of alms giving becomes the commodity exchange of consumption (see Appadurai 1986: 13). Alms money is donated individually, handled by *mae chee* and then kept and spent collectively through *mae chee* on behalf of the monastic community as a whole. Put simply, *mae chee* mediate much of the economic exchange between the monastery and lay society.

Arguably, *mae chee* are performing the role of laity in handling alms donations on behalf of the monastic community: a role that would be performed by lay devotees were there no *mae chee* in this monastery. My argument, however, is that in the context of monks and *mae chee* working to cultivate a perspectival capaxcity for the experience of religious truths, such duties are expressly understood as the responsibility of monastics. We have seen that all work in the monastery is more or less meritoriously accumulative. As we shall examine in the next chapter, *mae chee* understand their observance of hierarchy and their service to monks and the monastery as opportunities to cultivate selflessness and equanimity. It is in such a spirit that they understand the handling of the potentially problematic donations of money on behalf of the community.

The ambiguity of the position of *mae chee* means that their performance of monastic identity, understood as an act of giving, is central to their relationship with laity. Their involvement in the ritual process is dependent upon *mae chee*'s embodiment of the principles of mindful awareness. This is not commensurable with the involvement of monks, who hold formal ordination status and central roles in ritual. However, it is precisely this ambiguity that enables *mae chee* to handle monetary alms donations, something that is spiritually problematic for monks because they have monastic precepts expressly forbidding it.

It is important to emphasize that control of money does not necessarily provide an index of authority. Thai women (as women elsewhere in Southeast Asia) play an active role in economic and business responsibilities (cf. Busby 2000; Carsten 1989; Stirrat 1989). Kirsch (1985: 303) suggests that in both rural and urban settings it has been shown that women tend to 'have charge of the family purse strings and petty marketing, while men dominate whatever positions of authority or prestige exist'. Furthermore, it has been argued (Thitsa 1980: 5) that the sexual division of labour in Thailand lies between women engaged in economic activities and men engaged in bureaucratic activities, with ecclesiastical roles being ascribed a far higher status than money making activities, which are believed to be connected to the material, corporeal side of life. This theory is supported by the fact that monks have precepts forbidding them to handle money, which *mae chee* do not. However, as we have seen, all work in the monastery is understood as meritorious to a greater or lesser extent; there is no way in which working with money is particularly sterile (cf. Taussig 1980; Bloch and Parry 1989) for those who do not hold precepts expressly forbidding them to have contact with it.

Weiner's seminal work locates women's exchange practices as a component of larger exchange cycles (Weiner 1976; cf. Weiner 1988). She argues that exchange must be understood as expressing and producing hierarchy. Examining the gendered and political ramifications of exchange she demonstrates, contra Malinowski (1922), that not only are Trobriand women involved in exchange, but also that women's exchange in mortuary rituals (*sagali*) occupies a central role in the 'total system' of Trobriand social organization through which subclans (*dala*) reproduce themselves. Furthermore, she argues that men's autonomy is held in check, undermined or supported by women's economic presence and that power is constituted through rights and access to 'cosmological authentication'.[5] While it is a concern of this chapter to consider the ways in which practices of giving lead to heterogeneity and difference, a distinction between separate but articulating female and male domains (see Weiner 1976: 18) is unhelpful for understanding the continuities in *mae chee* and monks' involvement in gifting – continuities that, in the monastic context, are central to monastic and lay understanding of religious practice. All action and interaction in the Thai monastic context are more or less meritoriously accumulative: for the monastic this includes doing one's monastic duty, whether that be working in the monastery or providing a living exemplar of Buddhist ethics for the laity. Nevertheless, handling money presents spiritual pitfalls for monks. As such, by selflessly doing work that is spiritually problematic (by handling potentially dangerous gifts) yet remaining uncorrupted, *mae chee* are doing good and indeed meritorious work.

Mae chee are making merit by facilitating the merit making of others. This, coupled with alms donations and receiving alms from laity, suggests that the involvement of *mae chee* in this system of generalized exchange is highly qualified. The generalized reciprocity of alms giving, in which the recipient is occluded, is maintained when alms money is given to *mae chee* on behalf of the monastery. That it is possible for *mae chee* to perform this role suggests that they are viewed as monastics by the laity even though they are not officially recognized as part of the sangha. From the point of view of the laity, to see *mae chee* as separate from the monastic community would devalue the *dāna* that they give. Nevertheless, for *mae chee* to be able to handle alms money at all makes an implicit statement about their ordination status. Because of the proscription on contact with money for

---

[5] Weiner identifies the central concern of exchange as one of 'keeping-while-giving', arguing that what motivates exchange is 'the desire to keep something back from the pressures of give and take' (1992: 43). Central to this ongoing political struggle is the inalienable gift, understood as a set of social processes in which one's capacity to exchange and withhold is a marker of social strength and identity (Weiner 1992). Strathern has argued contra Weiner that the inalienability of things does not presuppose the inalienability of actors (1988: 283–4). Strathern argues that gifts reveal human value in the attributes of things: it is through gifts that persons and the social relations objectified in persons are continually remade (see Strathern 1984: 162–3). At issue for Strathern is an 'aesthetic', or 'the way in which people construe social action and make known the outcomes of their relations with one another' (1988: 341).

monks, *mae chee* suggest that their involvement facilitates the smooth running of the monastery. I do not want to suggest that the gifts given or received by *mae chee* are of a different order to those of monks. Because of the ambiguity inherent in their position, *mae chee*'s *behaviour* is central to their monastic identity more than is the case for monks. Nonetheless, the value of alms donations as free gifts is reflected in the performance of monastic identity by all monastics – a performance that is thought to begin and/or end with the realization of non-self. As such the gift may be understood as a vehicle for the ongoing process of renunciation.

CONCLUSION: THE GIFT OF RENUNCIATION

In Thailand alms donations (*dāna*) are understood as 'free gifts': they are non-reciprocal, renouncers are forbidden to express gratitude, and neither the gift nor the beneficiary is recognized as such (though the donor is understood to have given). In this context, to give is to gain: the flow of material resources is accorded little significance. Alms donations to monastics are understood as instances of generalized exchange.

As a field of merit monks are accorded ritual deference by *mae chee* and lay people. Tambiah suggests that this is because 'The Buddhist idiom of selfless giving of gifts, control of passion through asceticism, and renunciation of worldly interests is an idealization and extension of a contrast to the social norm of reciprocity' (1968a: 119). This is a situation in which people give to monks as a 'field of merit' rather than engaging in personalized relationships of reciprocal gift or commodity exchange. Strenski suggests that in the context of Buddhism, ritual giving (*dāna*) defines the relationship between the sangha and lay society: 'the monks are always receivers, the laity always givers' (1983: 470). Yet, *mae chee* give alms to monks *and* receive alms as monastics and on behalf of the monastic community. As such *mae chee* facilitate the smooth running of the monastery, and mediate relationships with the outside world.

When donating alms themselves *mae chee* are more closely associated with the laity than the sangha because, like the laity, they donate alms *to* the sangha. In contrast, in order to assume the mediating role of receiving alms *from* the laity individually and on behalf of the monastic community as a whole, *mae chee* are necessarily associated *with* the sangha. Handling alms money in Wat Bonamron is an area in which clear gender differences are maintained, but the meaning of these differences is only to be understood in the context of local ideas and representations. By donating alms to monks *mae chee* appear to be reaffirming their status of partial ordination yet in order for them to be able to receive alms from the laity they must see themselves, and be recognized by the laity, as an integral part of the monastic community. As such by facilitating the smooth running of the monastery through mediating the generalized exchange of alms donations *mae chee* earn merit and the monastery is understood as a community.

How are we to make sense of the different roles *mae chee* play in alms donations in relation to both the sangha and the laity? I argue that in this context social positions within the monastic hierarchy are negotiated and maintained through the giving and receiving of alms but that this is made possible because such exchanges are understood as non-reciprocal; the evidence for non-reciprocity is sought by the laity in monastics' demonstrable ability to remain removed from reciprocal social obligations. Selfless giving on the part of both laity (through the donation of alms) and monastics (through the embodiment of the soteriological message of Buddhist detachment) is both meritoriously accumulative and the result of personal merit. Through religiously meaningful practices *mae chee* are understanding themselves and being understood by others as monastic and this is consistent with the soteriological telos of an ideal Buddhist life – release from suffering and cutting attachment to a sense of self. In a community typified by sartorial neatness and physical control, striving for an ideal of non-self, the ultimate act of giving is of oneself and it is *through* the gift of the embodiment of renunciation that renunciation *becomes* embodied.

CHAPTER 8

Hierarchy, gender and mindfulness

As we have seen in the preceding chapters, *mae chee* are playing qualified roles in emblematic monastic practices and are an integral part of the community in Wat Bonamron. In this chapter I wish to examine the gendered hierarchy of the monastic community in more detail, taking into account prevalent understandings of gender and modernity in Thailand. If monastics are aiming to experience a sense of self as delusional, what implications does this have for the ways in which they relate to each other within a gendered hierarchy?

The ambivalence found in the roles and changing status of *mae chee* in a meditation monastery presents some interesting dilemmas for the anthropologist. On the one hand, *mae chee* are being recognized as religious professionals in previously male-defined spheres. They are being accorded considerable respect and prestige. On the other hand, the media through which such change is being enacted (through *mae chee* embodying moral norms such as humility, equanimity and servitude) engage precisely those idioms that have historically marked and ensured their subordination to male authority. Thus, the performance of the virtues of grace and modesty that are concomitant with being mindful may be understood as an enhancement of the virtues that mark their subordination.

In this chapter I will consider representations of *mae chee* in the literature and compare this with *mae chee*'s own accounts of their lives. As we shall see, *mae chee* have largely been portrayed negatively as disadvantaged and subordinate to monks. While I do not question that *mae chee* are hierarchically inferior to monks and that many *mae chee* lead challenging and economically disadvantaged lives, such accounts are in stark contrast to the ways in which the *mae chee* with whom I work understand their monastic duties and the institutional organization of Buddhist monasticism. That there is such a stark disjuncture between the account that *mae chee* give for their own choices and actions and how *mae chee* are understood in the literature encourages me to reflect upon alternative ways in which we might understand the lives of religious women in Buddhism without the primary significance of such religious practice necessarily being its ability to resist structures of male authority.

Mae chee argue that the service they provide in Wat Bonamron is a site in which they are able to develop experiential understanding of non-self and that with such insight the gendered hierarchy of the monastery becomes irrelevant because, as one sees through the delusional sense of self, one also sees that gender is a condition created by delusional attachment. As such, it is in the process of making oneself an ethical person through the embodied and virtuous practices of monastic tradition that one ideally comes to transcend gendered attachment. Importantly, if the ideal of non-self presents a religious telos by which monastics may measure their religious development, it is not necessarily a reality for all people at all times.

THE BROADER PICTURE OF *MAE CHEE* IN THAILAND

As we have seen, *mae chee* have ambiguous status because they have renounced lay life and yet are not able to take full ordination or be recognized within the sangha. There are large variances in the practice, behaviour and procedure of *mae chee* across Thailand. While there is still disparity in their lives and living conditions and a great deal of ambivalence in the status of *mae chee*, education and Buddhist practice have been important in *mae chee* gaining legitimacy as religious professionals in recent years. Over the last twenty years the status of *mae chee* has been improved through their devotion to Buddhist practice and access to religious education.

When *mae chee* appear in accounts of the Thai religious landscape it is often in negative terms. Tambiah reports that in the 1970s *mae chee* were considered as a 'peripheral' category of the monastic community:

in that they are normally allocated their living quarters away from the monks' residences in space that is technically associated with the laity (*kharawat*) and not the religious and that is also where the monastic kitchen is situated – and yet are, wherever they are found, some of the most assiduous practitioners of meditation. (1984)

In Bunnag's 1973 study of Thai Buddhist monasteries she also found that *mae chee* 'though subject to the authority of the abbot as the head of the community are, except in a few cases, outside the system properly speaking, and have little contact with the monks and novices in a *wat*' (1973: 99). It appears significant that in Bunnag's study the one monastery with a large number of *mae chee* (thirty-five) integrated into the community, Wat Yai Chai Mongkhon, was orientated towards meditation and the abbot was a renowned meditation teacher (Bunnag 1973: 87). The extent to which *mae chee* are integrated within a monastic community is dependent on the guidance of the abbot. Many monasteries have very few or no *mae chee* living in them.

Mae chee are not obliged to belong to a religious organization such as the sangha and there are variations in their practices and procedures. The Institute of Thai *Mae Chee*, founded in 1969 under the instruction of the Supreme Patriarch and patronage of the Queen of Thailand, was intended to establish a religious network and form of representation for those *mae chee* who joined. Barnes gives the goals of the Institute as 'uniting and organizing all *mae ji*, improving their status, providing religious instruction, and contributing to their social well-being' (1996: 268). However, the number of *mae chee* registered with the Institute remains limited and none of the *mae chee* in the monastery is a member despite many having been solicited personally.[1]

In a recent overview of the nuns' order in Buddhist Asia, Barnes (1996) describes '*mae ji*' as scattered throughout Thailand, with no cohesive organizational structure, whose activities and practices consequently vary widely. She paints a picture of poor *mae chee* barely subsisting through cooking and cleaning in exchange for minimal maintenance from monasteries. She suggests that many *mae chee* are elderly and lack familial support, that they are considered a 'nuisance' by many monks, and that the most fortunate live in nunneries. Quoting Chatsumarn Kabilsingh (1991: 36–9) she argues that 60 per cent of *mae chee* are from rural backgrounds and have received less than seven years education. While I would not dispute this, I would question the way in which educational attainment is used in this instance to portray *mae chee* negatively on terms which are not necessarily their own. As we saw in Chapter 5, monastic engagement with education is variously motivated. Barnes goes on to say that 'The *mae ji* are not yet in a position to serve society religiously or socially. Because of their social backgrounds and lack of education, few *mae ji* have even thought of trying to improve their situation' (1996: 268). Barnes presents *mae chee* as a social group in need of assistance, and attributes the founding of the Institute of Thai *Mae Chee* to the benefaction and concern of the Thai government and

---

[1] The reason given by many *mae chee* I spoke to was that the Institute's emphasis upon correct procedure, learning by rote and education was felt to contrast with the *mae chee*'s own emphasis upon meditation and insight.

senior monks. She conflates the duties of *mae chee* with social engagement and advancement. In short, *mae chee* 'live lives of hardship and poverty'; they are a group with 'serious problems' (Barnes 1996: 268). She suggests that the role of *mae chee* is, not surprisingly, unappealing to better-educated urban women.

For Penny Van Esterik (2000: 17), the lack of status accorded to *mae chee* is the result of assumptions about their lack of specialized knowledge and their demeanour. *Mae chee* have been known to beg on the streets of Bangkok (as have monks), they are often peripheral to the monastic compound and spend much time cooking and cleaning. She argues that many *mae chee* live in semi-starvation because few people offer food to them and that, apart from in a select few nunneries, few *mae chee* had time to study or meditate until very recently. Though the status of *mae chee* has changed significantly in recent years it must be noted that the position of *mae chee* throughout Thailand varies massively and there are still *mae chee* who struggle to meet their basic needs. However, *mae chee* are increasingly gaining access to *dhamma* study, Pali studies, *Abhidhamma* (and other) examinations, secular education and training in meditation equivalent to that of monks. The *mae chee* in Wat Bonamron have ritual duties (chanting *Abhidhamma* at wakes, receiving alms, meditation, teaching, *dhamma* talks), they have access to education (secular and religious) and they have ample chance to practise meditation and are encouraged to see this as an ongoing process in all daily activity (see also Cook 2009).

By comparison, Lindberg Falk stresses that, though *mae chee* have often been portrayed as broken-hearted, poor or widowed, their status is influenced by age, social background, educational level, aspirations and motives (Lindberg Falk 2002: 10). She cites examples of exceptional *mae chee* who have attained public recognition for their activities. Such *mae chee* are usually well educated and media savvy, appearing on television and radio programmes as well as in newspapers and magazines.[2] This has, to some

---

[2] One shining example of this is the internationally renowned Mae Chee Sansanee. Mae Chee Sansanee holds a Bachelor's degree and was formerly a PR executive; she became a *mae chee* at 27. She is the founder and Director of Sathira-Dhammasathan Centre, in Bangkok, from where she coordinates *dhamma* projects. She has been prolific in her spread of *dhamma* teaching through different media: for example, Sathira-Dhammasathan runs a monthly magazine, *Savika*, a live radio programme, which runs for an hour every Saturday and Sunday broadcasting her teaching; a two-minute television programme featuring her teaching every morning from Monday to Friday; a website, www.sansanee.org; and a film, *A Walk of Wisdom*, has recently been made about her life and work and featured in the Santa Barbara International Film Festival in February 2005. While the *mae chee* in Wat Bonamron are heavily involved in the propagation of *vipassanā* to the laity, other *mae chee* in Thailand are performing work focused upon social welfare and in some cases, as in the case of Mae Chee Sansanee, combining this with teaching meditation.

extent, acted as a corrective to the stereotype of *mae chee* as disadvantaged women. She also argues that where *mae chee* live will influence their status because of the huge variance in forms of practice, Buddhist teachings and temple rules. Her ethnography draws the conclusion that nunneries provide an 'appropriate platform for *mae chiis* who strive to fulfill their potential as Buddhist nuns' while monasteries do not, because in monasteries '*mae chiis*' activities are more centred upon the domestic realm even though they have left the worldly life' (Lindberg Falk 2002: 24). A great strength of Lindberg Falk's work is in her presentation of *mae chee* as a heterogeneous category, which has recently begun to gain religious legitimacy. There is clear variance in the situation, practice and duties of *mae chee* throughout Thailand.

Lindberg Falk's work focuses upon the development of self-governed nunneries in Thailand. For her, this development connotes a modification of male religious domains (Lindberg Falk 2002: 3). She suggests that in monasteries *mae chee* have a marginal status because they do not hold formal roles (2002: 8). Thus, it is a central plank of Lindberg Falk's thesis that the status of *mae chee* is improved by residing at a self-governed nunnery. While I do not question this, in my opinion it would do a disservice to her exceptional ethnography to posit an unproblematic correlation between residence patterns and the status of *mae chee*, especially given the variance in temples, teaching and practice that Lindberg Falk herself recognizes. Lindberg Falk concludes that *mae chee* 'assume an identity as ordained persons based on their celibate and disciplined monastic lifestyle recognized and attributed by lay people' (Lindberg Falk 2002: 95). Thus, it is through religious performance and agency that *mae chee* are challenging ideas of women as being associated with the lay realm.

Recent scholarship has contributed to a consideration of ambivalence in the roles and statuses of *mae chee*. In their account of *mae chee* teaching higher levels of Pali language and *Abhidhamma* in monastic education institutions in Bangkok, Collins and McDaniel (2010) are able to go beyond a binary distinction between 'lay' and 'ordained' and celebrate the lives of *mae chee* in Thailand who are highly respected and who, importantly, understand the life of a *mae chee* to be one of 'beauty': 'with meticulous and inspiring pedagogy, sophisticated learning and meditative expertise as goals and values *per se*, with intrinsic virtue as well as instrumental value in reducing suffering and leading to nirvana'. Such an approach does not undervalue the implications of the hardships of *mae chee*'s lives, discrimination in the Thai ecclesia, or the issue of full ordination; rather, it reveals that despite inequality and discrimination there are many opportunities for *mae chee* to study and teach the subjects considered to be the most difficult and prestigious for Buddhist monastics, and, furthermore, that the *mae chee* who Collins and McDaniel interviewed themselves understand their lives to be 'beautiful'.

Seeger (2009), similarly, reports on a sample of outstanding Buddhist women in the context of the rapidly changing socio-religious context of contemporary Thai Buddhism. He notes the shifts in status of *mae chee* as a result of changes in residence patterns, the increase in numbers of self-governed nunneries, increasing approximation of monks, roles in receiving alms and ordination procedures, and access to education, while also recognizing that most *mae chee* remain structurally disadvantaged and commonly hold low status when compared to monks. His work examines the high level of personal charisma that particular *mae chee* have built up and he uses this to underscore the plurality of statuses and practices to be found: 'Albeit still in a marginal position, women seem to be gaining more and more space in Thai Buddhism' (Seeger 2009: 810). He suggests that in conjunction with the debates surrounding the *bhikkhunī* ordination lineage (see below), and the approximation of roles between monks and *mae chee*, the accounts of widely acknowledged Thai women who excel as *dhamma* teachers, are esteemed for their social engagement, or who are revered as Buddhist 'saints' all indicate a demarginalization and redefinition of women's religious roles.

SPATIAL SEPARATION AND DOMESTICITY

As we have seen in Wat Bonamron, a monastic community comprising monks and *mae chee*, *mae chee* are adopting religious roles through the complex negotiation of monastery life while also being involved in the kinds of 'domestic' activities that in Lindberg Falk's analysis are understood as antithetical to renunciatory identity and the enhancement of religious status. Lindberg Falk argues that the role of *mae chee* in nunneries has become more analogous to that of monks, while the roles of *mae chee* in temples are more focused upon the 'domestic realm' (Lindberg Falk 2002: 24). This presents an interesting perspective from which to consider the lives of *mae chee* in Wat Bonamron. In the monastery *mae chee* have significant religious duties. As well as learning and teaching *dhamma*, practising and teaching meditation, receiving alms from laity, chanting *Abhidhamma* at wakes, *mae chee* in the monastery receive Pali names at ordination and are thus 'reborn' into the 'family of the Buddha' at ordination,[3] are requested to administer on

---

[3] This is in contrast to the women with whom Lindberg Falk works who retain their lay names after ordination (Lindberg Falk: personal communication, 25 September 2006).

religiously significant occasions by laity and are sought out by laity for counsel. However, they also have a considerable number of duties that would be considered 'domestic': they prepare all the food for the community, they clean the monastery, they serve monks, they occupy many of the administrative positions within the monastery, and, as we have seen, they play a qualified role in emblematic ritual practices such as the alms round and ritual duties. Thus, whereas the women with whom Lindberg Falk worked understood the alms round as central to their identities as monastics, the women with whom I work are debarred from going for alms though they do receive alms on other occasions. Of interest here is not the degree to which 'domestic' duties reaffirm *mae chee* subordination to monks but that such duties and behaviour are understood as religiously significant by *mae chee*.

Mae chee do not see the service they provide in the monastery as relegating them to a non-religious sphere. Rather, they understand their work in the monastery to be religiously significant. As we saw in Chapter 3, there is a clearly gendered division of labour within the monastery. The gendered hierarchy is also clearly reflected in the spatial layout of the monastery, the deference shown to monks by *mae chee* and the prohibitions on physical contact between monks and *mae chee*. *Mae chee* and monks maintain that such a spatial layout is necessary for them to observe formal proscriptions on physical contact. Gendered spatial separation in the monastery extends to a proscription on physical contact of any kind, including passing each other objects. One must put down the object before the other can pick it up. The spatial separation of monks and *mae chee* may be understood as a symbolic articulation of this proscription. As Mae Chee Sicam told me, '*Mae chee* live on one side of the monastery and monks live on the other side. We connect when we work. For living we are separate.'

Being aware of hierarchical self-placement and showing deference to others through physical comportment is a concern of all members of the community. To show deference to someone, one's head should be lower than theirs. The head is the highest part of the body, and it is a great insult to intentionally touch someone's head. It is rude to step over people, one must always go around them; particularly while they are eating one must shuffle with bent knees as low to the ground as is practically possible in order to get past, bowing as one goes. At all ritual and religious meetings monks sit on a small raised platform that runs down one wall of the main temple and the *sala*. All other men and novices sit on the floor with their heads at the same height as women and *mae chee*. This spatial organization demonstrates a distinction between monks and all other members of the congregation. In this respect *mae chee* are on the same level as the laity. At such meetings *mae*

Figure 10: Mae Chee Pon preparing floral offerings for senior monks

chee sit in a tight group in front of the Buddha statues, proximity to the Buddha connoting relative length of ordination. After chanting for approximately an hour on Holy Day (*Wan Phra*) the whole congregation goes out to the *stūpa*, which they circumambulate three times. Monks lead the procession followed by *mae chee* and laity after which the congregation places offerings of flowers, candles and incense on the *stūpa* before returning to the *vihāra* for a meditation session.

Mae chee are located as hierarchically inferior to monks in spatial organization, embodied performance and ritual responsibility. Such hierarchical placement is reflected in daily activity: for example, a *mae chee* must stop walking and wait for a monk to walk past, while he does so she must *wai* (a form of greeting and respect) and have her head lowered; *mae chee* serve monks; *mae chee* wait for monks to begin eating before they eat; *mae chee* sit below and walk behind monks. In short, *mae chee* strive to show deference to monks in all their activity, often trying to anticipate the needs of monks, serving them with deference and humility.

Why is it, then, that religiously defined women would choose to serve others in such a way? And, more generally, why do they choose to participate in those practices that appear to reaffirm their subordination to men? It has been argued by Penny Van Esterik that such activity is understood by *mae chee* as a means of improving their karmic status: 'With no feminist re-evaluation of their spiritual worth, some nuns are eager to acquire merit to improve their chances of rebirth as men, and see this as an excellent opportunity to do so' (2000: 77). While this is true to some extent, we have also seen that not all religious practice is interpreted in terms of its efficacy in accumulating merit. In Wat Bonamron, ideas about status are understood as secondary to the concerns of cultivating the virtues of humility, equanimity and non-self encouraged in all monastic practice. We have seen that all work in the monastery is considered to be meritorious, and accruing merit is a concern of monastics and laity alike. Significantly though, such concerns are adumbrated by the meritoriously rewarding project of ascetic discipline. The humility exhibited by *mae chee* is understood as morally virtuous and personally significant. For example, Mae Chee Pon responded to my concerns about inequality in the monastery by suggesting that she actually felt quite sorry for monks: 'after ordination their status is so high that they have a really hard time to be humble. They don't have the experience of *mae chee* to help them'.

Mae chee sit in-between lay people and monks during rituals, separating the two and drawing a white line between them. In this half place they are both ordained and lay. One *mae chee* told me that 'We are second class citizens in the monastery . . . sometimes'. I was told that *mae chee* are half-lay, like lay women who want to follow the Buddha's lifestyle:

It is because the rules for monks were given by the Buddha, but the rules for us weren't. People give to the monastery to give to monks, but *mae chee* can take as well. You can see it in the way the two behave. *Mae chee* talk and socialize with lay more; monks eat and sit separately. The way to improve the situation of *mae chee* is to work and practice to improve yourself. (Mae Chee Suat)

In Wat Bonamron I was continually told that the way to improve the status of *mae chee* in general was to meditate and guard one's precepts very well. This is evidenced through the performance of physical control and mindful comportment. The same level of physical control is not emphasized for monks because they are controlled by the 227 precepts of the *vinaya*, while the lack of formal rules for *mae chee* means that their performance of monastic identity is crucial in their self-placement between the sangha and the laity. Those *mae chee* who adopt the principles of *vipassanā* meditation in communities of practice are able to understand their bodily practices and performance as congruent with Buddhist notions of merit, mindfulness and morality. Through correct ascetic practice *mae chee* are making claims to religious authority and status by actively incorporating 'true Buddhism' in their lives. *Mae chee* in the monastery feel that partial ordination as *mae chee* is sufficient for them to lead religiously defined monastic lives. Without challenging either the hierarchy or doctrine of Thai Buddhism the embodiment of the principles of meditation in monastic practice is changing people's understandings of individual and group identity and thereby inserting *mae chee* into a strong position in relation to the laity and the sangha.

RECONSIDERING GENDERED MONASTIC PRACTICE

The practices and ideals that *mae chee* engage with are often recognized by academics as those which reaffirm the subordination of women in relation to men. The actions of *mae chee* may be understood as reinforcing the ways in which they are subject to hierarchical domination. As such it is possible to point to any example of assertion (for example, *mae chee* learning and chanting *Abhidhamma*) as evidence of opposition to dominant male authority, to the extent that a nascent feminist consciousness is read into the motivation of such actions. Alternatively, it is possible to search for the success that women's actions have, unintended or otherwise, in subverting or challenging patriarchal domination. For example, *mae chee*'s embodiment of the soteriological principles of Buddhism is leading to recognition of them as an integral part of the monastic community. It is a small step from this to understanding such practice in terms of the challenge it holds for dominant patriarchal norms. It is the case that *mae chee* are hierarchically inferior to monks and that this may quite comfortably be interpreted in a progressive political model of domination and subjugation, so much so that scholars are able to argue for what *mae chee* 'need' in order to counter such inequality. The duty of service that *mae chee* perform for monks appears to reflect the social conservatism, subjugation of women and cultural backwardness bemoaned by scholars who focus on the domination of women by men. What is striking and problematic about such approaches is the

Hierarchy, gender and mindfulness

absolute rejection of such ideas by the *mae chee* with whom I work. As the Head Mae Chee told me over tea,

> These rules, all the rules of the monastery, the way I have to behave, the service that I give to monks, this is all hard for people to understand. To them it looks like I live in a cage. For me, I understand it as a frame. Just as a picture looks better if it is in a frame, I can see myself better because I am framed by the monastery.

Interpretations of the gendered hierarchy of Buddhist monasticism have often been informed by a notion of human agency as that which challenges social norms. While such scholarly approaches have performed the necessary and valued task of calling our attention to the roles *of mae chee* and the hierarchy present in Buddhist monasticism, they have not accounted for the significance of asceticism and monastic duty *for mae chee*. It is possible that there are other forms of value, morality and agency in a given context that are not easily understood in terms of resistance and subversion of hegemonic discourse and social institutional structure. The structure of monasticism is often interpreted as the patriarchal chains that oppress *mae chee*. Such assumptions prevent us exploring the ongoing experience of shaping the self through ascetic practice: forms of practice in which the subject relates to their internal and external state as a means for and a measure of the extent to which they are able to create the self. It is not the case, necessarily, that political and moral autonomy will be conjoined in such a project.

Performance and non-social movement

The relationship between outward behaviour and the subjectivity that such behaviour enacts is key in our understanding of the significance of monastic practice for monks and *mae chee*. In this context the control of the body is central to the learning process by which monastics develop experiential realizations of religious ideals. The monastic duty to comport oneself mindfully at all times is not understood to be primarily performative. By this I mean that a difference between bodily performance and the internal state of the performer is not understood as a hypocritical inconsistency. Monks and *mae chee* believe that by performing their duties, including the duty to behave as religious professionals for the laity, they will learn to experience internally the states that they perform externally. Through a sequence of practices and actions one learns how to be enlightened. Though the condition of mindfulness may not be constant, it is through the continual performance of mindfulness that monastics intend to 'fill the robes from the inside'. Bodily acts – such as walking slowly, serving others, eating silently – are not performances detachable from an interiorized self. Rather, it is through such acts that internal responses are brought into line with external behaviour. Thus, such performances are the means and measures of spiritual development. Crucial here is the conceptualization of the role that the body plays in such formation. The outward behaviour of the body is the means by which idealized interiority is achieved. Thus, 'non-self' is sought after by monastics through the media of the body and emotions. Though it is not necessarily the day-to-day experience of monastics, an awareness of dissonance between ideal and experience is understood as a failure to apperceive the true nature of reality. The work of asceticism is understood as being ongoing and it is believed that one can read the degree of success one has in maintaining the experience of non-self through the body.

One effect of the monastic involvement of *mae chee* in recent years has been an improvement in their status and increased involvement in monastic duty and structure, but the ways in which such involvement is understood by women themselves suggest that we need to examine this in terms other than those of domination and resistance. Monastics anticipate effecting change in the world through the promotion of *vipassanā* both as a lay practice and a monastic discipline. Through retraining the 'self' monastics anticipate the development of new social and moral orders, and indeed given the prevalence of lay meditation practice in Thailand and abroad there is a degree to which this is already the case. But such a social movement is not predicated upon the politics of identity, rights and representation. Rather, as increasing numbers of people practise meditation it is thought that change will be effected because of the numbers of people using meditation to cultivate virtues. The changing status of *mae chee* as a result of the cultivation of the virtues of humility and equanimity is secondary to the primary motivation of the women involved to make themselves into certain kinds of spiritual and religious persons. Such social recognition is thought of as a happy consequence of being a disciplined monastic, but it is not the primary motivation for their practice.

This is illustrated in the view that most *mae chee* in the monastery take on the current *bhikkhunī* movement in Thailand. While *mae chee* in Wat Bonamron understand the cultivation of mindfulness through monastic duty to be central to their identity as monastics, concomitant changes are occurring in the status of Thai Buddhist women that are resulting in the assertion of women into positions of religious authority. Recently, a movement to establish a *bhikkhunī* sangha (community of fully ordained nuns) in Theravādan countries has gained force in Thailand. It has been argued that the Mahayana tradition may be traced back to the Theravāda *bhikkhunī* order in Sri Lanka and as such it is legitimate for Mahayana *bhikkhunī* to help revive the Theravādan lineage. On this basis Sri Lanka revived female ordinations in 1998, and in 2001 one Thai woman, Chatsumarn Kabilsingh, received full ordination in Sri Lanka as a *sāmaṇerī* (female novice monk) and returned to Thailand as a fully ordained novice. There have been many disputes in Thailand as to the legitimacy of her ordination but on 10 February 2002 Mae Chee Varangghana Vanavichayen became the first Thai woman ever to receive full ordination in Thailand, taking the name Dhammarakhita *Sāmaṇerī*.

Gellner and LeVine (2005) provide a thorough account of the movement to establish full ordination for nuns. They report that a few highly educated, mostly Western women of the Tibetan and Theravāda traditions, launched this movement understanding it as a necessary development if Buddhism was to expand (2005: 264):

Women of the calibre needed to build a sound institutional base for Buddhism in the West would only be willing to join an order that was strongly committed to social and gender equality. Full ordination for women and the status this conferred in the eyes of lay contributors was, they believed, essential to that commitment.

The Bodh Gaya Conference on Buddhist Women in February 1987 focused upon the status of nuns vis-à-vis monks and the ways in which it might be improved. This conference was organized by three eminent Buddhist women: the German-born Jewish American *dasa sil mata*[4] Ayya Khema, the American Karma Lekshe Tsomo and Chatsumarn Kabilsingh. Following the conference, the International Association of Buddhist Women was established and given the name 'Sakyadhita' ('Daughters of the Buddha'). The aims of the Association were: 1) to create a network of communications among Buddhist women of the world; 2) to educate women as teachers of Buddhism; 3) to conduct research on women in Buddhism; and 4) to work for the establishment of the *bhikkhunī* sangha where it did not currently exist (Gellner and LeVine 2005: 266).

The work of Chatsumarn Kabilsingh must be placed in context. Chatsumarn's very useful book *Thai Women in Buddhism* (1991) historically contextualizes the position of *mae chee* in Thai society and she devotes a chapter to the *bhikkhunī* movement in Thailand. She argues that *mae chee* suffer from a negative social image and a lack of self-esteem, which has resulted in low social and religious status. Her position is that *mae chee* are marginalized, alienated and uneducated. Chatsumarn's mother

---

[4] The *dasa sil mata*, founded in 1903 in Sri Lanka, observe ten precepts.

controversially took full ordination in Taiwan in 1970 and at the time of the 1987 conference was the only fully ordained Thai nun in the Theravāda tradition (Gellner and LeVine 2005: 265). Chatsumarn is one of the best-known advocates for the re-establishment of the *bhikkhunī* sangha in Thailand and her view of the reinstated *bhikkhunī* sangha is very particular. According to Barnes, 'Dr. Kabilsingh does not foresee a sangha of bhikshuni who would devote their time exclusively to meditation, however, or to religious observances. Bhikshuni would be able to work to solve some of the country's and the world's horrendous social problems, with the force of the venerable sangha behind them' (Barnes 1996: 269).

The current *bhikkhunī* movement is taking place in a political as well as a religious context in which women's claims are being taken seriously in religious terms. In recent years increasing numbers of women have taken *bhikkhunī* ordination in Thailand and as the order becomes more established we are likely to see a proliferation of foci and practices being adopted by religious women. Though this is at present a relatively small-scale movement it has important implications for the thousands of *mae chee* throughout Thailand living lives of renunciation without the official recognition of the sangha. The majority of *mae chee* in Wat Bonamron did not want full ordination. There were three reasons that *mae chee* gave for this: first, *mae chee* argued that ordination as a *mae chee* was sufficient for them to lead lives as renunciates; secondly, *bhikkhunī* ordination was not possible because the lineage had died out; and, thirdly, some understood the movement to reinstate the *bhikkhunī* lineage as a bid for status driven by delusion.[5] As one *mae chee* put it, 'Chatsumarn is a woman's rights campaigner. If lay people didn't pay attention to her she would disrobe and find another way to campaign.' The request for full ordination by the *bhikkhunī* movement was presented as antithetical to the emphasis on mindful reflection valorized by these *mae chee*. However, both the monasticization of *mae chee* and the *bhikkhunī* movement must be understood as part of a broader context in which women are increasingly being recognized in positions of privilege and respect. The concern of *mae chee* in the monastery is that such a movement, to demand either more recognition or religious responsibilities for women who chose to ordain, is in conflict with the ethical project of realizing non-self through ascetic discipline, as they understand it, be that in meditation or in observing the responses of

---

[5] The one *mae chee* who thought that she would possibly like to become a *bhikkhunī* reasoned that full ordination would make life easier because a *bhikkhunī*'s brown robes would be easier to keep clean than the white robes of a *mae chee*.

the mind and body as one does one's duty to others. However, the movement itself and the diversity of ways in which Thai Buddhist women are increasingly being recognized as religious professionals, including the diversity of foci for *mae chee* throughout Thailand, suggest that the antithesis recognized by these *mae chee* between alternative ways of being a female Buddhist renunciate is a potentially negotiable response to the shifting ways in which women are engaging with religious practice and identity in Thailand today.

RECONSIDERING ETHICS

In a compelling consideration of the women's mosque movement in Egypt, Mahmood (2005) argues against a search for a universal category of acts, such as those of resistance, which can be identified outside the ethical and political context in which such acts acquire their meaning, and for an uncoupling of the notion of self-realization from that of autonomous will. Mahmood's uncoupling of agency and autonomy is useful: it points towards a form of analysis that takes the ability to effect change in the world and within oneself to be culturally and historically specific and, thus, the agency identified by the analyst in a given context must emerge as a result of an exploration of the meaning of particular concepts and modes of being. In the light of this, what may be understood from a progressive political model to be passivity and submission to patriarchal forms of life on the part of *mae chee* may be reinterpreted as a form of agency by which the subject is formed: that is, the means by which an ethical project is enacted, inhabited and embodied.

In accounting for the aspirations, values and norms that are inhabited and embodied by monastics I have suggested that we must locate the wilful shaping of subjectivity in a matrix of power relations. Building on the Foucaultian analysis of asceticism developed in Chapter 4, I understand power as a necessary condition of the subject: power is not external to the subject, dominating the subject to a greater or lesser extent, but rather it is the condition for the subject's creation. Thus, agency is not understood as that which resists a power that is external to it. Agency is understood as necessarily already produced through power relations. The subject who resists power is no less produced through power relations; what Butler (1993: 15) has called the subject's 'productive reiterability'.

In questioning how the self is conceived and made we come up against the challenge recognized by Foucault. Such a project necessarily challenges an important premise of modern liberalism – that of the 'individual' as self-evident and natural – and suggests instead that the modern self is a historical product. By examining how 'self' is formed we can unpack the genealogy of the ethical subject and we must, therefore, accept the possibility that 'the self' may be made and constituted in different ways. In such an approach, freedom is not the unfettered exercise of the will; the will must be worked on to be created rather than a necessary and 'natural' precondition of identity. In focusing on the practice of taking the self as an object of reflection and action we can examine the significance of an ascetic and ethical ideal in providing a telos and a technology for cultivating such a reality, which subjects incorporate into their understandings of themselves and by which they constitute themselves as ethical subjects.

NON-SELF AND GENDERED EXPERIENCE

In the main office of the monastery in the late afternoon I sat with a group of *mae chee* and a monk sipping iced drinks in the heat. Phra Panyo sat on a higher chair and was served coffee by one *mae chee*, who prepared him a cup of his favourite iced coffee, placed the cup on his ceremonial cloth and *wai'*d respectfully before backing away on her knees. It was a lazy afternoon with no lay people coming in for information, and we discussed understandings of gender. I was told that perceiving male or female is the result of delusion, and that if I practised meditation sufficiently I would see that there is no male or female. As the monastic cuts attachment to a sense of self they are believed to become bodily and mentally less gendered, to the extent that emotional responses are minimized, men stop producing semen and women stop menstruating (See Falk and Gross 1980: 220–1). I was told of a disciple of the Buddha who was very advanced in meditation and kept changing the sex of his/her body. This proved very difficult for the sangha because every time he/she changed, he/she would have to re-ordain in the lineage that was appropriate to his/her current sex. Finally, he/she agreed to remain in a male body because that was the lineage that he was currently ordained in. The story was used to highlight the view held by *mae chee* and monks that the sex of the body is the result of delusion and impurity of the mind and that the closer one is to enlightenment the more uncertain and unclear is one's gender and sex. We then have a clear picture of contradiction: on the one hand, women are discriminated against, they serve men and are religiously disadvantaged, inasmuch as they do not seek full ordination. On the other hand, they argue that through ascetic discipline they are cultivating the virtues that will result in the experiential insight that a perception of the self as gendered is delusional.

Penny Van Esterik argues that a thorough understanding of the Buddhist textual tradition leads to the conclusion that gender is a moveable and changeable phenomenon. Referring to the canonical texts she writes:

> In the logic of Theravāda Buddhism, we come to realize that we hold the false belief that there are male and female humans with separate identities and selves ... It is an error of understanding, an instance of thinking on the ordinary level and not the karmic level, to think that there are fixed entities such as men and women. This is illusion and unreality. (2000: 79–80)

Van Esterik suggests that Thai gender is best theorized as a context-sensitive process. She argues that Thai conceptions of gender are a worldly accommodation of the Buddhist concepts of *anattā* (non-self) and *anicca* (impermanence), in which surfaces are transformable and temporary while the self remains hidden and unknowable (2000: 203). Bodies are impermanent but they are clues to karmic status and 'the stage upon which appearance and reality are played out' (Van Esterik 2000: 207). Thus, as we have seen, people speculate about the karmic status of others based upon the self that they body-forth. The well-composed, fragrant body is thought to be indicative of moral purity. But the body is also that which is to be detached from in the practice of meditation. For example, a well-known meditative technique is to meditate upon the images of decaying or mutilated corpses.[6] Observing the transience of beauty, the decay and impermanence of the body encourages detachment from physical form and the realization of impermanence as a condition of all phenomena (see Pattana 2007). Images of mutilated or decaying bodies are pedagogic aids in monastic practice and are commonplace in other areas of Thai society.

Penny Van Esterik suggests that understandings of the body and performance in Thailand may be read through the soteriological principles of Buddhism:

> gestures and acts, performative of gendered bodies, raise a very Buddhist question about the ontological status of the body apart from the masquerade which constitutes its reality. In fact, the politics of bodily appearances reinforces the Buddhist emphasis on non-self, impermanence, illusion and the deceptive nature of appearances. Bodies, like self and ego, are constituted as 'nothing but' appearance and illusion. (2000: 221)

While *mae chee* and monks refer to Buddhist teachings on non-self, attachment and meditative attainment that transcend gendered identity positions

---

[6] See Klima (2002) for an interesting discussion of this meditation technique (*asubha kammaṭṭhāna*).

(see Lindberg Falk 2002: 25), daily monastic life is replete with the concerns of maintaining a highly differentiated gender hierarchy.

In Charles Keyes' renowned account of Thai gender, women are understood to hold a 'spiritually inferior status' (Keyes 1984: 234). For Keyes the critical issue is that women are debarred from the privileged position of full ordination and indeed he links this to a position on 'private woman', 'public man':

> This difference bespeaks a basic unreflected assumption characteristic not only of Buddhist societies but most, if not all traditional societies: roles that define women in terms of their relations as wives or sex partners of men and as mothers of children while men's roles are defined in terms of public activities to which prestige attaches. (Keyes 1986: 86)

Keyes argues that ordination for men produces a new gender position, 'sangha-gender', because of 'the Buddhist ideal of renunciation ... that makes it possible to transcend "natural" sexuality' (1986: 86). For the period of their ordination monks are classed as members of a 'gender' or category of person (*phet yang song*) that is quite separate from that of lay men (*phet chai*).

This '*sangha*-gender' is not based on the attributes of the sexed body but is acquired through monastic discipline that enables the transcendence of sexuality. He suggests that such *sangha*-gender is only possible for men and states quite categorically that, 'Whatever significance female renunciation may have had at the time when an order of *bhikkhuni* existed in India or Sri Lanka (but never in Southeast Asia), no Northern Thai woman nor any other woman in the Theravadin societies of Southeast Asia can alter her gender identity by ordination' (1986: 86). I would argue that the 'making' of *sangha*-gender through monastic discipline that Keyes identifies as being the preserve of monks in the 1980s is of a kind with the discipline through which *mae chee* are gaining respect as renunciates. While *mae chee* may not be relying on dominant, non-religious, discourses on gender, their bodily practices are congruent with the Buddhist idioms of non-attachment and non-self.

Monastics strive in their practice and duties to experience the condition of non-self and, by extension, to experience themselves as non-gendered. However, this does not preclude the presence or significance of gender hierarchy in the community. Engagement in gendered relations is one way in which monastics endeavour to cultivate the condition of non-self. As monastics strive to cut attachment to a sense of self they employ their emotional, physical and mental response to gendered and hierarchical duty as a means and measure of this work. As such *mae chee* doing their duty by serving monks selflessly and equanimously becomes a measure of the powers of enlightenment present within the *mae chee*. The effect of this is, on the one hand, to reaffirm hierarchy and, on the other, to change hierarchy as the more that *mae chee* are able to behave virtuously the more they are recognized as meritorious monastics. The renunciate, as religious professional, is working towards such a state.

In an analysis of early Buddhist texts Sponberg argues that diverse views on women and the feminine should not be read as an inconsistent ambivalence but rather as a rich multivocality in which early Buddhists sought to reconcile the tensions that arose from accommodating critical social doctrines with the mundane demands of conventional social values (Sponberg 1992: 4).[7] He identifies four different attitudes in Mahayana and Theravāda texts, in some cases within the same text: soteriological inclusiveness, institutional androcentrism, ascetic misogyny, and soteriological androgyny (Sponberg 1992: 8). The contrast between the differing attitudes Sponberg identifies is striking. First, he highlights an attitude of soteriological inclusiveness; as a theory and method of liberation from suffering the earliest Buddhists held that one's sex, as with one's caste or class, was no barrier to attaining the goal of liberation from suffering. Not only is this path open to women, but it is the same path for men and women; sex and gender differences are soteriologically insignificant. However, he also identifies a contrasting attitude of ascetic misogyny – a fear of the feminine and its power to undermine male celibacy – and an attitude of institutional androcentrism, by which women may pursue a full-time religious career but only within a carefully regulated institutional structure that maintains social standards of male authority and female subordination (Sponberg 1992: 18), both of which appear to be basically in conflict with the spirit of such soteriological inclusiveness. Sponberg argues that such incongruity should not be played down, but, rather, it should be seen as an indication of conflicting interests within the early community (1992: 22). Thus, Sponberg argues that different and conflicting views towards women are present in the Buddhist texts and that this must be understood in the context of human affairs as the concerns of different factions in the early community.[8]

---

[7] As I go on to consider textual and narrative form in the monastery I wish to emphasize that my point is not to make Buddhist texts stand for the contemporary ethnographic context. I assume neither that textual accounts are faithful representations of cultural practices, nor that it is tradition as it is found in the text that is 'remembered' and performed through ascetic practice. Understanding textual narratives as multivocal, as a script with different players or voices, enables us to take into account the ways in which people engage with them in contemporary Buddhist contexts.

[8] The fourth attitude identified by Sponberg is less relevant to this discussion. Soteriological androgyny is the view that all beings consciously or unconsciously manifest all the characteristics normally understood as gender specific. Femininity and masculinity are, in this view, mutually complementary

Sponberg is keen to note that a position of soteriological inclusiveness does not imply that gender differences do not exist or are not hierarchically constituted, but rather that they are not presented as relevant for enlightenment. He underscores his point by noting that most contemporary Asian Buddhists feel that women have equal access to the *dhamma*, but argue that sexual differences are real and that the male sex is socially and spiritually superior to the female sex by nature (Sponberg 1992: 12). I cannot comment on how widespread such views are but they are certainly prevalent in Wat Bonamron. This, then, makes the use of a non-gendered narrative of spiritual achievement by *mae chee* and monks all the more interesting. I want to suggest that the hierarchy of gender prevalent in the monastery is effectively sidestepped by *mae chee* and monks through ascetic practice. They thereby employ the ideals of soteriological inclusiveness, without engaging with either institutional androcentrism or ascetic misogyny. While such views are present in the monastery and reflected in spatial separation, hierarchical duty and monastic performance, they are understood as irrelevant to the non-gendered narrative of spiritual achievement.

CONCLUSION

For *mae chee* in this monastery, the rationale of monastic practice is never understood in terms of resistance to male authority or the equality of women vis-à-vis men. Now, I could argue that irrespective of the intent of the women involved we may analyse their practices in terms of their effectiveness in reinforcing or undermining structures of male domination. However, such an analysis necessarily remains confined within an opposition of resistance and subordination that is not ethnographically relevant. It is a culturally particular understanding of how power works, tied to an equally ethnocentric notion of equality and 'liberation', and is inattentive to motivations and desires that are not in accord with such theoretical principles and imported political agendas. When considering the place of religious embodiment and moral virtues in contemporary debates I argue that it is through repeated acts that the self may be trained to behave according to established standards. Through monastic performance and meditative training the *mae chee* establishes both the 'critical markers' and 'ineluctable means' (Mahmood 2001: 214) by which she trains herself to be ethical. Of concern here is not primarily the regulation of the feminine body by male

and both necessary for the ideal state of androgynous integration. The feminine is affirmed but in such a way as to reject the dichotomy between traits identified as feminine or masculine (Sponberg 1992: 25–7).

religious authority but rather the processes of individual ethics by which a person is responsible for her own actions, and thereby her own self.

Theravāda Buddhism is a soteriology: a tradition that transmits and embodies 'a distinctive project of renunciatory self-fashioning, in pursuit of an ideal of liberation from embodied existence' (Laidlaw 2006: 219). The continuity of the tradition of Theravāda Buddhism is not a question simply of the transmission of a continuous content of shared beliefs, but also roles and relationships, narratives and practices (including bodily techniques) (Laidlaw 2006: 220) – as Carrithers calls it, a 'patterned flow of contingencies and aspirations, routines and imaginative responses' (1990: 141). Through the practice of meditation and mindfulness, in very specific ways, people perform a certain number of techniques on the body, thought and ways of being by which they intend to attain, in Foucault's words, 'a certain kind of state of happiness, purity, wisdom, perfection, or immortality' (2000d: 225) in accord with Thai Buddhist tradition. Such a focus on the practical ways in which people make themselves and make sense of themselves necessitates that we relocate power within a set of relations that form the conditions of the subject, rather than simply dominating it to a greater or lesser extent.

The rising status of *mae chee* over the last few decades has been in part due to their increasing access to education, the increase in prevalence of self-governed nunneries, an increase in public profile through institutions such as the Thai Nuns' Institute and through media representations of charismatic and articulate *mae chee*. Given these ongoing developments, in this chapter, I have tried to examine the ways in which *mae chee* understand their commitment to the gendered hierarchy of the monastic community. *Mae chee* teaching and practising meditation in Wat Bonamron present an interesting challenge to an approach that highlights gender equality: they are engaging with practices, ideals and institutions that have traditionally accorded women a subordinate status and in so doing they seek to cultivate virtues that are associated with passivity such as humility, patience and equanimity.

Monastic practice may actualize Buddhist ethical principles while simultaneously being located in local and historically specific social worlds. The performance of religious identity is one way in which the moral self is both formed and communicated: the embodiment of the principles of meditation is not only a means through which monastics cultivate detachment from a sense of self but it is also a monastic duty (and interpreted as indicative of spiritual attainment). Thus, the transformations that we are seeing in the position of *mae chee* in Thai monasticism must be considered with reference to the specific practices that make particular modes and presentations of subjectivity possible. *Mae chee*'s embodiment of the virtues of humility, selflessness and service may be understood as positive and affirmative ways of acting in the world. Such ethical self-formation necessitates the enactment of prescribed bodily behaviours within a given tradition. Such acts engage with historically specific social objectives in a manner that is socially and culturally recognized. Thus, embodied mindfulness is entirely culturally specific: it is the enactment of morality through quite rigidly prescribed behavioural idioms. In the pedagogic project of the monastery, both in the discipline of monastics and in the teaching of meditation to the laity, it is through the repeated performance of virtuous acts that the subject's will, emotions and body take on a particular form. It is through the enactment of religious performance that the monastic self is produced.

CHAPTER 9

Monasticization and the ascetic interiority of non-self

We have seen in the foregoing that while monastic identity and ascetic practices such as *vipassanā* meditation have historically been the preserve of monks, requiring full ordination and celibacy, this is not the case in contemporary Thailand. Furthermore, 'monastic' and 'lay' have never been uncomplicated or mutually exclusive categories in the Thai context.

I have argued that the involvement of *mae chee* in teaching and practising meditation is leading to the incorporation of women in religious and monastic roles; *mae chee* in Wat Bonamron are able to define themselves and be defined by others as monastics. As we saw in Chapter 8, there are different ways in which the office of '*mae chee*' is being understood and enacted in the broader context of the Thai religious landscape. We have also seen, however, that *mae chee* remain hierarchically inferior to monks, as evidenced by spatial separation between men and women in the monastery. *Mae chee* do not make claims to the monastic office of monkhood and understand their demonstrable respect for monks (as paragons of religious professionalism) to be meritorious.

While ideas about pollution and separation are clearly visible in the monastery there are ways in which they are balanced by the identity held by both monks and *mae chee* of 'ordinand' (*nak buat*). As we saw, in the *mae chee* ordination ceremony the significance of ordination for both monks and *mae chee* in Wat Bonamron is that it provides 'the opportunity to follow the Buddha's lifestyle and understand the true Buddhist teaching'. For both monks and *mae chee*, guarding the monastic precepts potentially enables them to free themselves from suffering. However, in order that these precepts 'come from the heart', they believe that it is necessary for them to practise meditation. The criteria by which different people constitute religious membership vary but the monastic rules remain the yardstick by which all measure their morality. While monks are controlled by the 227 precepts of the *vinaya*, the relative lack of formal rules for *mae chee* means that their *performance* of monastic identity here is crucial in their self-placement between the sangha and the laity.

Other developments have occurred during the recent decades of popularization of meditation including reformist critiques of Buddhism, and social and environmental movements based upon a Buddhist ethic. These are not separate from the propagation of meditation but, I have argued, they have occurred in tandem. In what I understand as 'Engaged Buddhism', a global socio-political position is incorporated within Buddhism to produce forms of Buddhist social activism and the validation of monastic work in the advancement of social and environmental welfare. The contrast between 'Engaged Buddhism' and those monasteries concerned exclusively with the propagation of *vipassanā* to the laity highlights the 'monasticism' of the meditation movement: while lay religious practice may be consonant with the social aspirations of a modernized and developed Thailand, monastic religious practice remains the ideal of moral perfection. The centrality of monasteries and the historical roles of monks have not been challenged by propagation of meditation to laity. Rather, their role has been augmented and the order is maintained by the aspirations of meditation students.

The religious resurgence that can be recognized in the increasing popularity of alternative forms of religiosity in Thailand, including the popularity of *vipassanā* meditation, represents forms of religious revival and institutional reform. The increasing prevalence of meditation practice for the laity and the changing roles of monastics who teach and practise meditation have occurred in tandem with a proliferation of alternative practices and movements.[1] This proliferation of religious movements in the contemporary context demands that we consider the degree to which previously demarcated analytic distinctions, such as this-worldly and other-worldly, sacred and secular, material and spiritual, are being transgressed by increasingly transnational and modernist discourses and religious movements. Through the propagation of meditation, growing emphasis is being placed on the interiorization and experience of soteriological Buddhist principles, which are increasingly the responsibility of more and more people, monastic and lay, as the meditation movement gains momentum.

---

[1] This is not to suggest that this presents a radical breach from religiosity as it has been historically practised in Thailand. For example, in the pre-modern period alternative forms of religiosity, such as spirit cults, Brahmanic practices and a wide variety of Buddhist pedagogies, flourished in the context of periodic elite reform movements (on this see McDaniel 2008).

Among all the calls for doctrinal reform and the involvement of laity in monastic practice there are no calls for a Protestant-like reform of Thai Buddhism. No lay Buddhists or *mae chee* have attempted to appropriate full religious authority to themselves. The greatest religious status remains with those who most strikingly follow the *vinaya* code, and that remains the monks. However, while a distinction between lay and monastic statuses is an important feature in Buddhist thought, this is variously interpreted in practice. While I understand the increasing numbers of people practising meditation and the changing status and responsibilities of *mae chee* as instances of the monasticization of modernist Buddhism, I do not propose such an interpretation in opposition to processes of 'laicization', but, rather, as one identifiable trend in the context of the plurality of practices and statuses in contemporary Thai Buddhism.

THE MONASTICIZATION OF THE LAITY AND THE DOMESTICATION OF THE SANGHA

As we saw in our discussion of alms donations, Carrithers (1979; 1984) understands the relationship between monastics and laity to be one characterized by reciprocity. Without revisiting this argument in detail here, I wish to explore the implications of Carrithers's theory of the domestication of the sangha in the light of the propagation of meditation to laity.

Carrithers argues that because of the organization of the sangha in small, localized groups in relation to the laity with whom they are interdependent, over time ascetic practices are gradually abandoned and lay values are adopted. Thus, the sangha is 'domesticated' as it is drawn into 'the values of everyday life' (1979). There is an inevitability about this that Carrithers returns to in a later work arguing that 'what pushes the sangha towards domestication is the sheer difficulty of remaining undomesticated' (Carrithers 1984: 322). The domestication of the sangha then is 'gradual, unconscious, apparently inevitable, and in these senses, natural' (Carrithers 1979: 296). Happily, this spiralling of moral degradation is held in check by the periodic enactment of ascetic ideals in reform movements:

The order of ascetics, separated from the world, gradually evolves towards the equilibrium state, the domesticated Sangha. Once this is reached, reformers may then arise from within the ranks, and though the majority of the Sangha remain domesticated, there appear groups, necessarily small because necessarily self-referring, of reform monks. As these settle and grow, they evolve towards domestication, and though associated in name with reform, come to entertain in fact the opinions of village literary specialists. Within these overgrown domesticated erstwhile reform groups there then appear further reformers ... and the process continues. (Carrithers 1979: 297)

Interestingly, Carrithers identifies those monastics who practise meditation as associated with reform, while those who do not live apart from society are associated with domestication. How then are we to make sense of the involvement of monastics with the laity in the propagation of meditation?

As we saw in Chapter 3, the need to accommodate large numbers of laity in the monastery has led to the structural bureaucratization of monastic duty and the monastery itself. The meditation centre requires different facilities in addition to the core monastic buildings and a large administrative organization to coordinate large numbers of meditation students. Under the leadership of the Abbot, the organization of the monastery is divided into different subordinate chairs, committees and offices. Furthermore, the monastery has developed both a mission statement and a constitution, reflecting national lay concerns about democracy and accountability. Is this, then, the domestication of the sangha? Alternatively, following Carrithers, it is possible to interpret the propagation and practice of meditation by the sangha as a reform movement that *legitimizes* the purity of the sangha, but we must still account for the widespread influence and adoption of this movement. While Carrithers's model has been apposite to understanding patterns of sangha reform and revival, the present situation does not appear to fit with the boom and the bust that Carrithers had in mind. Further, examining the reform of the sangha does not account for the adoption of ascetic practice by people outside the monastic hierarchy. However, we may see domestication in the structure whereby monastics and laity alike can adopt ascetic and ethical practice: that is, the context in which they become monasticized.

In Chapter 2, we saw that Buddhism has been incorporated as a representative marker of Thai national identity in both national discourse and international representation. Meditation practice is presented as an authentically Thai experience that is accessible to all people, Thai and foreign, monastic and lay. It is mainly propagated through the institutions of Buddhist monasteries. While the majority of Buddhist monasteries are not focused on the propagation of meditation, those that are, such as Wat Bonamron, are given over to this purpose and monastic structure, spatial layout, daily routine and hierarchy are all affected by such a focus. As we saw in Chapter 3, this monastery has been focused on the promotion of *vipassanā* as a monastic and a lay practice since it was founded in the early

1970s and is now a wealthy and popular establishment. I have argued that this has led to what may be understood as 'monasticization' for participants in the monastery: involvement in the religious institution and monastic practice is enabling those outside the sangha of fully ordained monks, such as *mae chee*, to self-identify and be defined by others as monastic. This has by no means led to a call for doctrinal reform, and distinctions between monastic statuses remain important. Forms of monasticization are one identifiable trend in the plurality of practices and foci in contemporary Thai Buddhism.

The propagation of meditation has had a significant impact on the monastic structure and daily routine of monasteries that are given over to its transmission. As we saw in Chapter 3, the monastery is designed to accommodate hundreds of laity for short periods in addition to the stable monastic community. Groups of lay students come to the monastery to be taught meditation by monks and *mae chee*. During their stay they are provided with teaching, food and bedding. This demands that the monastery have facilities in addition to the core monastic buildings and individual monastic's *kuṭis*, such as sleeping quarters, dining halls, large kitchens, shower blocks, meditation halls, and so on.

As well as individual duties, all monastics have the duties of meditating, learning *dhamma* and offering an example of monastic discipline to the laity. In this monastery this has had important implications for the involvement of women in the monastic community. The daily routine of all monastics is highly structured and is focused on the promotion of meditation and the maintenance of the monastery. The differences between monks and *mae chee* and the shared understanding that monastic life in this monastery is focused on meditation are highlighted in the two ordination ceremonies. Importantly, in both, ordination is formally presented as a personal opportunity for the ordinand to practise meditation. The monk and *mae chee* ordination ceremonies are thought to mark entry into the monastic community even though *mae chee* ordination is only partial and the significance of ordination is sermonized as providing the ordinand with the opportunity to gain insight into impermanence, suffering and non-self through meditative discipline.

The reasons people choose to ordain are varied but once ordained in Wat Bonamron all monks and *mae chee* come to understand their meditation and renunciation as an ongoing 'work'. This is in part self-selecting (those people who are not interested in meditation would be more likely to ordain in a different monastery) and in part the process of learning what it means to be a monastic in this context. The cultivation of 'mindfulness' through disciplined behaviour is an explicit focus for all monastics. As with the exhortation to act as a '*dhamma* friend' for those having doubts about their ability to maintain monastic discipline, the monastic's personal development through meditation was a concern that was shared at a community level. However, this remains the 'work' of individual monastics: through very specific meditative methods and practices monastics intend to alter their responses to internal processes and cultivate a capacity for discipline through which they may gain insight into religious truths.

This raises some important questions: what is the relationship between the social order of the monastic community and the ethical practice of asceticism? And, in what way may the relationship between the monastic community and the laity inform understandings of morality? Finally, where do individuality and personhood lie if the monastic body is intended to give an example of non-self to the laity?

THE BUDDHIST *MOI*

Marcel Mauss (1985) distinguishes between the social concept of the person (*personne*) and human self-awareness (*moi*). For Mauss, *personne* is the conception of the individual as a member of a collectivity – the individual's social identity. *Moi* is the individuality of the person, both physical and mental, interacting with other persons as moral agents. Mauss attempts to trace the historical trajectory of the concept of the social person but in so doing he also theorizes about individual self-awareness. He begins by setting out his examination in terms of social and legal history, rather than the psychic or philosophical '*moi*'. But as Carrithers (1985: 235) comments,

> What we naively take to be psychic, or inner, or spiritual, or at least a natural matter, our notion of our self, is revealed by Mauss to be something else altogether, a product of social history and a matter wholly explicable through sociological exegesis. Mauss had seemed to set the self aside only to retrieve and explain it triumphantly at the end.

Mauss argues that the modern notion of the person is basically a Christian one. (He suggests that because in Buddhist soteriology the self is divisible, the annihilation of which is sought by the monk [Mauss 1985: 13], this is an inappropriate place to search for *moi* theory.) By employing a Christian historical trajectory Mauss is able to trace the origins of *moi* theory while appearing to guide the reader through the origins of *personne*: 'From a simple masquerade to the mask, from a "role" [*personage*] to a "person" [*personne*], to a name, to an individual; from the latter to a being possessing metaphysical and moral value; from a moral consciousness to a sacred being; from the latter to a fundamental form of thought and action – the course is accomplished' (Mauss 1985: 22). Thus Mauss, with considerable chutzpah, follows a path from external religion through the collective, arriving ultimately at the individual. For Mauss, then, religion is replaced by the individual as the source of ultimate values. This is an evolutionary trajectory that, while allowing the presence of *personne* theories in complex societies, denies some the privilege of *moi* theories; strategically, this remains a moot point for Mauss himself as long as he professes to be emphasizing *personne* theories.

Carrithers (1985), in a thoughtful and stimulating article, responds to Mauss by postulating that Mauss's original premise – that it is possible to divorce thought about the individual in social life from 'conscious personality' or 'spiritual/physical individuality' – was in error. Contra Mauss, Carrithers suggests that Buddhism may be read as a *moi* theory par excellence. Buddhist understanding of 'non-self' (*anattā*) focuses on the psychophysical individual and relates this to a moral and cosmic order (Carrithers 1985: 245). In a project that echoes that of Mauss, Carrithers traces *moi* theory through different continents and ages, but whereas Mauss began with 'primitive societies' Carrithers begins with human beings alone: 'communing with Nature for the German Romantics, acting according to his own human nature for the Stoics, meditating in the forest for Theravāda Buddhists, struggling in one's room in prayer for Protestant Christians' (Carrithers 1985: 248). By revealing the wide distribution and narrative history of *moi* theories Carrithers is able to show that *moi* and *personne* views relate to each other both comparatively and by influencing each other. Consequently Carrithers concludes that collectivist sociology such as Mauss's cannot encompass the truth about human behaviour in its totality 'for it can never fully comprehend the place and representation of the psychophysical individual in social and cultural life, or in history' (Carrithers 1985: 255).

Carrithers argues that the Buddhist teaching of non-self cemented the *moi* as the paramount concern of human life: one that is essentially moral and social, and subject to analysis and discipline by each person. His discussion of co-dependent origination is particularly pertinent to our interests, since through this he reveals 'a thorough and thoroughly abstract conception of the individual mind and body' (Carrithers 1985: 253). Carrithers is quite right to point out that while the *moi* of Buddhism is aimed at one's own purposes, individual experience is understood from the viewpoint of whether it is morally good and psychologically wholesome;

thus it constitutes 'an opposition view which dwelt upon human mental and physical individuality in respect of the morally conceived social interaction of such individuals within a natural-spiritual order' (Carrithers 1985: 255). Taking a historical perspective, Carrithers demonstrates that the teaching of non-self contradicted prevalent views of the eternal Self. In response to Mauss's Christian origins of *personne* Carrithers counters that, 'If Roman law constituted a decisive step in human thought about humans as persons in a collectivity, Buddhism constituted a decisive step in human thought about humans in relation to their mental and physical individuality' (Carrithers 1985: 253).

Buddhist *moi* theory may be identified within the practice of *vipassanā* through which the principle of non-self (*anattā*) is intended to be realized as a psychological reality. The body is broken down into its constituent parts, the feelings are isolated and examined apart from their causes, bodily desire is subdued and the mind is quietened through the restriction of sensory stimulation. The implication of this is that, in this context, *anattā* is a state that is realizable for all people, lay or monastic. Thus, the monastic life may be entered for given periods of time, either as *upāsaka/upāsikā* (pious lay person) or as renunciate, in order to practise meditation as a form of mental training.

The practice is intended to bring about a change in the perception of the meditator. As I argued in Chapter 4, meditation may be understood as a 'technology of the self' by means of which Buddhist ethical principles become actualized through the bodies and minds of practitioners. The attainment of enlightenment is understood as a moral duty for all humans and the realization of non-self becomes a moral imperative. Thus, I have argued that transcendence of the self may be actualized in the body and mind of the practitioner through a process of continuous physical and mental discipline in which resolution may be achieved between the ideal of Buddhist soteriology and ascetic practice. This is reflected in the retreat process in the role of the teacher, whose duty it is to encourage the student to witness experiences as transient conditions. The reasons a student may think underlie meditative experiences are met with technical instruction. Thus the student develops the ability to detach herself from involvement with mental or emotional states and the ability to look at rather than look through them.

In Chapter 4 we examined in detail the meditation as it is taught to beginners, looking at the ways in which the technique builds up through the retreat and the emphasis placed on the religious tenets of impermanence, suffering and non-self. Practitioners seek insight into these religious truths in their mindful observation during meditation. As mindfulness develops, it is held, practitioners gain the perspectival capacity to recognize these truths in their own subjectivity. They seek to experience a particular religious subjectivity through specific techniques and patterns of reflection that lead to different ways of experiencing and relating to themselves and the world around them. Thus it is through the effort involved in ascetic practice that non-self is realized. The reduction of attachment to 'self' and consequent insight into the nature of the world ideally reach their telos in the final hours of the retreat when the self-identity of the practitioner is potentially extinguished. The possibility of cessation of self-control is implicit in the telos of non-self, but this is only to be experienced as a result of dedicated and willed discipline.

In the meditation monastery, the lived experience of monasticism is caught up with the transformative effect that meditation is intended to have. As we saw in Chapter 4, the process of learning to be a monastic involves routinization through the repeated process of intensive meditation retreat. I have interpreted this as a social learning process: the cognitive categories of Buddhism are imbued through socially taught methods and are sought and identified in the experiences of the meditator. Through the ongoing observation of internal and external sensory phenomena, the practitioner learns to reinterpret subjective experiences and to alter his or her subjectivity. Meditation, a solitary activity if ever there was one, has important social dimensions, which are collectively taught and understood, including technique and intended effects. It is through the repeated practice that religious tenets become the ground from which responses are appraised.

As mindfulness develops the meditator both observes and experiences changes in their subjective state. Importantly, these changes in subjectivity must be understood in the context of broader ideas about the nature of knowledge and wisdom. In Chapter 5 we examined the ways in which the work that monastics do on themselves relates to broader understandings of language and experience in meditation and in social interaction. In this monastery, Pali language in chants and meditation is thought to have bodily effects upon those who chant and hear it. Pali words are incorporated into the retreat process as a method by which people may develop the capacities to perceive religious truths in their meditative experiences. The psychophysical conditions that arise as a result of the use of Pali are then to be responded to using mindful observance. Through the development of the capacity to observe the conditions of the words the practitioner is able to correctly 'understand' the truths of these experiences. Perception of religious tenets is progressively cultivated through intentional practice: through retraining his or her relationship to the senses the practitioner cultivates the ability to perceive religious tenets in his or her self-identity. Renunciation is taken as a process of becoming that is not achieved through the act of ordination alone. The process of renunciation involves the stated and intended perspectival shift towards an ascetic subjectivity that is achieved through specific socially shared understanding and pedagogic methods.

So far, so *moi*. But as we have seen, monastics have clear conceptions of what it means to be a member of a religious community that vary as monastics understand themselves in relation to themselves, the laity and other monastics. It appears that the individuality of ascetic practice, while present in the monastery, may not be understood in isolation from the location of the monastic as a member of a social order. Indeed, the two are understood as mutually supportive in the monastic project: the *moi* project of the renunciate will always be located within the *personne* project of a community of practice. For example, while ordination marks footfalls on the path to release from the wheel of rebirth it also marks the noviciate's entry into the monastic community and hierarchy: he or she is reborn in the 'family of the Buddha'. Similarly, through *vipassanā* practice, understandings of the psychophysical individual are related to a moral and cosmic order. 'Non-self' as it is actualized by monastics is located in the context of a monastic's social identity as a member of a collective.

Building on the work of Carrithers, Collins demonstrates that the monastic order and Buddhist community are not defined in terms of Buddhist first principles; that is, the Buddhist order *cannot* be understood as typified by either *moi* or *personne* theory alone; it must be understood as incorporating both theories. The *moi* system of non-self identified by Carrithers is moral but it is not restricted to a specific social system, or to the person defined in relation to others or the collectivity. As a soteriological premise it is applicable to all persons irrespective of their agency or social arrangements (see Collins 1994: 67–8). But, as Collins argues, ordination means a change in status and social role in traditional Buddhist societies: 'to be ordained as a monk is, on the formal level at least, to change one's social identity from that enabled and constrained by one's place in a specific kinship group, patron–client matrix, or other local relationships, to that afforded by the translocal, universal monastic role' (Collins 1994: 68). Buddhist renouncers remain social agents and 'unitary and enduring persons' (Collins 1994: 69) though not the same 'persons' that they were before renunciation. However, monastic rank, sect, affiliation to a monastery and teaching lineage all influence the *personne* one becomes after ordination; nonetheless, one does become a *personne*. What is expected of or valorized for renunciates is socially stipulated and as such renouncers and laity alike recognize the 'individuality' of renouncers, typified by the absence of demonstrations of a sense of self or amoral behaviour. Indeed, this is in accord with Tambiah's view that 'the renouncer's life is an exemplary one which had to be respected, admired and supported by the society at large whose troubles, obsessions and vices it transcended' (1982: 307). Thus, adherence to *vinaya* discipline by renouncers is a focus for renouncers and laity alike and the way of life of the renouncer makes sense in contradistinction to that of the householder (cf. Burghart 1983; Tambiah 1982: 306).

While the non-self of Buddhist soteriology is intended to be applied by the Buddhist renouncer to monastic practices such as duties and meditation this does not dispense with social responsibility or membership of a religious community. As Collins writes, 'There is, in principle, an analysis of such agency which can dispense with reference to persons, but such a reductionist discourse cannot serve the social, legal, or behavioural purposes of the nonreductionist discourse which it can, in principle, replace' (1994: 69). He argues that,

> Not-self is a secondary theory. In Buddhism human beings are 'directly given' as embodied persons and social agents, both monastic and lay; the ultimate truth of the changing, transmigrating flux of consciousness and karmic causality is hidden, and must be discovered through meditation ... the occasions when secondary theory actually replaces primary theory are necessarily those of specialized practices conducted by trained experts: exorcisms and spirit lore, laboratories and academic publications, and in the Buddhist case the monastic practices of meditation and scholarly textual activity. (Collins 1994: 73)

The religious professionals with whom I work are striving to actualize such secondary theory as an embodied, ongoing reality. Such a project provides a telos in the ongoing training of the monastic self. As we saw in Chapter 6, monastics have a moral duty to behave in an appropriate way. Sartorial and emotional composure are not only the means through which monastics cultivate detachment from a sense of self but they are also a monastic duty (and interpreted as indicative of spiritual attainment). In Chapter 6 I located the monastic duty to behave selflessly and offer a 'spotless performance' to the laity in the context of monastic hierarchy and ritual duty. I argued that lay moral expectations of monastics are defined in absolute terms. In contrast, the expectations and constraints on behaviour between monastics are defined relationally and moral judgments are influenced by social role and position. Deportment is a morally weighted issue; furthermore, it is meritoriously accumulative to witness a monastic behaving mindfully – that is, behaving morally. The transfer and accumulation of merit makes it appropriate for mindful *mae chee* to bear witness to the alms donations of the laity. Monastic behaviour, then, becomes a question of social responsibility as well as individual morality, and the polite and mindful presentation of the monastic self may mask conflicting emotions experienced within the person.

I will pause for a moment to consider the seminal work of Louis Dumont on renunciation and 'individuality' before considering the ways in which the social responsibilities of monastics living in community are related to the cultivation of specific perspectival capacities in an ethical project of self-formation. In an acclaimed structural correlation between the renouncer and the man-in-the-world, and between individualism and holism, Dumont famously identified renouncers as the source of individualism and religious change in Hinduism, Buddhism and Jainism. While this volume has had a very different theoretical focus, Dumont's theory and the scholarship it generated provide an important foundation for any analysis of renunciation and individuality.

DUMONT'S RENOUNCERS AND THE BEGINNINGS OF INDIVIDUALISM

In a far-reaching essay entitled 'World Renunciation in Indian Religions' Dumont (1980 [1966]: appendix B) attempts to draw an overarching picture of the role of the 'renouncer' in Hinduism. He argues that there are two kinds of men in Indian society: those who live in the world and those who have renounced it. For Dumont, the institution of world-renunciation allows full independence from the social interdependence of the caste system.[2]

---

[2] For Dumont the fundamental institution in Indian society is the caste system: an essentially religious system based hierarchically upon 'the complementarity of the pure and the impure, of the superior and the inferior' (1980: [1966] 270). Hinduism for Dumont is the religion of caste, and he accounts for modifications of Hinduism through the 'addition' of sectarian movements. He uses a unitary definition of Hinduism and argues that while many heretical innovations have occurred the survivors have been those that have not denied caste and thus they have been absorbed easily within the system.

Dumont argues that Indian society imposes interdependence upon each person and group within it. He argues that caste society is characterized by a hierarchy of values and a system of relations between groups, the value of which is reckoned by the role that any element plays in relation to the society as a whole. There can therefore be no 'individual' as he defines it in this system. As he writes, 'To say that the world of caste is a world of relations is to say that the particular caste and the particular man have no substance: they exist empirically, but they have no reality in thought, no

Thus it is through the 'individuality' of the renouncer that all innovation in Indian religion has occurred (Dumont 1985). He suggests that a dialogue exists between the renouncer and the 'man-in-the-world'. The renouncer does not deny the religion of the man-in-the-world, but rather his discipline becomes additional to it. Through distance from the world the renouncer is able to 'relativize' life in the world while the lay man is only privy to a 'relative ethic': to be generous to monks and avoid self-abasing actions (1985: 95). Dumont writes that, 'In leaving the world he [the renouncer] finds himself invested with an individuality which he apparently finds uncomfortable since all his efforts tend to its extinction or its transcendence. He thinks as an individual, and this is the distinctive trait which opposes him to the man-in-the-world and brings him closer to the western thinker' (Dumont 1980 [1966]: 274–5). For Dumont, then, the world-renouncer is the only Indian figure comparable with the individual in the Western sense of an autonomous agent. In this way the individualized religion of

Being' (1980: [1966] 272). Thus he is challenged by his own assertion to account for the existence of any kind of substantialist perspective in India which may be identified as a concept of the individual.

Dumont suggests that 'individualism' is an ideology unique to the modern West according to which 'every man is, in principle, an embodiment of humanity at large, and as such he is equal to every other man and free' (Dumont 1977: 3–6, cited in Tambiah 1982: 299). The individual in this formulation is independent and autonomous, and irreplaceable in his singularity. The individual is a person conceived of as 'having universal value, as being a complete manifestation of the essence of man or as embodying so to speak humanity in one biological individuum' (Dumont 1965: 9, cited in Tambiah 1982: 299).

Homo Hierarchicus was for Dumont the beginning of a project to explore not only holism, which he felt typified societies in which paramount value was placed upon society as a whole, but also the individualism found in Western societies. He sought to read against 'the ideology of the caste system' something important about the history of Western values, bringing the two, as he saw them, distinct societal ideologies into discussion with each other.

In his examination of the Christian origins of modern individualism Dumont (1985) further argues that the religious conception of the individual ('outworldly') was incorporated into the secular ('inworldly') and that this transformed the 'traditional holistic type' of society into the universe of 'modern individualism'. He argues that early Christianity was of the same sociological type as India in which the individual was antagonistic to the world, in part because for both Indian renunciatory traditions and early Christianity the concern for the individual was founded on devaluation of the world (1985: 96–7). Again, tracing 'universes of thought' and historical trajectories Dumont explores the way in which individualist value becomes adapted to worldly ethics creating the 'inworldly individual':

If I could draw a figure, it would represent two concentric circles, the larger one representing individualism in relation to God, and within it a smaller circle standing for acceptance of worldly necessities, duties and allegiances: that is to say, the accommodation to a society, pagan at first and later Christian, which has not ceased to be holistic ... encompassing the antithetical worldly life within the all-embracing primary reference and fundamental definition, and subordinating the normal holism of social life to outworldly individualism. (1985: 100)

Thus the institution of renunciation, which had conquered the world, is itself ultimately condemned to become 'inworldly'. In a similar way, for Dumont, Hinduism becomes imbued with asceticism as a general orientation and as a way of salvation (Dumont 1980 [1966]: 273).

the renouncer, based upon choice, autonomy and reflection, is added on to the religion of the group and of caste, based upon hierarchy, mutual interdependence and social persons. Interestingly, Dumont speculates that Hinduism integrated ideas of transmigration and karma (moral retribution) within itself but that these were essentially the values of the renouncer. It has been observed that in Dumont's analysis the complementarity of the 'man-in-the-world' and 'world-renouncer' is reflected in the Buddhist soteriology of *saṃsāra* and *mokkha*, rebirth and release (Collins 1982: 164). Thus Dumont is able to demonstrate a way in which transmigration represents social reality.

There have been many ways in which Dumont has been criticized but his work provides us with more than a simple structural dualism.[3] We will now examine Dumont's theory of the renouncer as 'individual outside the world'. I intend to argue that, while there are some valid criticisms of this view, it nonetheless provides us with an important stepping-stone on our way to understanding the significance of ascetic practice.

THE RENOUNCER: COMMUNITY AND AMBIVALENCE

Dumont suggests that because Hinduism limits periods of renunciation to the last stage in the life of the Brahman, there is a degree of ambivalence to renunciation. This 'subdued hostility' appears in contrast to the transformative effect on Hinduism that Dumont attributes to renunciation as it was integrated into the religion. This perspective has been questioned by the work of Das (1995) and Madan (1987), who respectively argue that such textually located practices might not be actualized in reality and that ambivalence to renunciation may be felt while genuine renunciation is simultaneously valorized.

Tambiah (1982) suggests that the founding of sects, recognized as an important feature of the Indian religious landscape by Dumont, must also

---

[3] For Dumont the cognitive and symbolic thought structuring the social system is formed with paired oppositions, beginning with the complementary principles of purity and pollution. Understanding these underpinning values reveals the universal processes of symbolism and cognition. Thus, Dumont is able to give a complete explanation of Hindu civilization by accounting for what he identifies as its core values. Dumont's theory generated an intense and often heated academic debate concerning theories of caste (see Bayly 1999; Burghart 1983; Daniel 1984; Das 1995: 33; Dirks 1987; 1989; Heesterman 1985; Inden 1976; 1990; Inden and Nicholas 1977; Madan 1987; Marriott 1976a; 1976b; 1989; 1990; Ostor *et al.* 1992; Raheja 1988a; 1988b; 1989). A useful list of literature stimulated by Dumont's work can be found in the second English edition of *Homo Hierarchicus* (1980 [1966]: xiii). A full bibliography of Dumont's writing up to 1980 can be found in Madan (1982), with supplements after that date in Strenski (2008).

include the monastic orders and communities to which Dumont's 'world-renouncers' belonged. In so doing he questions the renouncer's 'individualism' as discussed by Dumont, for it is not the case that 'outworldly individuals' (Dumont 1985: 95) commonly live outside of all society. It is worth quoting Tambiah at length:

> we are called upon to judge the logic of renouncer's 'personal' quest which nevertheless was thought to be best undertaken as a member of a collectivity subject to a communal discipline, and to explore the contours of the 'individuality' of a renouncer who leaves his family, goes from home into homelessness, only to have himself initiated into, and then submit and merge himself in a 'total institution' ... the sangha, which is an organized commonalty, whose central pillar is a disciplinary code, the *vinaya*. In this sense, early Buddhism confronts us not so much with the dichotomy of householder versus individual ascetic as with that of the lay household and the religious monastic community. (Tambiah 1982: 303–4)

Dumont himself comments that a renouncer 'may live in solitude as a hermit or may join a group of fellow-renouncers under a master-renouncer, who propounds a particular discipline of liberation' (1985: 85). Nonetheless, the picture of the religious community is unclear in his discussion of individualism. While the Buddhist path of liberation, its conceptions and techniques, are all the focus of the individual renouncer who must depend upon their own efforts for progress and ultimately salvation, emphasis is also placed on the importance of individual renouncers practising within the confines of a monastic community and its social and moral precepts. As the ethnography in this volume demonstrates, contemporary renunciates in the Buddhist countries of South and Southeast Asia often live in elaborately structured orders as members of corporate groups, obeying the law of the land and local customs as well as the overarching *vinaya* rules.

To discuss the renouncer in this instance only as individual would be to miss the complex layers of social organization, hierarchy and location in which the person is found. Burghart (1983) makes a further point that by focusing upon renunciation from the perspective of Brahmanical theorizing Dumont entirely overlooks the field of intersectarian ascetic relations:

> in the intersectarian discourse concerning the nature of transience some ascetics might find themselves classified by others as 'householders', householders as 'ascetics', and indeed the very category of householder might be neutralized so that it no longer stands in any specific relation to ascetic. Thus the only general statement which one can make concerning asceticism in the religious traditions of south Asia is that all ascetics see themselves as followers of some path which releases them from the transient world (*not* the social world) and that all ascetics distinguish themselves from non-ascetics who do not seek such release. (Burghart 1983: 643)

Tambiah (1982) takes up the question of Brahmanic ambivalence in a continued consideration of the issues opened up by Dumont. He suggests that Brahmanic ambivalence to Buddhism was directed towards the organization of renouncers in a community rather than towards the individual renouncer as recluse (Tambiah 1982: 317). He suggests, following Dumont, that the most important development in Hinduism was the 'including and hierarchising' of new components. While Tambiah is right to redress the balance between renouncer-individual and renouncer-community left by Dumont one must be aware at this point that what was hierarchized and included within Hinduism for Dumont was the individual, while for Tambiah it appears to be the community.

ALTERNATIVE INDIVIDUALITY

Dumont's model defines individual and hierarchy as opposites whose interaction, with the inclusion of *saṃnyāsa* (renunciatory) practices within the 'caste religion', is necessary for Hindu society as a formulation of pure and impure, which reflects the roles of householder and renouncer in relation to each other.

Mines (1994) draws our attention to the limitations of a dichotomous model such as that developed by Dumont. Ultimately, his model will only allow for an either/or: Either people are socially constructed or they are individuated. The only room for slippage is through the incorporation of *saṃnyāsa* elements into the dominant religion, but in his formulation this is performed by 'religions' rather than persons. While Dumont's theory is engaging he overplays his hand in saying that 'the society must submit and entirely conform to the absolute order, that consequently the temporal, and hence the human, will be subordinate, and that, while there is no room here for the individual, whoever wants to become one may leave society proper' (Dumont 1980 [1966]: 286). In my reading of Dumont it appears that he grants renouncers individuality without agency. The people of caste have no value, of themselves, whereas the renouncer qua individual does. Nonetheless, sociologically it is not important what singular renouncers do. As this volume demonstrates, in contemporary Thailand the performance of monastic identity and ascetic practice is in diverse ways absolutely crucial in the creation and valorization of renunciation and the ascetic self. The renouncer, in Dumont's description, does have a singular agency, which he does not problematize. For him, renouncers are paragons of religiosity; while they are individuals it is as though the process of renunciation were accomplished once and for all through the act of retreat from the world. They appear as perfect individuals, which, as renouncers know better than anyone, is a rare thing indeed.

As we have seen, Dumont's is a daring structuralist argument about a critical discussion between Indian Holism (the ideology of the caste system, in which the parts are subordinate to the whole), Indian Individualism (the individual-outside-the-world) and Western Individualism (autonomous and singular) (see Dumont 1985). Dumont himself was sometimes hesitant about his own characterization of 'outworldly' and 'inworldly' persons:

> The (western) individual is a man in the world, enjoying property as one of his necessary attributes. Therefore my compound may be objected to. It means only that he shows some important characteristics of the individual, although he differs from him in other respects. Here again the vocabulary is imperfect, but the perception it is meant to convey, of the situation of the renouncer in relation to the man of caste, on the one hand, and in comparison to the Western individual on the other is the main thing. (Dumont 1965: 92, fn. 9)

I agree with Mines that Dumont's analysis creates 'a myth of the Indian as Other, the radical antithesis of the Western individual' (Mines 1994: 6; cf. Obeyesekere 1992: 15–17) – the focus of which is not the way in which individuality is formed or the process by which renunciation is realized.

Louis Dumont's intention in drawing a distinction between the self-conscious physical entity on the one hand, and the idea of the individual as a cultural value on the other was to focus his analysis on the 'individual' as an idea that may or may not be valued in a given society and thus 'avoid making him a universal unit of comparison' (Dumont 1980 [1966]: 9, cited in Mines 1994: 4). Yet one could question further Dumont's idea of the self-conscious physical entity by asking if the person and the self are understood as the same or distinct in this formulation. The idea of the individual in Dumont's reading must be more than an idea of greater or lesser cultural value, for individuality to be *experienced* by persons, be they renouncers or men-in-the-world, and value to be thereby attributed *to* the individual. Though renouncers are socially marked out as 'outside-the-world', and thus are psychophysically distinct from laity, they nonetheless do not always adhere as closely as they might wish to the ascetic ideal. For example, in the Thai context the cultivation of non-self provides the social and psychological space for the renouncer to progress in meditation, but the way in which individual renouncers employ this opportunity is varied and, paradoxically, dependent upon the agency of the individual.

For Dumont individuality is understood as an achievement that is *applied* to the religion of caste. Behind Dumont's analysis of the caste system and Western individualism is, of course, his division of the world on a binary axis: East and West, collective and individual, hierarchy and equality, them and us. It follows from this that religion belongs to the collective and individuality to the renouncer, though the *saṃnyāsa* elements incorporated into the religion of caste are necessarily religious. Thus, Dumont robs himself of a way of analysing the collectivity of the renouncer. The balance Dumont identifies between what we might call 'fission and fusion', between the renouncer and society, ultimately does not account for the agency of individual renouncers. The unique position of the renouncer identified by Dumont makes no account of the society in which the renouncer finds himself, and yet presupposes just that society, for the religion of the individual to have impacted upon Hinduism to such an extent.

INDIVIDUALITY AND COMMUNITY

Through the foregoing we have seen that the categories of monastic and lay are not fixed or mutually exclusive and, furthermore, that members of the community are relationally located through distinctions such as ordination lineage, education, age, time in robes. In focusing on *mae chee*'s involvement in monastic hierarchy and practice I have attempted to draw out the changing roles of women, their engagement with hierarchy and involvement in religious practice. I have argued that *mae chee* are becoming monasticized while remaining hierarchically inferior to monks. This was shown through the examination of alms donations in Chapter 7. *Mae chee* receive alms from laity as monastics and on behalf of the monastic community, and thereby perform the religious duties of monastics. However, they also donate alms to monks and as such they engage in emblematically lay religious practices. I have argued that *mae chee* mediate in a relationship of generalized reciprocity between the monastic community and lay society. Giving and receiving alms is meritoriously accumulative but monastics also understand it to be an important arena for the cultivation of virtues such as generosity and non-attachment. Through service to the monastery and observance of hierarchy, *mae chee* are involved in emblematic religious practices in qualified ways. As we saw in Chapter 6, for monastics to strive towards an embodiment of the soteriological message of Buddhist detachment is understood as an act of giving and it is through such religiously meaningful practices that *mae chee* are being recognized as monastics.

This raises some important questions about the role of community and hierarchy in the process of renunciation. The monastic community in Wat Bonamron is rigidly hierarchical and *mae chee* are always located as inferior to monks. *Mae chee* are being recognized as religious professionals in previously male-defined spheres but this is being enacted through their embodiment of the virtues of equanimity, humility and service – idioms that have historically marked their subordination. *Mae chee* are involved in 'domestic' activities such as cooking, cleaning and office work. They also have important religious duties such as learning and teaching *dhamma*, practising and teaching meditation, receiving alms and administering to the laity. Importantly, *mae chee* understand all their work in the monastery to be religiously significant. This includes their deference to monks in spatial separation, embodied performance and ritual responsibility, which are understood as important for cultivating the virtues of humility, equanimity and insight into non-self.

Mae chee have been progressively recognized as religious professionals in recent years as a result of easier access to education, the establishment of self-governed nunneries, increasing public profile and increasing access to monastic practices such as meditation. For the women with whom I work the changing public perception of *mae chee* is understood as a happy consequence of ethical practice: of the efforts of individuals to make themselves into certain kinds of moral and religious persons. In meditative practice and in monastic duty, *mae chee* strive to cut attachment to a sense of self and in so doing they employ their responses to gendered and hierarchical duty as a means and measure of this process.

Mae chee in this monastery never account for their own choices or practice in terms of their ability to resist structures of male authority. That women who choose to live as religious professionals understand their commitment to a gendered hierarchy to be itself religiously significant is understood here as one way in which the moral self is created and presented. *Mae chee*'s embodiment of humility and equanimity may be understood as a positive way of acting in the context of a pedagogic project of the monastery. Thus, it is through exploring the creation of the kind of person, located in a matrix of social and community concerns, they think they ought to become that accounts for the 'individual' (*moi*) and 'collective' (*personne*) significance of asceticism and renunciation for monastics themselves. It is through a social learning process that the self is trained to accord with established standards. Through the performance and control of the body the learning process leading to experiential realizations of religious ideals occurs; the ethical self is formed through the duty to be mindful.

ASCETIC INTERIORITY

Following Dumont, Collins recognizes renouncers as being in a unique position to perceive themselves as individuals, a perception which is encouraged by lay recognition. Thus the conception of non-self may provide the Buddhist specialist with a pattern of self-perception and psychological analysis and, as the instrument by which he achieves his goal, the realization of non-self and nirvana (Collins 1982: 12). Collins writes of renouncers that 'the orientation towards a purely personal and immaterial goal both differentiates them from the laity, bound up in networks of material concern, and creates the actual behavioural space in which the subjectivized interiority inculcated by meditative practices can take place' (Collins 1994: 76).

Collins analyses the co-operation between laity and renouncers in what he calls 'their mutually performed socioreligious theater' (Collins 1994), and discusses the self-analysis which is the basis of mindful reflection. He argues that monastic discipline, meditation on the body and effort to eradicate desire create cognitive space within the practitioner for individualized, privatized and subjectivized analysis. Also, he holds that the social position of the monastic order, in theory and practice, enables monks to be construed, by themselves and others, as 'independent, autonomous, and individual agents' (Collins 1994: 76). Collins's discussion is revealing in that he tries to show how 'not-self' becomes a practice in which truth is realized: 'a practice which might be summarized as a certain kind of textualized meditative introspection, occurring within a specific, performed social and behavioural environment' (Collins 1994: 79).

In the Buddhist context salvation depends upon the efforts of the individual person and as such the actions a person has performed and the resultant wisdom and *kamma* that have accrued are important. Though negative actions may be the result of bad *kamma*, and negative responses may be the result of defilement, the effort to behave well and meritoriously is the responsibility of the individual actor. As we saw in Chapter 4, one's actions become a demonstration to others of what/who one is and what one has done, both in this life and previous ones. Focusing on what the employment of non-self and individuality in public life *says*, as well as what it *does*, provides us with a way of understanding hierarchy in our discussion of Thai monastic personhood. It also provides us with a way of understanding the individuality of the renouncer. This is a unique form of individuality, a neo-individuality, which is both the vehicle and the goal of Buddhist practice that, apparently paradoxically, locates the individual firmly within the social context. Meditative accomplishment may be thought of as the development of an individual set of skills but it is through those skills that the self becomes divided. Through mindfulness the self is divided and dissolved into different stances of self or self-positions. As we have seen, *vipassanā* practice identifies a self that feels and a self that observes feeling. This leads finally and ideally to non-identification with any of these stances of self; it is more than the displacement of the centre of control of the self. Like a vanishing trick, the self is revealed to be in none of the places it at first appeared. The self-willed practice of the monastic is enhanced by the moral expectations of others and it is in the seeming paradox of monastic performance – one's awareness of oneself as a spectacle of asceticism and the reality of one's own imperfection – that the monastic ideal may be actualized.

By teaching meditation monastics make it possible for laity to engage comfortably in both worldly involvement and clerical ideology. It is in this way that Wat Bonamron has become a place of utmost relevance to the laity within a period of modernization and social change. Furthermore, it is in this context that *mae chee* are able to sit comfortably between monks and laity, working, meditating and teaching meditation in the monastery, thereby ascribing to themselves new kinds of religious authority and prestige without calling into question the religious authority of monks, yet being identified as monastic. The visual icon of the *mae chee* becomes closely connected to contemporary patterns of Buddhist focus and organization, as through the behaviour of *mae chee* one is ideally presented with an ideal embodiment of mindfulness. Through working for the monastery both monks and *mae chee* incorporate the material activity that ensures the running of the monastery and the community's well-being and religious practice while walking the path to *nibbāna*.

As we have seen from our discussion of Carrithers and from the ethnography presented above, in the Buddhist *moi* we have a highly sophisticated account of subjectivity. The experience of '*moi*' in this context occurs through routinization, pedagogy and private 'work'. Renunciation may not fruitfully be understood as that which is achieved through the act of ordination. Rather, it requires effort and dedication. For this reason it is not assumed that all monastics will be equally meritorious and laity seek signs of disciplined attainment in the behaviour of monastics. The way in which the monastic understands the self that he or she progressively produces is located in a community of practice. The social position of monastics means that they may be constructed by themselves and others as independent and autonomous. Through the practice of non-self and the social negotiation of identity within a hierarchical Buddhist community renouncers experience a very particular individuality. It is in Mauss's terms to focus on '*moi*' theory in the context of '*personne*'. At the same time the obverse is true: while the practice of non-self enables the renunciate to realize Buddhist soteriological truth it also becomes a way to relate to others within the monastic hierarchy.

Vipassanā has been propagated to the laity in Thailand since the 1950s; large numbers of laity now enter this monastery as meditation students for short periods and accept monastic precepts for the duration of their retreat; and the subsequent monasticization of social religion is enabling *mae chee* in such monasteries, though outside the ordained sangha, to define themselves and be defined by others in ways which are religious, ascetic *and* associated with prestige. The adoption of *vipassanā* as ascetic practice by laity and *mae chee* in contemporary Thailand reveals that not only is asceticism a vibrant and relevant practice in modernity but also that ascetic practice may be adopted by those outside the religious order valorized in textual Buddhism. The propagation of meditation to laity has resulted in the monasticization of popular Buddhism at the same time as such propagation is used by monastics as a means of renunciation. Through the practice of this historicized and contested tradition it becomes the responsibility of all in this monastery to develop the subjective individuated interiority of non-self.

APPENDIX

Ordination transcript for an eight-precept nun (mae chee)

Arahaṃ sammā-sambuddho bhagavā
The Blessed One is Worthy and Rightly Self-awakened.
Buddhaṃ bhagavantam abhivādemi
I bow down before the Awakened, Blessed One.
[Prostrate one time]
Svākkhato bhagavatā dhammo
The *dhamma* is well-expounded by the Blessed One.
Dhammaṃ namassāmi
I pay homage to the *dhamma*
[Prostrate one time]
Supaṭipanno bhagavato sāvaka-saṅgho
The sangha of the Blessed One's disciples has practised well.
Saṅghaṃ namāmi
I pay respect to the sangha.
[Prostrate one time]
Namo tassa bhagavato arahato sammā-sambuddhassa [repeat three times]
Homage to the Blessed One, the Worthy One, the Rightly
   Self-awakened One.
[Prostrate three times]
*Esāhaṃ bhante, sucira-parinibbutaṃ pi taṃ bhagavantaṃ saraṇaṃ
   gacchāmi, dhammañ ca bhikkhu-saṅghañ ca, pabbajjitaṃ maṃ bhante
   saṅgho dhāretu, ajjatagge pāṇupetaṃ saraṇaṃ gataṃ*
Venerable Sir, I take refuge in the Blessed One – though he long ago
   attained liberation – together with the *dhamma* and the *bhikkhu*
   sangha. May the sangha henceforth regard me as one gone forth,
   having attained refuge from this day forward.
Dutiyaṃ pi esāhaṃ bhante . . .
Venerable Sir, a second time . . .

> *Tatiyaṃ pi esāhaṃ bhante* . . .
> Venerable Sir, a third time . . .
> [Prostrate three times, change robes outside and return]
> [Prostrate three times]
> *Ahaṃ bhante, ti-saraṇena saha aṭṭha sīlāni yacāmi*
> Venerable Sir, I request the Three Refuges and the Eight Precepts.
> *Dutiyaṃ pi ahaṃ bhante* . . .
> Venerable Sir, a second time . . .
> *Tatiyaṃ pi ahaṃ bhante* . . .
> Venerable Sir, a third time . . .

The monk then recites the following passage three times, after which the *mae chee* repeats it three times:

> *Nammo tassa bhagavato arahato sammā-sambuddhassa*
> Homage to the Blessed One, the Worthy One, the Rightly
>   Self-awakened One.
> [Prostrate three times]

The monk then recites the following passages line by line, with the *mae chee* reciting line by line after him:

1. *Pāṇātipātā-veramaṇī sikkhāpadaṃ samādiyāmi*
   I undertake the precept to refrain from destroying living creatures.
2. *Adinnādānā-veramaṇī sikkhāpadaṃ samādiyāmi*
   I undertake the precept to refrain from taking what is not given.
3. *Abrahmacariyā-veramaṇī sikkhāpadaṃ samādiyāmi*
   I undertake the precept to refrain from any kind of erotic behaviour.
4. *Musāvādā-veramaṇī sikkhāpadaṃ samādiyāmi*
   I undertake the precept to refrain from incorrect speech.
5. *Surāmerayamajjapamādaṭṭhāna-veramaṇī sikkhāpadaṃ samadiyāmi*
   I undertake the precept to refrain from intoxicating liquor and drugs, which lead to carelessness.
6. *Vikālabhojanā-veramaṇī sikkhāpadaṃ samādiyāmi*
   I undertake the precept to refrain from eating at the wrong time.
7. *Naccagītavāditavisūkadassana-mālāgandhavilepanadhāraṇa-mandanavibhūsanaṭṭhāna-veramaṇī sikkhāpadaṃ samadiyāmi*
   I undertake the precept to refrain from dancing, singing, music, going to shows, wearing garlands and beautifying oneself with perfumes and cosmetics.
8. *Uccāsayana-mahāsayana-veramaṇi sikkhāpadaṃ samadiyāmi*
   I undertake the precept to refrain from lying on high or luxurious sleeping beds.

Imāni aṭṭha sikkhāpadāni samādiyāmi [repeat three times]
I undertake these eight precepts [repeat three times]
    Leader:
Imāni aṭṭha sikkhāpadāni silena sugatiṃ yanti silena bhogasampadaṃ silena nibbutiṃ yanti tasmā silaṃ visodhaye
These Eight Precepts have morality as a vehicle for happiness, good fortune and liberation. Let morality therefore be purified.
    [Prostrate three times]

Bibliography

Abhisit, V. 2009. 'Statement by His Excellency Mr. Abhisit Vejjajiva Prime Minister of the Kingdom of Thailand at the General Debate of the 64th Session of the UN General Assembly New York.' 29 September. www.un.org/ga/64/generaldebate/pdf/TH_en.pdf (accessed 13/2/10).

Adiele, F. 2004. *Meeting Faith: The Forest Journals of A Black Buddhist Nun.* New York: Norton.

Alter, J. 2004. *Yoga in Modern India: the Body Between Science and Philosophy.* Princeton, NJ and Oxford: Princeton University Press.

Anisa, S. and W. Krittaya. 2004. 'Thailand: Centre of Buddhist Learning and Traditions'. *Tourism Authority of Thailand, e-magazine.* www.tatrans.org/common/print.asp?id=2146 (accessed 30/6/08).

Appadurai, A. 1986. *The Social Life of Things: Commodities in Cultural Perspective.* Cambridge: Cambridge University Press.

(Phra Khru) Arunthammarangsri. 1999. *Monpithi plae samrap Phra Phiksusamanen lae Buddhasasanikachon tua bai.* Bangkok: Mahamakut Monastic University Press.

Bailey, F. G. 1983. *The Tactical Uses of Passion.* Ithaca, NY and London: Cornell University Press.

Barnes, N. J. 1996. 'Buddhist Women and the Nuns' Order in Asia'. In C. S. Queen and S. B. King (eds.), *Engaged Buddhism: Buddhist Liberation Movements in Asia.* Albany, NY: State University of New York Press, pp. 259–94.

Bayly, S. 1999. *The New Cambridge History of India.* Vol. IV, pt 3. *Caste, Society and Politics in India from the Eighteenth Century to the Modern Age.* Cambridge: Cambridge University Press.

2004. 'Conceptualizing from Within: Divergent Religious Modes from Asian Modernist Perspectives'. In H. Whitehouse and J. Laidlaw (eds.), *Ritual and Memory: Toward a Comparative Anthropology of Religion.* Walnut Creek, CA: AltaMira, pp. 111–34.

Beatty, A. 1999. 'On Ethnographic Experience: Formative and Informative'. In C. W. Watson (ed.), *Being There: Fieldwork in Anthropology.* London and Sterling, VA: Pluto Press, pp. 74–98.

Benjamin, W. 1997 [1916]. 'On Language as Such and On the Language of Man'. In *One-Way Street.* New York: Verso.

Benson, S. 2000. 'Inscriptions of the Self: Reflections on Tattooing and Piercing in Contemporary Euro-America'. In J. Caplan (ed.), *Written on the Body: The Tattoo in European and American History*. London: Reaktion Books, pp. 234–54.

Blackstone, K. 1998. *Women in the Footsteps of the Buddha: Struggle for Liberation in the Therīgāthā*. Richmond: Curzon.

Bloch, M. 1998. *How We Think They Think: Anthropological Approaches to Cognition, Memory, and Literacy*. Boulder, CO: Westview Press.

Bloch, M. and J. Parry. 1989. 'Introduction: Money and the Morality of Exchange'. In J. Parry and M. Bloch (eds.), *Money and the Morality of Exchange*. Cambridge: Cambridge University Press, pp. 1–32.

Boellstorff, T. and J. Lindquist. 2004. 'Bodies of Emotion: Rethinking Culture and Emotion through Southeast Asia'. *Ethnos*, vol. 69, 437–44.

Brown, P. 1988. *The Body and Society*. New York: Columbia University Press.

Brown, S. 2001. *The Journey of One Buddhist Nun: Even Against the Wind*. Albany, NY: State University of New York Press.

Bunnag, J. 1973. *Buddhist Monk, Buddhist Layman: A Study of Urban Monastic Organization in Central Thailand*. Cambridge: Cambridge University Press.

Burghart, R. 1983. 'Renunciation in the Religious Traditions of South Asia'. *Man*, vol. 18, 635–53.

Busby, C. 2000. *The Performance of Gender: An Anthropology of Everyday Life in a South Indian Fishing Village*. London and New Brunswick, NJ: Athlone Press.

Butler, J. 1993. *Bodies that Matter: On the Discursive Limits of 'Sex'*. New York: Routledge.

Carrier, J. 1995. *Occidentalism: Images of the West*. Oxford: Clarendon.

Carrithers, M. 1979. 'The Modern Ascetics of Lanka and the Pattern of Change in Buddhism'. *Man (N.S.)*, vol. 14.

   1983. *The Forest Monks of Sri Lanka: An Anthropological and Historical Study*. Delhi: Oxford University Press.

   1984. 'The Domestication of the Sangha'. *Man (N.S.)*, vol. 19, 321–2.

   1985. 'An Alternative Social History of the Self'. In M. Carrithers, S. Collins and S. Lukes (eds.), *The Category of the Person: Anthropology, Philosophy, History*. Cambridge: Cambridge University Press, pp. 234–57.

   1990. 'Jainism and Buddhism as Enduring Historical Streams'. *Journal of the Anthropological Society of Oxford*, vol. 21, 141–63.

Carsten, J. 1989. 'Cooking Money: Gender and the Symbolic Transformation of Means of Exchange in a Malay Fishing Community'. In J. Parry and M. Bloch (eds.), *Money and The Morality of Exchange*. Cambridge: Cambridge University Press.

Chatsumarn, K. 1991. *Thai Women in Buddhism*. Berkeley, CA: Parallax Press.

Chatterjee, P. 1993. *The Nation and Its Fragments: Colonial and Postcolonial Histories*. Princeton, NJ: Princeton University Press.

Chirasombutti, V. and A. Diller. 1999. '"Who am 'I' in Thai?"–The Thai First Person: Self-reference or Gendered Self?' In P. A. Jackson and N. M. Cook (eds.), *Genders and Sexualities in Modern Thailand*. Chiang Mai: Silkworm Books, pp. 114–33.

Coleman, S. 2006. 'Materializing the Self: Words and Gifts in the Construction of Charismatic Protestant Identity'. In F. Cannell (ed.), *The Anthropology of Christianity*. Durham, NC and London: Duke University Press, pp. 163–84.

Collins, S. 1982. *Selfless Persons: Imagery and Thought in Theravada Buddhism*. Cambridge: Cambridge University Press.

  1994. 'What are Buddhists Doing When They Deny the Self?' In F. Reynolds and D. Tracy (eds.), *Religion and Practical Reason: New Essays in the Comparative Philosophy of Religions*. Albany, NY: State University of New York Press, pp. 59–86.

  1997. 'The Body in Theravada Buddhist Monasticism'. In S. Coakley (ed.), *Religion and the Body*. Cambridge: Cambridge University Press, pp. 185–204.

Collins, S. and J. McDaniel. 2010. 'Buddhist "Nuns" (Mae Chi) and the Teaching of Pali in Contemporary Thailand'. *Modern Asian Studies* (published online 21 April).

Cook, J. 2008a. 'Tattoos, Corporeality and the Self: Dissolving borders in a Thai monastery'. *Cambridge Anthropology*, vol. 27, no. 2, 20–35.

  2008b. 'Alms, Money and Reciprocity: Buddhist Nuns as Mediators of Generalized Exchange in Thailand'. *Anthropology in Action Special Edition: Gift Exchange in Modern Society*, vol. 15, no. 3, 8–21.

  2009. 'Hagiographic Narrative and Monastic Practice: Buddhist Morality and Mastery Amongst Thai Buddhist Nuns', *Journal of the Royal Anthropological Institute*, no. 15, 2, 349–64.

Copeman, J. 2005. 'Veinglory: Exploring Processes of Blood Transfer Between Persons'. *Journal of the Royal Anthropological Institute*, vol. 11, no. 3, 465–85.

Daniel, E. V. 1984. *Fluid Signs: Being a Person the Tamil Way*. Berkeley, CA: University of California Press.

Darlington, S. M. 1998. 'The Ordination of a Tree: The Buddhist Ecology Movement in Thailand'. *Ethnology*, vol. 37, no. 1, 1–15.

  2000. 'Rethinking Buddhism and Development: The Emergence of Environmentalist Monks in Thailand'. *Journal of Buddhist Ethics*, vol. 7. Online.

Das, V. 1995. *Critical Events: An Anthropological Perspective on Contemporary India*. Oxford and New York: Oxford University Press.

Derrida, J. 1992. *Given Time 1: Counterfeit Money*. Chicago, IL: University of Chicago Press.

Diller, A. 2002. 'What Makes Central Thai a National Language?' In C. J. Reynolds (ed.), *National Identity and its Defenders: Thailand Today*. Bangkok: Silkworm Books, pp. 71–107.

Dirks, N. B. 1987. *The Hollow Crown: Ethnohistory of an Indian Kingdom*. Cambridge: Cambridge University Press.

  1989. 'The Original Caste: Power, History, and Hierarchy in South Asia'. *Contributions to Indian Sociology (N.S.)*, vol. 23, 79–101.

Drougge, P. 2007. 'Almost Homeless – Emerging Forms of Buddhist Monasticism'. Paper presented to Meeting of the Society for the Anthropology of Religion. 13–16 April. Phoenix, AZ.
Drummond, S., G. Brown, J. Gillin, J. Stricker, E. Wong, and R. Buxton. 2000. 'Altered Brain Response to Verbal Learning following Sleep Deprivation'. *Nature* 403, 655–57.
Dumont, L. 1965. 'The Functional Equivalents of the Individual'. *Indian Sociology*, vol. 8, 85–99.
  1977. *From Mandeville to Marx*. Chicago: University of Chicago Press.
  1980 [1966]. *Homo Hierarchicus: The Caste System and its Implications*. Chicago, IL and London: University of Chicago Press.
  1985. 'A Modified View of our Origins: The Christian Beginnings of Modern Individualism'. In M. Carrithers, S. Collins and S. Lukes (eds.), *The Category of the Person: Anthropology, Philosophy, History*. Cambridge: Cambridge University Press, pp. 93–122.
Falk, N. A. and R. Gross. 1980. *Unspoken Worlds: Women's Religious Lives in Non-western Cultures*. San Francisco, CA: Harper & Row.
Fernandez, J. and M. Herzfeld. 1998. 'In Search of Meaningful Methods'. In H. Russell Bernard (ed.), *Handbook of Methods in Cultural Anthropology*. Walnut Creek, CA: AltiMira Press, pp. 89–130.
Flood, G. 2004. *The Ascetic Self: Subjectivity, Memory and Tradition*. Cambridge: Cambridge University Press.
Foucault, M. 2000a. 'The Battle for Chastity'. In P. Rabinow (ed.), *Essential Works of Michel Foucault*. Vol. 1. *Ethics: Subjectivity and Truth*. London: Penguin Books, pp. 185–98.
  2000b. 'On the Genealogy of Ethics: An Overview of Work in Progress'. In P. Rabinow (ed.), *Essential Works of Michel Foucault*. Vol. 1. *Ethics: Subjectivity and Truth*. Penguin Books, pp. 253–80.
  2000c. 'Polemics, Politics, and Problematizations: An Interview with Michel Foucault'. In P. Rabinow (ed.), *Essential Works of Michel Foucault*. Vol. 1. *Ethics: Subjectivity and Truth*. London: Penguin Books, pp. 111–20.
  2000d. 'Technologies of the Self'. In P. Rabinow (ed.), *Essential Works of Michel Foucault*. Vol. 1. *Ethics: Subjectivity and Truth*. London: Penguin Books, pp. 223–52.
Freiberger, O. 2006. 'Introduction: The Criticism of Asceticism in Comparative Perspective'. In O. Freiberger (ed.), *Asceticism and Its Critics: Historical Accounts and Comparative Perspectives*. Oxford and New York: Oxford University Press, pp. 3–24.
Geertz, C. 1973. *The Interpretation of Cultures*. New York: Basic Books.
Gellner, D. and S. LeVine. 2005. *Rebuilding Buddhism: The Theravada Movement in Twentieth-Century Nepal*. Cambridge, MA: Harvard University Press.
Gombrich, R. 1971. *Precept and Practice*. Oxford: Oxford University Press.
Gombrich, R. and G. Obeyesekere. 1988. *Buddhism Transformed: Religious Change in Sri Lanka*. Princeton, NJ: Princeton University Press.
Gregory, C. A. 1982. *Gifts and Commodities*. London: Academic Press.

Harris, I. 1995. 'Getting to Grips with Buddhist Environmentalism: A Provisional Typology'. *Journal of Buddhist Ethics*, vol. 2, 173–90.
Hastrup, K. and P. Hervik (eds.). 1994. *Social Experience and Anthropological Knowledge*. London: Routledge.
Heelas, P. 1991, 'Cults for Capitalism: Self Religions, Magic and the Empowerment of Business'. In P. Gee and J. Fulton (eds.), *Religion and Power, Decline and Growth*. London: British Sociological Association, Sociology of Religion Study Group, pp. 28–42.
  1992. 'The Sacralization of the Self and New Age Capitalism'. In N. Abercrombie and A. Warde (eds.), *Social Change in Contemporary Britain*. Cambridge: Polity Press, pp. 139–66.
  1996. 'Introduction: Detraditionalization and its Rivals'. In P. Heelas, S. Lash and P. Morris (eds.), *Detraditionalization: Critical Reflections on Authority and Identity*. Oxford and Cambridge, MA: Blackwell, pp. 1–20.
  2002. 'The Spiritual Revolution: From "religion" to "spirituality"'. In L. Woodhead, P. Fletcher, H. Kawanami and D. Smith (eds.), *Religions in the Modern World: Traditions and Transformations*. London: Routledge, pp. 357–77.
Heesterman, J. C. 1985. *The Inner Conflict of Tradition: Essays in Indian Ritual, Kingship, and Society*. Chicago, IL: University of Chicago Press.
Herdt, G. 1994. *Third Sex, Third Gender*. New York: Zone Books.
Hewison, K. 2000. 'Resisting Globalization: A Study of Localism in Thailand'. *The Pacific Review*, vol. 13, no. 2, 279–96.
  2001. 'Nationalism, Populism, Dependency: Southeast Asia and Responses to the Asian Crisis'. *Singapore Journal of Tropical Geography*, vol. 22, iss. 3, 219–36.
Hick, J. 1995. 'Foreword'. In V. Wimbush and R. Valantasis (eds.), *Asceticism*. New York and Oxford: Oxford University Press, pp. ix–x.
Hirschkind, C. 2001. 'The Ethics of Listening: Cassette-sermon Audition in Contemporary Cairo'. *American Ethnologist*, vol. 28, no. 3, 623–49.
  2006. *The Ethical Soundscape: Cassette Sermons and Islamic Counterpublics*. New York: Columbia University Press.
Holt, J. 1991. 'Protestant Buddhism?' (review of Gombrich and Obeyesekere 1988). *Religious Studies Review*, vol. 17, no. 4, 307–12.
Houtman, G. 1990. 'Traditions of Buddhist Practice in Burma'. PhD: School of Oriental and African Studies (University of London).
Humphrey, C. and J. Laidlaw. 1994. *The Archetypal Actions of Ritual: A Theory of Ritual Illustrated by the Jain Rite of Worship*. Oxford: Clarendon Press.
Inden, R. 1976. *Marriage and Rank in Bengali Culture*. Berkeley, CA: University of California Press.
  1990. *Imagining India*. Oxford: Basil Blackwell.
Inden, R. and R. W. Nicholas. 1977. *Kinship in Bengali Culture*. Chicago, IL: University of Chicago Press.
Ishwaran, K. (ed.). 1999. *Ascetic Culture: Renunciation and Worldly Engagement*. Leiden: Brill.

Jackson, P. A. 1999. *Buddhism, Legitimation and Conflict: The Political Functions of Urban Thai Buddhism*. Singapore: Institute of Southeast Asian Studies.
  1997. 'Withering Centre, Flourishing Margins: Buddhism's Changing Political Roles'. In K. Hewison (ed.), *Political Change in Thailand: Democracy and Participation*. London: Routledge, pp. 75–93.
  2003. *Buddhadasa: Theravada Buddhism and Modernist Reform in Thailand*. Bangkok: Silkworm Books.
Jordt, I. 2007a. '"What is a "True Buddhist"?: Meditation and the Formation of Knowledge Communities in Burma'. *Ethnology*, vol. 45, no. 3, 193–208.
  2007b. *Burma's Mass Lay Meditation Movement: Buddhism and the Cultural Construction of Power*. Athens, OH: Ohio University Press.
  2008. 'Transnational Buddhism and the Transformations of Local Power in Thailand'. Paper presented to The 10th International Conference on Thai Studies, 9–11 Jan. Thammasat University, Bangkok, Thailand.
Karim, W. J. 1990. *Emotions of Culture: A Malay Perspective*. Singapore: Oxford University Press.
Kelty, C. 2002. *Hau to Do Things with Words*. Creative Commons Public License.
Keyes, C. F. 1978. 'Ethnography and Anthropological Interpretation in the Study of Thailand'. In E. B. Ayal (ed.), *The Study of Thailand: Analyses of Knowledge, Approaches, and Prospects in Anthropology, Art History, Economics, History, and Political Science*. Athens, OH: Ohio University Center of International Studies, pp. 1–66.
  1981. 'Death of Two Buddhist Saints in Thailand'. In M. Williams (ed.), *Charisma and Sacred Biography*. Chico, CA: Scholars Press, pp. 149–80.
  1983. 'The Study of Popular Ideas of Karma'. In C. F. Keyes and E. V. Daniel (eds.), *Karma: An Anthropological Inquiry*. Berkeley, CA: University of California Press, pp. 1–24.
  1984. 'Mother or Mistress but Never a Monk: Buddhist Notions of Female Gender in Rural Thailand'. *American Ethnologist*, vol. 11, 223–41.
  1986. 'Ambiguous Gender: Male Initiation in a Northern Thai Buddhist Society'. In C. W. Bynum, S. Harrell and P. Richman (eds.), *Gender and Religion: On the Complexity of Symbols*. Boston, MA: Beacon Press, pp. 66–96.
  1999. 'Buddhism Fragmented: Thai Buddhism and Political Order since the 1970s'. Keynote Address, Seventh International Conference on Thai Studies, 4–8 July, Amsterdam.
Kirsch, A. T. 1977. 'Complexity in the Thai Religious system: An Interpretation'. *Journal of Asian Studies*, vol. 36, no. 2, 241–66.
  1985. 'Text and Context: Buddhist Sex Roles/the Culture of Gender Revisited'. *American Ethnologist*, vol. 12, 302–20.
Klima, A. 2002. *The Funeral Casino: Meditation, Massacre, and Exchange with the Dead in Thailand*. Princeton, NJ and Oxford: Princeton University Press.
  2004. 'Thai Love Thai: Financing Emotion in Post-crash Thailand'. *Ethnos*, vol. 69, 445–64.
Kornfield, J. 1993 [1977]. *Living Buddhist Masters*. Kandy, Sri Lanka: Buddhist Publication Society.

La Loubere, S. D. 1986 [1691]. *The Kingdom of Siam*. Oxford: Oxford University Press.

Laidlaw, J. 1995. *Riches and Renunciation: Religion, Economy, and Society among the Jains*. Oxford: Clarendon Press.

  2000. 'A Free Gift Makes No Friends'. *Journal of the Royal Anthropological Institute*, vol. 6, 617–34.

  2002. 'For an Anthropology of Ethics and Freedom'. *Journal of the Royal Anthropological Institute*, vol. 8, 311–32.

  2005. 'A Life Worth Leaving: Fasting to Death as Telos of a Jain Religious Life'. *Economy and Society*, vol. 34, 178–99.

  2006. 'A Well-disposed Social Anthropologist's Problems with the "Cognitive Science of Religion"'. In H. Whitehouse and J. Laidlaw (eds.), *Religion, Anthropology, and Cognitive Science*, Durham, NC: Carolina Academic Press, pp. 211–46.

  2008. 'The Generality of Well-being: The Concept of "Well-being", and the Encounter of Jain Ascetic Non-violence with Utilitarian Animal Liberation and Environmentalism'. In A. Corsin Jimenez (ed.), *Culture and Well-being: Anthropological Approaches to Freedom and Political Ethics*. London: Pluto Press, pp. 156–79.

Lave, J. and E. Wenger. 1991. *Situated Learning: Legitimate Peripheral Participation*. Cambridge: Cambridge University Press.

Lester, R. 2005. *Jesus in Our Wombs: Embodying Modernity in a Mexican Convent*. Berkeley, CA and London: University of California Press.

Lindberg Falk, M. 2000. 'Thammacarini Witthaya: The First Buddhist School for Girls in Thailand'. In K. L. Tsomo (ed.), *Innovative Buddhist Women: Swimming Against the Stream*. Richmond: Curzon.

  2002. *Making Fields of Merit: Buddhist Nuns Challenge Gendered Orders in Thailand*. Goteborg University, Department of Social Anthropology: Kompendiet.

  2007. *Making Fields of Merit: Buddhist Nuns and Gendered Orders in Thailand*. Copenhagen Nias Press. (Originally published as a thesis, 2002.)

Luhrmann, T. 1989. *Persuasions of the Witch's Craft: Ritual Magic and Witchcraft in Present-Day England*. Oxford: Basil Blackwell.

  2000. *Of Two Minds: The Growing Disorder in American Psychiatry*. New York: Alfred A. Knopf.

  2009. 'What Counts as Data?' In J. Davies and D. Spencer (eds.), *Emotions in the Field: The Psychology and Anthropology of Fieldwork Experience*. Stanford, CA: Stanford University Press.

Lutz, C. 1988. *Unnatural Emotions: Everyday Sentiments on a Micronesian Atoll and their Challenge to Western Theory*. Chicago: University of Chicago Press.

Lutz, C. and G. White. 1986. 'The Anthropology of Emotions'. *Annual Review of Anthropology* 15, 405–36.

MacIntyre, A. 1988. *Whose Justice? Which Rationality?* London: Duckworth.

Madan, T. N. 1982. *Way of Life: King, Householder, Renouncer: Essays in Honour of Louis Dumont*. New Delhi: Motilal Banarsidass.

1987. *Non-Renunciation: Themes and Interpretations of Hindu Culture*. Delhi, New York and Oxford: Oxford University Press.
Mahmood, S. 2001. 'Feminist Theory, Embodiment, and the Docile Agent: Some Reflections on the Egyptian Islamic Revival'. *Cultural Anthropology*, vol. 16, 202–36.
  2005. *Politics of Piety: the Islamic Revival and the Feminist Subject*. Princeton, NJ: Princeton University Press.
Malinowski, B. 1922. *Argonauts of the Western Pacific: An Account of the Native Enterprise and Adventure in the Archipelagos of Melanesian New Guinea*. London: Routledge.
Marriott, M. 1976a. 'Hindu Transactions: Diversity without Dualism'. In B. Kapferer (ed.), *Transaction and Meaning*. Philadelphia, PA: Institute for the Study of Human Issues.
  1976b. 'Interpreting Indian Society: A Monistic Alternative to Dumont's Dualism'. *Journal of Asian Studies*, vol. 36, 189–95.
  1989. 'Constructing an Indian Ethnosociology'. *Contributions to Indian Sociology (N.S.)*, vol. 23, 1–39.
  1990. *India Through Hindu Categories*. New Delhi, Newbury Park and London: Sage Publications.
Mauss, M. 1966. *The Gift: Forms and Functions of Exchange in Archaic Societies*. London: Cohen and West.
  1985. 'A Category of the Human Mind: The Notion of the Person; the Notion of the Self'. In M. Carrithers, S. Collins and S. Lukes (eds.), *The Category of the Person: Anthropology, Philosophy, History*. Cambridge: Cambridge University Press, pp. 1–26.
McCargo, D. 2001. 'Populism and Reformism in Contemporary Thailand'. *South East Asia Research*, vol. 9, 89–107.
  2004. 'Buddhism, democracy and identity in Thailand'. *Democratization*, vol. 11, no. 4, 155–70.
McDaniel, J. 2006a. 'Buddhism in Thailand: Negotiating the Modern Age'. In S. Berkwitz (ed.), *Buddhism in World Cultures: Comparative Perspectives (Religion in Contemporary Cultures)*. Santa-Barbara, CA: ABC-CLIO Ltd, pp. 101–28.
  2006b. 'Liturgies and Cacophonies in Thai Buddhism'. *Aseanie*, vol. 18, 119–50.
  2008. *Gathering Leaves and Lifting Words: Histories of Buddhist Monastic Education in Laos and Thailand*. Seattle, WA and London: University of Washington Press.
Mills, M. B. 1999. *Thai Women in the Global Labor Force: Consuming Desires, Contested Selves*. New Brunswick, NJ: Rutgers University Press.
Mines, M. 1994. *Public Faces, Private Voices: Community and Individuality in South India*. Berkeley, CA: University of California Press.
Morris, R. C. 2000. *In the Place of Origins: Modernity and Its Mediums in Northern Thailand*. Durham, NC and London: Duke University Press.
Nietzsche, F. 1996. *On the Genealogy of Morals: A Polemic*. Oxford: Oxford University Press.

Nyanaponika, T. 1973. *The Heart of Buddhist Meditation*. New York: Samuel Weiser Inc.

Obeyesekere, G. 1992. *The Apotheosis of Captain Cook: European Mythmaking in the Pacific*. Princeton, NJ: Princeton University Press; Bishop Museum Press.

Ockey, J. 2005. *Making Democracy: Leadership, Class, Gender, and Political Participation in Thailand*. Honolulu, HI: University of Hawaii Press.

Olivelle, P. 2006. 'The Ascetic and the Domestic in Brahmanical Religiosity'. In O. Freiberger (ed.), *Asceticism and Its Critics: Historical Accounts and Comparative Perspectives*. Oxford and New York: Oxford University Press, pp. 25–42.

Ostor, A., L. Fruzzetti and S. Barnett. 1992. *Concepts of Person: Kinship, Caste, and Marriage in India*. Delhi: Oxford University Press.

Pandita, S. U. 2002. *In This Very Life: Liberation Teachings of the Buddha*. Somerville, MA: Wisdom Publications.

Parkin, D. 1985. 'Reason, Emotion, and the Embodiment of Power'. In J. Overing (ed.), *Reason and Morality*. London: Tavistock Publications.

Parnwell, M. and M. Seeger. 2008. 'The Relocalization of Buddhism in Thailand'. *The Journal of Buddhist Ethics*, vol. 15, 79–176.

Parry, J. 1985. 'The Brahmanical Tradition and the Technology of the Intellect'. In J. Overing (ed.), *Reason and Morality*. London and New York: Tavistock Publications, pp. 200–25.

  1986. 'The Gift, The Indian Gift and the "Indian Gift"'. *Man (N.S.)*, 21, 453–73.

  1989. 'On the Moral Perils of Exchange'. In J. Parry and M. Bloch (eds.), *Money and the Morality of Exchange*. Cambridge: Cambridge University Press, pp. 64–93.

Pattana, K. 2005a. 'Beyond Syncretism: Hybridisation of Popular Religion in Contemporary Thailand'. *Journal of Southeast Asian Studies*, vol. 36, no. 3, 461–87.

  2005b. 'Magic Monks and Spirit Mediums in the Politics of Thai Popular Religion'. *Inter-Asia Cultural Studies*, vol. 6, no. 2, 209–26.

  2007. 'Bodies in Thai Buddhism'. Paper presented to Syncretism in South and Southeast Asia: Adoption and Adaptation. 26 May. Mahidol University, Nakhon Pathom, Thailand.

Peletz, M. G. 1996. *Reason and Passion: Representations of Gender in a Malay Society*. Berkeley, CA: University of California Press.

Pilcher, J. and A. Huffcutt. 1996. 'Effects of Sleep Deprivation on Performance: A Meta-analysis'. *Sleep*, vol. 19, 318–26.

Raheja, G. G. 1988a. 'India: Caste, Kingship, and Dominance Reconsidered'. *Annual Review of Anthropology*, vol. 17, 497–522.

  1988b. *The Poison in the Gift: Ritual, Prestation, and the Dominant Caste in a North Indian Village*. Chicago, IL: University of Chicago Press.

  1989. 'Centrality, Mutuality and Hierarchy: Shifting Aspects of Intercaste Relationships in North India'. *Contributions to Indian Sociology (N.S.)*, vol. 23, 79–101.

Reynolds, C. J. 1972. 'The Buddhist Monkhood in Nineteenth Century Thailand'. PhD: Cornell University.
　1999. 'On the Gendering of Nationalist and Postnationalist Selves in Twentieth-century Thailand'. In P. A. Jackson and Nerida M. Cook (eds.), *Genders and Sexualities in Modern Thailand*. Chiang Mai: Silkworm Books, pp. 261–74.
Robbins, J. 2004. *Becoming Sinners: Christianity and Moral Torment in a Papua New Guinea Society*. Berkeley: University of California Press.
Rosaldo, M. 1980. *Knowledge and Passion: Ilongot Notions of Self and Social Life*. Cambridge: Cambridge University Press.
　1984. 'Toward an Anthropology of Self and Feeling'. In R. A. Sweder and R. A. Levine (eds.), *Culture Theory: Essays on Mind, Self, and Emotion*. Cambridge: Cambridge University Press.
Samuels, J. 2004. 'Toward an Action Oriented Pedagogy: Buddhist Texts and Monastic Education in Contemporary Sri Lanka'. *Journal of the American Academy of Religion*, vol. 72, no. 4, 955–71.
Sanitsuda, E. 2001. *Keeping the Faith: Thai Buddhism at the Crossroads*. Bangkok: Post Books.
Sayadaw, M. 1971. *Practical Insight Meditation: Basic and Progressive Stages*. U. P. Thin and M. U. Tin (trans.). Kandy, Sri Lanka: Buddhist Publication Society.
　2000. *The Fundamentals of Insight*. Bangkok: Buddhadhamma Foundation.
Seeger, M. 2009. 'The Changing Roles of Thai Buddhist Women: Obscuring Identities and Increasing Charisma'. *Religion Compass*, vol. 5, no. 3, 806–22.
Silananda, U. 1990. *The Four Foundations of Mindfulness*. Boston, MA: Wisdom Publications.
Silanandabhivumsa, A. 1982. *The Venerable Mahasi Sayadaw: Bibliography*. Trans. U Min Swe. Rangoon, Burma: Buddha Sāsanā Nuggaha Organization.
Smalley, W. A. 1988. 'Thailand's Hierarchy of Multilingualism'. *Language Sciences*, vol. 10, 245–62.
Soma, T. 1999 [1941]. *The Way of Mindfulness: The Satipatthana Sutta and its Commentary*. Kuala Lumpur: The Buddhist Publication Society.
Sperber, D. 1982. 'Apparently Irrational Beliefs'. In M. Hellis and S. Lukes (eds.), *Rationality and Relativism*. Oxford: Basil Blackwell.
Spiro, M. E. 1970. *Buddhism and Society: A Great Tradition and Its Burmese Vicissitudes*. New York: Harper & Row.
Sponberg, A. 1992. 'Attitudes Toward Women and the Feminine in Early Buddhism'. In J. I. Cabezon (ed.), *Buddhism, Sexuality, and Gender*. Albany, NY: State University of New York Press, pp. 3–36.
Stirrat, R. L. 1989. 'Money, Men and Women'. In J. Parry and M. Bloch (eds.), *Money and the Morality of Exchange*. Cambridge: Cambridge University Press, pp. 94–116.
Strathern, M. 1984. 'Subject or Object? Women and the Circulation of Valuables in Highlands New Guinea'. In R. Hirschon (ed.), *Women and Property – Women as Property*. London: Croom Helm, pp. 191–209.

1988. *The Gender of the Gift: Problems with Women and Problems with Society in Melanesia*. Berkeley, CA: University of California Press.

Strenski, I. 1983. 'On Generalized Exchange and the Domestication of the Sangha'. *Man (N.S.)*, vol. 18, 463–77.

2008. *Dumont on Religion: Difference, Comparison, Transgression*. London: Equinox.

Swearer, D. K. 1991. 'Fundamentalistic Movements in Theravāda Buddhism'. In M. E. Marty and R. S. Appleby (eds.), *Fundamentalisms Observed*. Chicago, IL: University of Chicago Press, pp. 628–90.

1995. *The Buddhist World of Southeast Asia*. Albany, NY: State University of New York Press.

1996. 'Sulak Sivaraksa's Buddhist Vision for Renewing Society'. In C. S. Queen and S. B. King (eds.), *Engaged Buddhism: Buddhist Liberation Movements in Asia*. Albany, NY: State University of New York Press, pp. 195–236.

Taffinder, N., I. McManus, Y. Gul, R. Russell and A. Darzi. 1998. 'Effect of Sleep Deprivation on Surgeons' Dexterity on Laparoscopy Simulator'. *The Lancet*, vol. 352, 155. 1, 191.

Tambiah, S. J. 1968a. 'The Ideology of Merit and the Social Correlates of Buddhism in a Thai Village'. In E. Leach (ed.), *Dialectic in Practical Reason* (Cambridge Papers in Social Anthropology, no. 5). Cambridge: Cambridge University Press.

1968b. 'The Magical Power of Words'. *Man*, vol. 3, 175–208.

1970. *Buddhism and the Spirit Cults in North-East Thailand* (Cambridge Studies in Social Anthropology, no. 2). Cambridge: Cambridge University Press.

1976. *World Conqueror and World Renouncer: A Study of Buddhism and Polity in Thailand Against a Historical Background*. Cambridge: Cambridge University Press.

1982. 'The Renouncer: His Individuality and his Community'. In T. N. Madan (ed.), *Way of Life: King, Householder, Renouncer; Essays in Honour of Louis Dumont*. New Delhi: Motilal Banarsidass, pp. 299–321.

1984. *The Buddhist Saints of the Forest and the Cult of Amulets: A Study in Charisma, Hagiography, Sectarianism, and Millennial Buddhism*. Cambridge: Cambridge University Press.

Tanabe, S. 1991. 'Spirits, Power, and the Discourse of Female Gender: The Phi Meng Cult of Northern Thailand'. In M. Chitakasem and A. Turton (eds.), *Thai Constructions of Knowledge*. London: School of Oriental and African Studies, pp. 183–212.

Tanabe, S. and C. F. Keyes. 2002. 'Introduction'. In *Cultural Crisis and Social Memory: Modernity and Identity in Thailand and Laos*. London: RoutledgeCurzon, pp. 6–25.

TAT. 2004. www.tourismthailand.org/about_thailand/overview/religion.php (accessed 30/6/08).

Taussig, M. T. 1980. *The Devil and Commodity Fetishism in South Africa*. Chapel Hill, NC: University of North Carolina Press.

Taylor, J. L. 2001. 'Embodiment, Nation, and Religio-politics in Thailand'. *South East Asia Research*, vol. 9, no. 2: 129–47.
Thitsa, K. 1980. *Providence and Prostitution: Women in Buddhist Thailand* (Women in Society). London: Change International.
Thomas, M., H. Sing, G. Belenky, H. Holcomb, H. Mayberg, R. Dannals, H. Wagner, D. Thorne, K. Popp, L. Rawland, A. Welsh, S. Balwinski and D. Redmond. 2000. 'Neural Basis of Alertness and Cognitive Performance Impairments during Sleepiness: Effects of 24h of Sleep Deprivation on Waking Human Regional Brain Activity'. *Journal of Sleep Research*, vol. 9, 335–52.
Thompson, V. 1941. *Thailand and the New Siam*. New York: Macmillan.
Tiyavanich, K. 1997. *Forest Recollections: Wandering Monks in Twentieth-Century Thailand*. Chiang Mai: Silkworm Books.
UNDV Conference Volume 2552/2009. *Buddhist Approaches to Economic Crisis*. Bangkok: Mahachulalongkornrajavidyalaya University.
Van Esterik, J. L. 1977. 'Cultural Interpretation of Canonical Paradox: Lay Meditation in a Central Thai Village'. PhD: University of Illinois.
  1996. 'Women Meditation Teachers in Thailand'. In P. van Esterik (ed.), *Women of Southeast Asia* (Center for Southeast Asian Studies, Monograph Series on Southeast Asia, Occasional Paper no. 17). Dekalb, IL: Northern Illinois University.
Van Esterik, P. 2000. *Materializing Thailand*. Oxford: Berg.
Walters, J. 2003. 'Communal Karma and Karmic Community in Theravāda Buddhist History'. In J. Hat, J. Kinnard and J. Walters (eds.), *Constituting Communities: Theravāda Buddhism and the Religious Cultures of South and Southeast Asia*. Albany: Suny Press, pp. 9–40.
Weber, M. 1948. *From Max Weber: Essays in Sociology*, H. H. Gerth and C. Wright Mills (eds.). London: Routledge & Kegan Paul.
Weiner, A. 1976. *Women of Value, Men of Renown: New Perspectives in Trobriand Exchange*. Austin, TX and London: University of Texas Press.
  1988. *The Trobrianders of Papua New Guinea*. Belmont, CA: Thompson Wadsworth.
  1992. *Inalienable Possessions: The Paradox of Keeping-While-Giving*. Berkeley, CA: University of California Press.
Wikan, U. 1990. *Managing Turbulent Hearts: A Balinese Formula for Living*. Chicago, IL: University of Chicago Press.
Williams, G. 2008. *Struggles for an Alternative Globalization: An Ethnography of Counterpower in Southern France*. London: Ashgate.
Wilson, L. 2004. *Charming Cadavers: Horrific Figurations of the Feminine in Indian Buddhist Hagiographic Literature*. Chicago, IL: University of Chicago Press.

Index

Abhidhamma 27, 34, 105, 122, 154, 160
  and meditation 32, 33
Abhisit Vejjajiva 38
Adiele, F. 6
Alms donations (*dāna*) 67, 73, 117
  and generalized exchange 14
  Offerings 62, 74, 117
  and *mae chee* 135–50
  and self-cultivation 140–1
  on alms round 59
  in envelopes 143
  Public 144–5
  Money trees as 144, 145
  and merit 149
Alter, J. 2
Anisa, S. and W. Krittaya 37
Appadurai, A. 146
arahant 29, 88, 106
Asian Financial Crisis 1997 37
Asceticism 15–18
Ascetic Interiority 13, 192–4
asubha kammaṭṭhāna 24, 167
Ayutthaya 31
Ayya Khema 163

Bailey, F. G. 126
Barnes, N. J. 5, 153, 164
Bayly, S. 42, 186
Beatty, A. 24
Belief 10, 23, 42, 96, 100, 107
  and meditation 113
Benjamin, W. 100
Benson, S. 132
bhikkhunī 4, 64, 67, 162–5
Bhumibol Adulyadej (Rama IX), King 38
Blackstone, K. 81
Bloch, M. 110
Bloch, M. and J. Parry 147
Boellstorff, T. and J. Lindquist 126
Brown, P. 16

Brown, S. 6
Buddhadasa 42
  and Buddhist modernism 42
  and *vipassanā* meditation 42
Buddhaghosa 27, 118
Buddhism
  in Thailand 1–2
  and reform 3–4, 26, 32, 43
  and localism 3, 35–40
  and understandings of self 7
  variety of focus in 15, 27, 35–45, 174–5
  Royal reformist movements 27, 30
  Demythologizing the *dhamma* 28
  and sangha unification 28
  and scientific rationality 35, 41–2
  and capitalist success 35
  and 'crisis of modernity' 36
  and Thai nationalism 36, 38, 43
  Decline and hybridity 43–5
  Lay concern for monastic purity 43
  Magical monks and spirit medium cults 44
  Monasticization and laicization 45
  Democratization of religious practice 35
  Commoditization of religion 35
  and development programs 41
  Six internal and external sense bases 91, 104
  and gender 166–7
  Engaged Buddhism 40–3, 174
  Gender and religious attainment 15, 169–70
  Sectarianism and centralization 27–31
  and spirit cults 174
Bunnag, J. 31–2, 152
Burghart, R. 48, 183, 186, 187
Burma 27
  monastery and meditation centre 45–7, 58
Busby, C. 147
Butler, J. 165

Cambodia 41
Carrier, J. 37

Index

Carrithers, M. 119, 136, 137, 171, 175–6, 178, 179–80
Carsten, J. 147
Chakri dynasty 27
Chanting 22, 52, 59, 60, 97, 98, 104, 113, 118, 121, 122, 136, 158, 181
    blessings (*hai pon*) 66
Chatsumarn Kabilsingh 153, 163
Chatterjee, P. 37
Chirasombutti, V. and A. Diller 125
Chulalongkorn, King (Rama V) 27, 28, 29
Co-dependent origination 8
Coleman, S. 35
Collins, S. 118, 132–3, 182–3, 186, 192
Collins, S. and J. McDaniel 4, 5, 6, 105
Communism 41
Community of practice 13, 133, 182, 194
Cook, J. 89, 135, 154
Copeman, J. 139

dāna, see alms donations
Daniel E. 186
Darlington, S. 41
Das, V. 186
dasa sil mata 163
Defilements (*kilesa*) 29, 71, 80, 109, 127, 192
Derrida, J. 139
Determination (*attitan*) 89–94
dhamma friends (*kalyāṇamittatā*) 69
Diller, A. 29
Dirks, N. 186
Domestication of the sangha 175–6
Drougge, P. 49
Drummond, S. 90
Dumont, L. 15, 184–90
    Renouncer and community 186–8
    and individuality 188–90

Education 105
    through monasteries 28
    Religious curricula 30
    and *mae chee* 105
Enlightenment
    Levels of 91
    Behaviour after 88

Falk, N. and R. Gross 166
Fernandez, J. and M. Herzfeld 21
Flood, G. 13, 16–17
Foucault, M. 17, 171
    and self-formation 11
    and confession 83
    and technologies of the self 86
    on ethics and freedom 87
    and the battle for chastity 86, 93, 94
Freiberger, O. 16

Geertz, C. 24, 126
Gellner, D. and S. Levine 3, 4, 163, 164
Generalised reciprocity 190
Globalization 55
    and meditation 37–8
Gombrich, R. 122
Gombrich, R. and G. Obeyesekere 1, 3, 4, 27, 33, 42, 47–9
Gregory, C. 137, 142

Harris, I 42
Hastrup, K. and P. Hervik 20
Heart/mind (*jai*) 10, 91, 104, 141
Heelas, P. 35
Heesterman, J. 186
Herdt, G. 126
Hewison, K. 38
Hirschkind, C. 11, 106–7
Holt, J. 49
Houtman, G. 3, 20, 21, 45–7, 58
Humphrey, C. and J. Laidlaw 78

Impermanence (*anicca*) 8, 24, 26, 65, 70, 73, 103, 140, 167, 177, 180
Inden, R. 186
Inden, R. and R. Nicholas 186
Individuality 13, 130, 178, 179, 182, 184–190
    and renunciation 15, 193
Institute of Thai *Mae Chee* 153
Ishwaran, K. 16

Jackson, P. 35, 36, 41, 42, 43, 44, 110
Jainism 43, 65, 78
Jordt, I. 27, 107–8

Karim, W. 126
kamma 112, 122–31, 138, 140, 159, 192
karma, see *kamma*
Kelty, C. 139
Keyes, C. 5, 29, 43, 44, 123, 168
Kirsch, A. 2, 44, 147
Klima, A. 24, 123, 167
Knowledge 99, 104, 110, 120
    Attitudes towards 10
    and meditation 21, 92, 95
    and wisdom 97, 105–8, 114, 181
Kornfield, J. 27
Kotelawala, Sir John 27

La Loubere, S. 5
Laidlaw, J. 43, 65, 78, 92–3, 94, 134, 138, 139, 140, 171
Language 28, 29, 96–7, 104, 113–15, 125–6, 181
    in ritual 10
    in meditation 10, 110–11

Language (cont.)
  in daily life 109–11
  Right speech 109
  see also Pali language
Laos 41
Lave, J. and E. Wenger 120
Learning 7–9, 11, 19, 60, 68, 105, 106, 110, 114, 119, 120, 156, 161, 177
  as social process 70–1, 181, 192
Lester, R. 11, 86
Lindberg Falk, M. 5, 6, 117, 135, 154, 155, 156, 168
Localism 37–40
Luang Ta Mahabua 39
Luang Phibunsongkhram 29
Luhrmann, T. 21, 35, 70, 112–13
  and psychoanalysis 83–5
Lutz, C. 126
Lutz, C. and G. White 126

MacIntyre, A. 70
Madan, T. 186
Mae chee, 4–6, 151–72
  Status of 4
  and monastic identity 4, 6, 191, 193
  and meditation 4, 6
  and alms donation 14, 121, 137, 142–50, 190
  pi liang 67
  Ambivalence in status and roles of 151–2, 191
  Duty and self-formation 152, 191–2
  and education 154, 155
  and monastic duty 154, 156
  and spatial separation 156
  and comportment 159–60
  and hierarchy 190
  and monasticization 190
  Ordination transcript 195–7
Maha Chakri Sirindhorn, Princess 100
Mahanikai 3, 26, 27, 53
Mahāsatipaṭṭhāna Sutta 27
Mahmood, S. 11, 165, 170
Malinowski, B. 147
Marriott, M. 186
Mauss, M. 138, 139, 178–9
McCargo, D. 36, 37, 38, 39, 43
McDaniel, J. 6, 29–30, 32, 35, 97, 174
Meditation, *see vipassanā, samatha*
Methodology and experiences of fieldwork 19–25
Merit 12, 14, 29, 42, 43, 47, 59, 65, 66, 67, 72, 98, 121–4, 127, 136, 137, 142–50
  and generalized reciprocity 137–42
  and monastics 142
  making 97, 118, 140
  and mindful deportment 123–4
Mills, M. B. 6, 44

Mindfulness 8, 10, 11, 14, 18, 21, 69, 101, 118, 141, 142, 161, 171, 172, 181, 193
  and monastic comportment 13, 119–20, 131–3
  Four foundations of 27, 70
  and non-self 78–80
  Cultivation of 85–6, 88, 95, 102, 103, 107, 114, 162
  and social relations 133–4
Mines, M. 188, 189
Moi and *personne* 178–82, 193–4
Monastic code, *see vinaya*
Monasticism
  as ethical project 73, 132–3
  and renunciation as process 182
Monastic duty 116–21
  and the laity 12
  and comportment 15, 118–19
  and performance 126–8, 183–4
Monastic identity
  and performance 6, 12, 13
  and *mae chee* 6
  and self formation 170–2
  and status 47
Monastic economy 136, 145–6
Monastic precepts 4, 6, 196
Monastic purity
  Lay interest in 3, 43, 124
Monastic community 6
  and meditation 7, 13
  and *mae chee* 13–15
  Doubt and guidance in 68–9
  and hierarchy 124–6, 182, 191
  and gender 14–15, 151–70
  and self-cultivation 160–2
  and monastic identity 173–4
  and mindful comportment 12, 129–31
Monasticization 4, 6, 177
  and laicization 47–50
Mongkut (Rama IV), King 27, 28, 34
Morality (*sīla*) 12, 13, 43, 49, 123, 124, 130, 132, 133, 160, 172, 173, 178, 184
Morris, R. 44, 99

Nepal 4, 27
Nietzsche, F. 16
Non-self (*anattā*) 8, 9, 11, 12, 18, 24, 26, 70, 73, 85, 86, 94, 103, 112, 140, 167, 179, 180, 182
Novices 55, 56, 57, 60, 65, 96, 125, 136, 152, 157, 163
Nyanaponika, T. 27

Obeyesekere, G. 189
Ockey, J. 6
Olivelle, P. 18
Opening ceremony 75

Ordination 2, 4, 6, 12, 14, 19, 28, 62–7, 162–5, 168, 177, 182, 195
  Temporary 20
  Reasons for 67–8
Ostor, A. 186

Pali language 10, 27–9, 30, 31, 61, 96, 155
  in ritual 63, 64, 65, 75, 97
  Effects of 98, 119–20, 181
  Suttas 99, 121
  in the meditation retreat 17, 91–3, 101–3, 111, 113–15
  and self-cultivation 102–4, 107
  in sermons 97
Paradox
  Ascetic 16–17, 181
  and performance 12–13
  of monastic performance 131–3
pāramī (Thai: *baramī*) 140
  dāna 140, 142
  khanti 88
Parkin, D. 126
Parnwell, M. and M. Seeger 37, 39–40
Parry, J. 99, 138, 139, 141
Pattana, K. 36, 44, 167
Peletz, M. 126
Phra Ajharn Man Bhuridatto 35
Phra Ajharn Sao Kantasilo 35
Phra Ajharn Thet 34
Phra Khru Arunthammarangsri 97
Phra Phimolatham 26, 27, 30–1
Phra Siwichai 28–9
Phra Thepsiddhimuni 31
Pilcher, J. and A. Huffcutt 90
pīti 98, 104, 112
Protective amulets/tattoos 89

Raheja, G. 186
Rains retreat (*Khao Phansa*) 56
Reynolds, C. J. 27, 37
riap roi 119–20
Robbins, J. 11
Rosaldo, M. 126

Sakyadhita 163
samādhi 33, 42
samādhi-maran 92–3, 94
samatha 23, 32, 33
Samuels, J. 22, 119
sangha 3, 5, 6, 27, 29, 34, 35, 36, 41, 45, 48, 49, 56, 58, 119, 137, 138, 141, 149, 150, 160, 162, 164, 175–6
  and hierarchy 4
  Council of Elders 30
  and moral crisis 43
  Gender 168
Sangha Act 1902 28, 29, 34
Sangha Act 1941 29
Sangha Act 1962 30, 41
Sanitsuda Ekachai 5, 38
Sansanee, Mae Chel 154
Santi Asoke 36
  Phothirak and 36
Sarit Thanarat 30, 41
Śāstra textual tradition 98–9
Sayadaw, M. 27, 52
Sayadaw U Pandita 72
Seeger, M. 5, 156
Self-formation 11, 14, 18, 104, 133, 165–6
  and cultivation of virtue 14
  and subjectivity 14
  and renunciation 15, 177–8
  and hierarchy 168–9
  and meditation 180–2
  and service 159
  Technology of the self 180
sīla, *see* morality
Silananda, U. 27, 80, 91, 98
Silanandabhivumsa, A. 27
Sleep deprivation 90
Smalley, W. 29
Soma, T. 27
Somdet Phra Mahawirawong 30
Sperber, D. 100
Spiro, M. 33, 61, 122, 123, 136, 141
Sponberg, A. 169–70
Sri Lanka 1, 4, 27, 42, 47, 49, 119, 123
Stirrat, R. 147
Strathern, M. 148
Strenski, I. 138, 149, 186
Subjectivity 2, 7, 9, 13, 14, 71, 86, 161, 165, 172, 182, 193
Suffering (*dukkha*) 8, 9, 11, 24, 26, 65, 70, 72, 140, 143, 150, 155, 169, 173, 177, 180
Sufficiency economy 38
Sulak Sivaraksa 42
Swearer, D. 36, 42, 52

Taffinder, N. 90
Tambiah, S. 5, 20, 28, 29, 30, 31, 32, 34, 41, 48, 52, 61, 89, 98, 102, 113, 149, 152, 183, 185, 186–7, 188
Tanabe, S. 44
Tanabe, S. and C. Keyes 36
Taussig, M. 147
Taylor, J. 36, 39, 44
Thailand
  and Buddhism 1–2
  Development of middle class 31

Thailand (cont.)
　and social and cultural changes 36
　Internal Security Operations Command 38
　Linguistic diversity and unification 29
　Nationalism/identity 37
thammacarik program 41
thammathud program 41
Thammakaai 36
Thammayut 27, 28, 30, 34
Therīgāthā 81
Thitsa, K. 147
Thomas, M. 90
Thompson, V. 29
The three characteristics 8, 65, 84, 90, 103, 167
　in meditation 8
　see also Impermanence, Suffering, Non-self
Thudong monks 31, 34
　Forest tradition 34
Tipiṭaka 6, 27, 118
Tiyavanich, K. 27, 28, 29, 34
The Triple Gem 62, 63, 64, 65, 75, 117
Tsomo, Karma Lekshe 163

upacha (Pali: *upajjhāya*) 64
upāsikā 5, 57, 62, 64, 65, 74, 128, 180

Van Esterik, J. 27, 32, 33–4
Van Esterik, P. 6, 154, 159, 167
Vietnam 4, 41
vinaya 6, 50, 132, 160, 173, 175, 183, 187
vipassanā meditation 33, 71–3
　Propagation of 1, 15, 26–7, 32, 45
　and scientific theory 3
　and monastic structure 7, 177
　and perception 7, 9
　Technique 7–8, 27
　and spontaneity 8, 92, 113
　and attainment 17, 87–95, 167
　as sole practice 23
　and Buddhist reform 26
　and lay involvement 32, 33–4
　and the Three Characteristics 9, 180
　and monastic identity 9
　and subjectivity 9, 10, 181
　and Pali language 10
　and tourism in Thailand 36
　as a social learning process 70–1
　Social dimensions of 71
　Retreat process 73–81
　Role of the teacher 81–5
　as ethical self-formation 6, 7, 8, 87
　and Bodily purity 88, 89
　and Sleepless period 88
　Experience of 91, 111–12
　and monasticization 174
　and Thai identity 176
　Teaching meditation 193
　and *phalasamāpatti* 91
　Phenomenon of arising and ceasing 91
　and *dap* 91
Visuddhimagga 118

Wachirayan, Prince 28, 29
wai 51, 117, 159, 166
Walters, J. 123
Wan Gon 57, 60, 61
Wan Phra 31, 56, 57, 60, 61, 103, 123, 136, 158
Wat Doi Suthep 29
Wat Bonamron 2, 4, 21, 49, 51, 183
　Meditation in 18–19
　Founder of 70, 72
　History of 52–3
　Spatial layout of 53–4
　Meditation students at 54–5
　Structural bureaucratization of 55–8
　Daily schedule in 58–61
　Monastic duties in 60
　Meditation retreat schedule in 60–1
Wat Bovonniwet 28
Wat Mahathat 26, 32, 52
　Satellite branches of 31
　Propagation of meditation by 32
Wat Phra Singh 53
Wat Yai Chai Mongkhon 153
Weber, M. 48
Weiner, A. 147, 148
Wikan ,U. 127–8, 129
Williams, G. 39
Wilson, L. 6

Yoga 2
yogi 46–7, 55, 56, 57
Yot Chiang Rai, King 52–3

Printed in Poland
by Amazon Fulfillment
Poland Sp. z o.o., Wrocław